BOBBY ROBSON

Bobby Robson (signature)

BOBBY ROBSON

WITH BOB HARRIS

My Autobiography

An Englishman Abroad

MACMILLAN

First published 1998 by Macmillan

an imprint of Macmillan Publishers Ltd
25 Eccleston Place, London SW1W 9NF
and Basingstoke

Associated companies throughout the world

ISBN 0 333 73484 X

3 5 7 9 8 6 4 2

A CIP catalogue record for this book is available from
the British Library.

Typeset by SX Composing DTP, Rayleigh, Essex
Printed and bound in Great Britain by
Mackays of Chatham plc, Chatham, Kent

Every effort has been made to trace copyright holders of material
reproduced in this book, but if any have been omitted the publishers
will be glad to make restitution at the first opportunity.

You'll find the road is long and rough,
    with soft spots far apart
Where only those can make the grade
    who have the Uphill Heart
And when they stop you with a thud
    or halt you with a crack
Let Courage call the signals as
    you keep on coming back

Keep coming back, and though the world
    may romp across your spine
Let every game's end find you still
    upon the battling line:
For when the One Great Scorer comes
    To write against your name
He marks not that you won or lost –
    But how you played the game!

Grantland Rice

Acknowledgements

Bobby Robson and Bob Harris would like to thank their long-suffering families; Jonny Dexter; José Mourinho; Don Howe; Dan Archer; Huw Davies; Artur Woolf and Jonathan Harris.

Contents

1

Flirting with Death

Some might say that I shook hands with the devil, but I prefer to think I was touched by angels in August 1995 when, with a little nagging from my wife Elsie, an instant diagnosis from consultant surgeon Mr Huw Davies and a successful operation by Mr Dan Archer at the Royal Marsden Hospital in London undoubtedly saved my life.

It looked as though my career was over as Mr Archer told me: 'Quite frankly Mr Robson, at your age you should not work again. Simply, people do not go back after this particular operation.'

But he did not know me at the time, and neither did most people: I had already overcome another threatening cancer shock three years earlier.

To this day even my closest friends believe that I took three months away from my job at PSV Eindhoven to undergo stomach surgery. That was, quite simply, a cover-up; I went into St Anne's hospital in Geldorf, Holland to have a cancerous tumour removed from my colon.

I could have ignored the first signs so easily. I was passing a little blood but not a lot, and I put it down to a touch of piles. I mentioned it, almost in passing, to the club's medical consultant Mr Artur Woolf; he examined me and discovered the truth and the tumour was quickly removed. He told me I would be out for some time. It was my second season at PSV and the club was very protective, announcing to the world that I would be absent from my job as coach because of a medical problem which required surgery. I was out for three months, didn't bother with convalescence and came straight back. I would have been back sooner but for the fact that I suddenly felt a sharp pain in my chest through to my back. I thought I had pulled a muscle while heaving myself up straight, but it transpired that I had an embolism and I had to stay for an extra eight days while they thinned down my blood. Frank Arnesen and the youth coach Huub Stevens, who went on to coach Schalke 04 in Germany, had kept things ticking over at Eindhoven and we went on to clinch the Championship for a second successive season. The club was excellent. They could easily have panicked and brought in another coach to keep the season going, but they didn't – they supported me.

That was a big enough warning, but it was almost minor compared to my return match three years later. This time it was an especially nasty little strain situated high up on my face between my nose and my left eye. It was certainly more than the 'nasal problem' that had been concerning me and fully justified Elsie's demands that I should go and have it looked at while I was briefly at home in England, just before the beginning of a new Portuguese season with champions Porto.

It had all begun with a blow on the nose many years ago in my first week as Ipswich manager. It is the sort of injury that is run-of-the-mill to a professional footballer and it left me with very little sense of smell and continual nasal problems which always seemed to flare up on cold winter nights or long aeroplane flights – both occupational hazards in my chosen profession! A quick sniff on a Vick's inhaler usually provided relief, but Elsie was aware that it had gone on long enough and that it was time I had something done about it. I finally gave in, more to satisfy Elsie than out of any concern of my own, and my local GP in Ipswich, Dr Keeble, referred me to an ear, nose and throat specialist, Mr Ian Lord, who gave me a scan and detected a slight blockage that needed cleaning out. And that, he promised, would be the end of it.

As fate would have it, Porto were due to arrive in London after a pre-season training camp in Sweden to play a testimonial for former Chelsea player Paul Elliott, whose career had been prematurely ended by injury after a challenge with the then Aston Villa player Dean Saunders. Elliott had taken the case to court, lost out and had been forced to pay heavy costs. We had agreed to a game not only to help the lad out but also because it suited our preparations.

The decision also saved my life. When the team flew back to Portugal I took the opportunity to have the minor operation in England. I confess I did it with some bad grace and I moaned about having unnecessarily to waste time when I was so busy, and I told Elsie she was making a fuss. After all, I had undergone a scan in Portugal which had given me a clean bill of health as recently as February 1995, and I told her: 'I know what is wrong with me – I have chronic sinusitis. I wish you wouldn't interfere. I don't have time for all this nonsense.' But I went through with it all the same.

It was nothing. A breeze. It was, as promised, a one-day job in Ipswich, successfully achieved as the surgeon, Mr Lord, cleaned me out and took a sample of my mucus for a biopsy just to be sure. He told me it looked fine and would confirm as much in three weeks' time. I explained that Porto were in the middle of pre-season training and that I would be grateful if he could get the tests processed as a matter of urgency so that I could concentrate on football as soon as possible. He assured me he would do his best and discharged me the next morning.

I returned to my home in Ipswich for a relaxing day on my own, recuperating from the effects of the anaesthetic. That night, six or seven hours later, the telephone rang as I was packing for my return to Portugal the next morning. It was the surgeon, who stopped me in my tracks by saying, 'I have to come and talk to you. I know where you live, just sit tight and wait for me.'

I hesitated, and explained that I had to be on a plane in the morning, but he said, 'I don't think you will be – but please sit tight and wait until I come.' Even then I did not feel the full impact of what he was saying. I assumed there were complications with my sinus and that at worst I'd be facing a little more minor surgery.

Mr Lord was with me in ten minutes flat, and that should have told me my own diagnosis was somewhat short of the mark. He told me to sit down, saying: 'I have to talk to you. I have some grave news. I pushed the biopsy through quickly as you asked and what you have is a malignant melanoma in the face and, to be honest, I don't know how long it has been there.' I sat there, desperately trying to think what a malignant melanoma was! My medical knowledge as a football man is limited to cartilages, hamstrings, tendons and the like. It certainly sounded serious and I could tell from the tone of his voice that it was something worse than a head cold. But even then I couldn't comprehend what he was about to tell me because I felt no pain, I was fit, I had no symptoms – I didn't even have a blocked sinus after the operation. He confirmed the urgency of the situation when he told me that he had already spoken to a specialist and had arranged an appointment for me the very next morning in Ipswich. 'Are you sure?' I asked, more in hope than anger. 'I really have to get back to work.' He replied that he couldn't stop me, but I would be very foolish if I did not keep the 9.30 a.m. appointment with the consultant surgeon who dealt specifically with head and neck cancer. That was it. He had spelt it out. We were talking about the Big C.

He left me on my own in the lounge wondering what the hell was happening. I rang Elsie in Dorset, where she was staying with friends, told her what had been said and she immediately made plans to return. I think I watched a little television to take my mind off it, but I couldn't remember what I had watched five minutes later, never mind now. I am lucky in that I have always been able to sleep whatever the circumstances, and that night was no exception. I was worried but, strangely, not afraid, even though it was evident that this was a serious situation.

I was prompt for my appointment when I met Huw Davies for the first time. He was a likeable Welshman whom I took to immediately, so much so that he later brought his wife to Spain for a holiday with us. He was the expert, the consultant surgeon for several hospitals in the area, and I was prepared to listen to what he had to say. He explained that I had been unlucky to contract such a rare form of the disease, that I had this malignant melanoma under the left eye and unless it was removed it would undoubtedly spread. At that precise moment they weren't sure how long I had had it or how widespread it was and, just in case I was still thinking about going back to Porto, he put me in no doubt when he said straight out: 'You can ignore it and return to Portugal – but I have to tell you that if you do you will not see the season out. It is a two per cent melanoma, it is very rare, but leave it alone and it will spread into the eye and then into the brain.'

He then explained in detail just what he had to do to get it out. I couldn't believe it was happening to me and, again, my first words were, 'Are you sure?' What I really could not understand was why I was apparently so close to death yet felt so fit. I had just come out of our pre-season training camp, getting up at the crack of dawn, breakfasting by 7.30 and running with the players in two training sessions every day. Here I was in my sixties keeping up with super-fit young footballers and living a ridiculously healthy lifestyle. 'Look at me,' I said, 'I have no problems, no pain! I am fitter than you.' He had, of course, seen and heard it all before and he told me gently: 'I know it is hard to take. I can assure you that what I am telling you is right. I will do the operation myself. I will get you through it. I would like the privilege of looking after you and getting you fit again.'

Even then I was still sceptical. I couldn't comprehend that I had a serious problem in my face when there were no obvious signs, and I asked him if it were possible to have a second opinion. There was no offence meant nor taken, and he not only said yes but told me that the man he would recommend, Dan Archer, was the very top man in the field and that he would accompany me to the appointment. Chillingly, he added: 'You need an operation and you need it now if your life is to be saved.'

There was clearly no time to be wasted and I was in London the next day with Mr Archer, who turned out to be a typical Liverpool lad who was more keen to talk about football than the operation. He explained that he had performed between two and three hundred operations of a similar nature and knew what needed to be done and, more importantly, how soon. We decided that I should undergo surgery in London as he felt that I could be protected more from the media there than in Ipswich. Mr Archer was aware enough to know that this would have been a nice little story for some journalist and they were more used to handling the situation at the Royal Marsden.

Strangely, that awareness of the outside problems gave me a great feeling that here was a man who knew what he was doing. Both of them made it abundantly clear to me that there was no time to lose. I needed surgery and I needed it immediately.

Porto were on the verge of kicking off the new season, defending the Portuguese title we had won the previous year and making an assault on the European Champions League. I was quickly in touch with my assistant José Mourinho, the president Jorge Pinto Da Costa and the club physician Dr Gomez, who had arranged the scan six months earlier. They were naturally concerned and told me to take all the time I needed.

At that stage there were no thoughts about my future. As far as I was concerned it was nothing more than a temporary blip; I would convalesce and get back to work. I was in great physical condition for a man of sixty-two, mentally I was strong and I knew that I was in the best possible hands. I believe it also helped that I was such a competitive person after a lifetime in football. It becomes engrained. Life as a footballer and a coach is a constant battle against the opposition, out-thinking and outwitting your rivals and always striving to win. This situation was really no different at all: the cancer was the opposition and I had to beat it. It was never in my mind to quit what I loved doing the most. Prior to surgery I had only one aim and that was to return to my job.

I had the operation within forty-eight hours of consulting Mr Archer and, as promised, he and Huw Davies were quick and skilful. Happy with their handiwork they declared it a complete success, but they were adamant that I should now rest on my laurels and forget all about returning to Porto or, indeed, to any other club. They pointed out that I had nothing left to prove and that I should take it easy for the rest of my life. I was having none of that. I didn't want to retire. I didn't want to stop working. My brush with death had, if anything, made me appreciate even more what I had. The game still enraptured me and I couldn't imagine a life without it.

During my recuperation Porto could not have been better to me. My assistant José Mourinho, the doctor and the president Pinto Da Costa and his wife Philomena came over both before and after the operation. It was all very relaxed and far from doom and gloom. In fact I took them to see *Phantom of the Opera* (an ironic choice under the circumstances, although it didn't cross my mind that I might have to wear a face mask after my operation) and we lunched at Chelsea Harbour. They were exceptionally supportive and there was never any mention from them about my not returning after the operation.

The operation, not surprisingly, left me with a horrendous face. To reach the cancer they had had to extract my top teeth, cut the bone in my left nostril and go through the roof of my mouth. I must confess I didn't look in the mirror too often, but I wasn't too concerned as both Dan Archer and Huw Davies told me that within a year the scars would hardly be noticeable. In fact it was much earlier than that. They not only did a thorough job in ridding me of the little pest, but also contrived to do an excellent cosmetic job as well.

Elsie, my family and my friends tried to persuade me to call it a day, but I remained obstinate. The addiction was still there and I needed the daily injection of adrenalin that football gave me. By November I was back in the saddle. It was probably a month or two too early, but it was my own decision - there was no pressure from Porto or anyone else. I felt well and wanted to get back. I went to see Porto play Nantes in the European Champions League, more to say hello to the players and to show that I was up and running rather than to take any sort of control. I left that to my capable assistants. Strangely enough I bumped into Arsenal director David Dein, manager Bruce Rioch and his assistant Stewart Houston who had read about my being apparently close to death and were clearly surprised to see me out there. I went to see the boys in the hotel, and while they were obviously pleased to see me, they couldn't help but stare at my misshapen face.

Having sat through a goalless draw I knew I needed to get back to the action, and especially the Champions League. It wasn't as if I was feeling unwell. Naturally the operation had taken something out of me but I was improving with every day and I seriously wanted to resume my career. I wasn't bored in the meantime, though: I took the chance to catch up on some reading, watched sport on television and went for walks. But most of all I wanted to get back. I was forever on the telephone to Portugal checking to see what was happening with my team and my plans, and my enthusiasm was further fired by another visit from the club president Pinto Da Costa. Again he refrained from asking when I would be back. Although his English was limited and my Portuguese no better, we talked a lot through his wife and made our plans for the future. We had a very sound relationship, which made it all the sadder when it soured at the end of my stay with Porto.

My decision to return to the game I love so dearly has proved to be fully justified. Not only did I win another League Championship with Porto, but I then moved on to take over the coaching reins at probably the biggest club in the world, Barcelona, who at the time were going through one of the most turbulent periods in their volatile history. The first of my two years in Spain was probably the most demanding in my career, even more so than the eight years at the helm of England, as I was caught up in something which at the time was beyond my ken. But I not only survived, I prospered, winning three trophies and a coveted place in the Champions League by finishing second to a Real Madrid team who had nothing but the Spanish title to concentrate upon that season.

Football is important to me and I can't give it up, but my struggle with cancer definitely helped put things into perspective. Anything that is a concern can now be dismissed or coped with so much more easily. There is no doubt at all that it helped me cope at Barcelona, and I will always remember that first year with pride as the second most successful season in the last hundred years of the club's history. Things never got on top of me because I had been in far greater and more real peril and come through it. Nothing at the Nou Camp could ever approach the battle I had won on the operating table.

I can also say that without a doubt I appreciate my wife Elsie and my family more than before. Managing or coaching a football team is, by nature, a selfish job and the family tend to be pushed to one side. I could so easily have died and never seen my kids again, but I am alive and I now relish the opportunity to spend more time with my family. For a football man Christmas and New Year at home is an unheard-of luxury, but during my second year at Barcelona a new role allowed me to enjoy the celebrations and see in 1998 in the bosom of my family.

The change of job from coach to director also enabled me to reduce the weight of pressure on me, and that was clearly the right thing to do. Dan Archer and Huw Davies both firmly believed that the cancer could easily have been a symptom of the stress I had been under for so many years – in all probability it was a contributory factor – and that is why they told me to take steps to reduce the pressure after the operation. After all, it was hardly taking his advice when I signed my contract for the

Barcelona job! I did not hide it from him, I told him what I was doing and he retorted: 'I told you to *de*crease – not *in*crease the pressure.' But even though he was something of a football student he did not realize the nature of the job I had until he visited Barcelona. Then he knew he had saved the life of a deranged man.

Cancer is a personal matter, and while my second bout became public knowledge, my first brush with the Big C, as I've mentioned, was kept under wraps, known only by my family and a handful of trustworthy people at Eindhoven. So why talk about it now? Easy. Because I have come to appreciate that by talking about it I can help ease the fear of an awful lot of people. Medicine has moved on so much that cancer need not be the dreaded news it used to be. It need no longer be a sentence of imminent death – far from it. Caught early, many of the forms of cancer are curable and I advocate a check-up if you're in the slightest doubt. I was twice saved by early, instant diagnosis, and when Huw Davies asked me to co-operate with a cancer awareness programme in Ipswich he explained to me that there are many thousands of people walking around with the disease unaware of it, and that the only way to discover and treat it is by examination. I joined in the campaign, appeared on television and 800 people turned up for their free examinations when the remainder of the country was pulling in forty or fifty people. Eight of them were carrying one form or another of cancer. Those eight lives were saved. As was mine. I shall be forever grateful to those instrumental in the detection and elimination of my cancer because it has allowed me to enjoy my life in a clearer and more fulfilling way, and to continue my involvement in a sport I love, and have always loved.

2

Geordie Boy

The perception of the north-east of England, particularly after the war, was that a football manager needed only to whistle down the pit to find a centre-forward. Certainly the area was, is and always will be a hotbed of the sport, but I never had the opportunity to play organized football at any of my schools. My father Philip, a miner all his life, was not a footballer but he loved the game with a passion and took me to watch our beloved Newcastle United when I was big enough to walk, and then encouraged me throughout my career as both player and manager.

I was born Robert William Robson in the heart of the north-east mining community in the village of Sacriston, County Durham on 18 February 1933. Within a few months of my birth the family moved to a little two-bedroom terraced house in Langley Park where my dad and my mom, Lillian, brought up their five boys: Tom, Philip, Ronald, Keith and myself. As the old song goes, 'We were poor but we were happy', and no different from the other families who lived on our street or, indeed, in the village. Clothes were passed down from child to child and money was tight – tight but never desperate, because in fifty-one years on the coalface my dad missed only one shift. That was important to us because if you did go missing, so did your wages. No show, no pay. There was no extra salary coming in to help my dad either, for women simply didn't have careers in those days and my mother stayed at home to cook, wash and mend, as did the majority of the women in the village. Neither did he waste his hard-earned cash on booze and fags for he didn't drink alcohol or use tobacco like so many of his workmates. Indeed, Mom and Dad were strong Methodists and were keen to bring up their five boys the right way, to respect authority and family values.

There were, of course, no televisions around then and the youngsters entertained themselves by kicking a ball around or playing cricket up against a dustbin with a piece of wood and an old tennis ball. When there was no ball to kick we used a piece of coal, and when that broke up there was always another lump lying around because that was one commodity that was not in short supply. For the adults there were was not a lot more: a couple of football pitches, the same number of cinemas, several pubs, a working men's club, an ice-cream parlour and a dance hall, although it was the radio that was every family's main source of entertainment. Dad didn't use the clubs as he was a teetotaller, but he did later in life when he retired, playing dominoes, whist and bridge. His strong influence meant that few of the family indulged in strong drink or tobacco. Tom was the only brother who smoked, and he stopped later in life. I have enjoyed the very occasional cigar and the odd glass of wine with meals, but I have never been a compulsive drinker like so many of our British footballers – something, I hope, that is changing these days under the influence of foreign coaches and players.

Our pride and joy at our house in Langley Park was a glorious radiogram, a combined radio and record player housed in a huge wooden cabinet which dominated our lounge. It was treated with tender loving care, polished almost daily, and if you were to mark it in any way there was hell to pay. Now and again my brothers and I would go into Durham and buy one of those old breakable 78 rpm records of Frank Sinatra, Nat King Cole, Bing Crosby, Lena Horne, Judy Garland or one of the other great singers of the day.

It was no big deal that the indoor plumbing served us only with cold water. Such luxuries as indoor toilets; plumbed baths and hot water on demand were not only unknown to us but unknown to the neighbourhood until, much later, the coal board went round replacing one of the bedrooms with a real bathroom. Before that major ablutions were confined to a big zinc tub in the front room with the water heated up by the roaring coal (of course) fire. The loo was down the back garden, making chamberpots essential in that part of the world in the depths of the icy winters.

My dad saved the family even more money by cobbling our shoes. He had his own shoemaker's last and would buy sheets of leather and cut them to fit our boots and toe caps which I continually kicked through playing football. His sensible accounting meant that we were always well fed, well clothed *and* rewarded with an annual summer holiday, first in local Whitley Bay and then, as we became more affluent, Blackpool. They used to run special buses from Durham to the famous resort where we would luxuriate in a boarding house and enjoy that massive expanse of sandy beach. Philip Robson taught me the true value of a penny and his lessons stood me in good stead later in life, particularly when I was managing Ipswich, treating every pound note the club spent as though it was my own. Every purchase I made had to be right because I could not afford to be wrong, and every season until the last, when the club was paying for new stands, we finished in the black. It was a question of balancing the books, for me an important, if not crucial, part of the job. There were no billionaire financiers around then to prevent a bankrupt club going to the wall.

My life revolved around football as far back as I can remember. We didn't play competitive football at my junior school, and the headmaster at my secondary school, Waterhouses Modern Intermediate, rest his soul, didn't like the game everyone else in the area loved and refused to enter a team in the local schools league. Ron was the clever one of the family; he passed for the local grammar school while I took my place with the majority at a comprehensive. I wasn't the dummy of the class by any stretch of the imagination, but football was more important to me than maths and very few children in those days passed what was then called the eleven-plus examination. I compensated for this lack of organized football at school by kicking my tennis ball or lump of coal around every waking minute. As soon as we returned home from class we would play 'headies' or bang a ball against the outside toilets, breaking off for tea, then supper, and eventually and reluctantly for homework.

It was thanks to my PE teacher David Gilliland that I was introduced to match-based football and cricket. In the absence of competitive games at the school he would take it upon himself to find us opposition and arrange games. But they were few and far between. The one benefit I gained from this absence of real football was that it gave me time to hone my skills. I was always working with a ball, be it a real football or a tennis ball. These days, I feel, kids are forced into the rough and tumble of competitive soccer far too early, playing games all the time rather than working on their basic technique.

Although the school had no teams, the village did, and as soon as I was able I was playing for Langley Park Juniors, often with lads two and three years older than me. By then I was receiving presents in the shape of football boots and a real leather ball for Christmas and birthdays, and I already had no doubts that I wanted to be a professional footballer. Football dominated my life and I became expert at blowing up and lacing my own leather football. No problem these days, but then you had to pump up the bladder and carefully fold and tie the little air tube before pressing it under the leather of the ball and lacing it up tight with a leather thong and a needle designed especially for the job. They were wondrous things those old footballs, particularly when they were wet: the weight doubled from three pounds to almost seven pounds on bad days, and the leather lace could be sharp enough to cut your forehead if the ball had been tied up incorrectly. No wonder centre-halves had bullet heads and talked like retired boxers! It was like heading a shot-put.

I was also a competent cricketer, playing in the Durham County League for Langley Park, but that was never a professional option. We didn't have a first-class county in the area as both Durham and Northumberland were involved in minor county cricket. In those days it was not unusual for all-round sportsmen to follow both codes as professionals and, indeed, my eventual Fulham team-mate Johnny Haynes was offered a contract with Middlesex as a wicketkeeper-batsman.

My urge to become a professional footballer was heightened by my visits to St James's Park. I turned out for Langley Park on a Saturday morning between the ages of eleven and fifteen, and then it would be off to watch Newcastle in the afternoon if they were at home. When at the age of fifteen I began to play for the under-18s the chances of watching were a little bit more limited, but I still went when I could although playing the game was by then far more important than watching it. It was seventeen miles (to St James's) and seventeen miles back by local bus and we were always at the ground early enough to be at the front of the queue for the big games to watch the likes of Len Shackleton, Jackie Milburn, Albert Stubbins, Charlie Wayman, Alf McMichael, Bob Cowell and the rest. They were my idols. I would watch them and then rush home to try to emulate what I had seen. They were, I suppose, the role models who began to shape my career, and they weren't inspirational only to me: the area was a real hothouse for developing football and every bit of grass or waste ground would hold an improvised match. We would climb over the fence to play on our local pitch, leaving someone to keep watch in case the village policeman or the groundsman should turn up.

Like most of the kids who left school between the ages of fourteen and a half and fifteen in that part of the world, I was involved in the mines by the time I was fifteen. It was no problem for me to get a job at the local colliery where Dad, by this time, was an overman and brother Tom the engineer. I didn't work on the coalface like my dad had done as I was found a 'cushy' number as a trainee electrician. This didn't excuse me from going down the pit with the rest, for I was down there every day for a year and a half in my helmet, boots and lamp, repairing the lights and other electrical fittings. It did me no harm and taught me to value my successes in years to come and to appreciate the fact that I was able to earn my living doing something I loved. When I was manager at Ipswich I took chairman and vice-chairman John and Patrick Cobbold and other members of the board to a pit in Swaddlincote before a game against Derby County. Brother Tom was by this time making rapid progress in his career, eventually becoming chief engineer for the National Coal Board for the Nottingham and Kent areas, and he arranged for permission for us all to go down to the coalface. We dressed them out in overalls, lamps and hard helmets and took them for a look at the other side of life. I remember it making a great impression on them, too.

Because of the footballing traditions of the area there were always scouts from clubs all over the country watching games, and I was invited to both Middlesbrough and Southampton for trials in 1948 when I was fifteen. The Saints followed it up but it was Boro who signed me on schoolboy terms. I might well have joined them at a later date but I didn't feel they showed a great deal of interest, not inviting me to Ayresome Park that often for training and so on. When I turned seventeen and they wanted to take me on as a professional, I told them no. There were plenty of other opportunities and I had no doubts that was where my future lay, although Mom and Dad insisted I maintained my career as an electrical engineering apprentice. Sunderland, Southampton, Lincoln, York, Blackpool, Huddersfield and Fulham all came knocking on our door, but the obvious choice was my adored Newcastle United. I bled black and white just like my dad and I am still amazed, almost half a century on, that I didn't crawl straight to St James's Park on my hands and knees.

Instead I opted to go south to Fulham, a popular London side at the time that had just won promotion to the top division. The manager, Bill Dodgin, was a persuasive talker and convinced me that I would have a much better chance of breaking through with a club like his where youngsters were encouraged and promoted rather than a big-spending set-up like Newcastle where they brought in the big-name stars. My decision certainly surprised my dad, but he was Newcastle United. I liked Bill because he took the trouble to travel north himself to see me and my parents and sat outside the house until the opportunity arose to talk to me. There was, of course, a great debate within the family and it was decided that I should go on the strict proviso that I kept up my career as an electrical apprentice just in case I didn't make the grade as a professional. Fortunately Fulham agreed, even though it meant my training in the evening as a part-timer rather than during the morning with the first-team players.

I wasn't the only one from our little village to go to a professional club when the time came. George Johnson and Dickie Brankstone went to Lincoln, Leo Dale to Doncaster and one of the Kilkenny brothers joined Newcastle, but unfortunately none of them followed it through to make the grade. But the numbers showed the depth of potential talent in the area.

Moving to London in 1950 was a major culture shock for me. I was found digs in Inglethorpe Street right next to the club and I shared with another young player, Tom Wilson, who has remained a true friend to this day. Each of us was best man at the other's wedding, and Tom went on to do extremely well in his business life, becoming chairman of a massive auctioneers and surveyors company which dealt mainly in industrial property. He went to the top and stayed there. Tom also became a Fulham director and with another former team-mate of ours, Jimmy Hill, successfully negotiated the lease, helping to ensure that Fulham stayed at Craven Cottage. I doubt that Fulham, Mohammed Al Fayed and Kevin Keegan would be there now but for Tom Wilson and his efforts.

Almost as soon as I arrived Bill Dodgin himself took me to Lloyds Bank in Putney High Street where he made me open an account with a pound note. I am still with Lloyds to this day. Bill was a kind and thoughtful man who encouraged positive thinking and attractive, attacking football. He would regularly shout at us, 'The ball is round – pass it around,' and he also used to urge us, 'Happy when you win, smile when you lose.'

Tom and I stayed in our digs, so close to the ground that we could walk and save on bus fares, until we split up to get married to our respective partners. It was all a bit special for me living in London with the running hot water, indoor toilet and bath. I felt like a king. The digs provided us with breakfast and an evening meal as well, but Tom and I always made sure that every day we had a proper three-course lunch with soup, meat and two veg and a pudding at the White Horse in Putney or somewhere similar. Then the family would eat together at 7.30 when the landlady's husband returned home from his job in the city. We certainly didn't go hungry.

There was still no television and our entertainment revolved around the radio, cinema and the theatre. We both liked the stage and would save up to go to a show or to see one of the top stars of the day – Sinatra, Sammy Davis Jr or Nat King Cole at the Palladium. That was a real treat, a trip to the Dilly, strolling from Leicester Square to Piccadilly Circus looking at the neon lights and the people and the tourists in their fancy gear, maybe stopping off for a coffee or an ice-cream.

When I first arrived in the capital I was found a job with an electrical company based at Victoria which had a contract to work on the Festival of Britain. One of my jobs was to go with one of the senior electricians to work at the Festival Hall itself to install the lighting and heating. Another cushy number? Forget it. I watched in horror one day as my partner stepped backwards and fell headlong over the unmade balcony onto the concrete floor below; he survived but he was rushed to hospital with multiple injuries. It frightened me because I thought it could easily have been me. Had it been, that would have been the end of my footballing aspirations there and then.

It was a hard day by any standards. I was up at six a.m. at my digs in Fulham and caught the bus to Victoria from where I was ferried to the Festival Hall by van. By the time I had made the return journey it was often seven o'clock in the evening before I was back in my digs, and three nights a week I would then have to go to training. When Saturday came round I was shattered. It was too much. I tried hard to keep it up but I was tired and it was affecting my progress as a footballer. The club was also concerned that I was trying to do too much. I told Mom and Dad that it was too heavy a workload for me and that if I kept it up I was going to be a good electrician and a very poor footballer. The club was on my side, they could see what it was doing to me, and when Mom and Dad came down to see Bill Dodgin he was able to persuade them that I should give my football career a real go. Dad wanted me to see through my apprenticeship, which would have meant living this double life until I was twenty-one, but he reluctantly agreed that I should be a full-time footballer and put my other career on the back-burner.

Even full-time I was only on seven pounds a week and, after paying for my lodgings and my food, there was nothing left to send home. I did, however, save up and on my first Christmas back home I proudly presented Mom and Dad with a seven-day chiming clock which Dad looked after religiously, making certain it was fully rewound every Saturday night. It lasted for years and years.

At the end of the season, when I returned home to the north-east to play cricket, I had a bit more spare cash because in those days we were paid a close-season salary of six pounds, a lot more than the four pounds I was earning down the pit as an electrician.

Switching to full-time football was the making of me. I was a bit of a prodigy and I was in the first team by the time I was eighteen. Because I had worked I never had to go through the boot-boy bit, cleaning the toilets or painting the stands. I was never an apprentice professional, signing full forms when

I was seventeen. When I started at Craven Cottage, Johnny Haynes was working in the offices licking stamps and posting letters while Tosh Chamberlain, Bos Taylor, Tony Barton and Roy Dwight were working apprentices from the ages of fifteen to seventeen. I certainly enjoyed the thrill of playing first-team football at such an early age and one of my memorable moments of that first season was when we were drawn against Chelsea at Stamford Bridge in the fifth round of the FA Cup. We held them to a 1–1 draw and then crushed them 3–0 in the replay at Craven Cottage – suddenly we were fantasizing about Wembley. Blackpool promptly exploded that little dream in the next round and went on to reach the final. We were relegated the next season, but it was not nearly as dramatic an event as it is now and it made little difference to me or my ambitions. It was almost expected of Fulham to bounce up and down like a yo-yo, and our comedian chairman Tommy Trinder used to joke: 'What's black and white and keeps going down? Fulham Football Club!'

Fulham was a nice club and everyone was helpful. There were few of the petty jealousies you hear of at other clubs and I was lucky that the senior professionals were all supportive. I remember players like Eddie and Reg Lowe, Ian Black, Robbie Lawler, Bobby Brennan, Bedford Jezzard, 'Big' Jim Taylor, Charlie Mitten, Harry Freeman and Dougie Platt. They were a good crowd of blokes and capable enough on the field to attract 26,000 to 27,000 a week to Craven Cottage and give any team in the country a game on their day.

But maybe we were too happy-go-lucky. We never achieved as much in the six years I was there as we should have done. It was a homely little club, but with one or two extra players we could have been more successful. Lots of showbiz stars came to watch us because of the close proximity to London and the fact that Tommy Trinder was our chairman, and that seemed to compensate for the lack of prizes. Fulham did not have a big staff and players' wages were capped, but we had big crowds every week. It makes me wonder all these years later, whatever happened to the money that must have been pouring in? But I was happy there. I made 152 League appearances and weighed in with sixty-eight goals from my attacking midfield position before my transfer in 1956 to West Bromwich Albion.

It was a sad day for me in many ways. As I said, I was very happy at the club, and although my international career took off after I left Fulham I had played for the under-23s and the England B side, so I never felt as though I was being held back. I learned a great deal from Bill Dodgin, and playing alongside such outstanding footballers as Haynes, Jezzard, Jimmy Hill, Tom Wilson, Mitten, Tony Macedo, Jimmy Langley, Bobby Keetch and other great characters was always instructive. There were some real eccentrics among them; Mitten, who had been kicked out of Old Trafford by Matt Busby, kept the dressing room in stitches with his antics and tales of his time in South America. He was not alone: Tosh Chamberlain and Tony Macedo were just as daft, and the late Bobby Keetch lived the life of a toff with his rich friends and his champagne lifestyle.

It was also at Craven Cottage that I first became interested in the coaching side of the game.

Jimmy Hill was one of England manager Walter Winterbottom's blue-eyed boys and a full badge coach. Typically, Jimmy wanted to use his knowledge by having our training sessions altered. I was also greatly influenced by another of our players, a certain centre-half named Ron Greenwood who was to become the England manager directly before I assumed control. Even then he was a deep-thinking football man who was listened to and respected whenever football was discussed.

I went with a group of like-minded fellow professionals from Fulham to watch the great Hungarian team bury England at Wembley in 1953, stripping us of our unbeaten Wembley record and our dignity with a wonderful 6–3 victory. It affected me deeply, and soon afterwards I began attending FA coaching courses along with Hill and Greenwood at Paddington Street.

Despite all the brains and skill at Fulham we stayed in the Second Division and that, presumably, had an effect on the finances; when West Bromwich Albion came in with a £25,000 bid – the record at the time was only £34,000 – they quickly accepted and I found myself, somewhat reluctantly, on my way to the Midlands. I had no thoughts of moving at the time. My career was still on the upward trend despite not being a First Division player, a fact that was emphasized when I was selected in 1955 for a close-season FA tour to the Caribbean, playing in Trinidad, Jamaica, Bermuda and Curaçao, and shortly after my return from that tour I married Elsie. I had met her in my Durham village in 1952 when I was eighteen, and we courted at the local dance hall and at the flicks. She was working at Sunderland Infirmary while I was in London. It was all a bit different in those days – especially as she was a good Catholic girl – and on the odd occasion she was allowed to visit me in London she had to have permission from her parents and my landlady just to stay in the spare room, with Tom Wilson acting as my chaperon. There was no thought of sneaking off to each other's bedrooms, it was simply something that was not done. We were wed in the local village church during the close season, honeymooning at the famous Waverley Hotel in Edinburgh for a few days before joining our friends Don and Helen Sinclair on a boat on the Thames in Kingston, motoring through the locks to Oxford and back.

It was while on our honeymoon that I saved Elsie's life, a

favour she was to repay when she prodded me into having that minor operation on my nose which revealed the malignant melanoma in my face. One day we were tied up at the river bank where we decided to take advantage of the sunshine to dine alfresco on the river bank, carrying the food, a little stove, crockery and cutlery down the gangplank and on to the grass. We had just settled down to eat when we realized we had forgotten the butter, and Elsie promptly offered to go to fetch it while we carried on chatting. On her way back the boat shifted on its moorings and Elsie tumbled into the water between the boat and the bank. I heard a faint plop but it did not register, and no one noticed that she was in serious trouble. She couldn't swim at all in those days and, in fact, is not much better now. I don't know what made me glance across to the boat, but whatever it was it certainly saved Elsie. All I could see was a hand holding a pack of butter. I rushed over and hauled her out. We had been married for just a week and I was almost a widower. She was lucky not only that I turned round in time to see her hand gradually disappearing, but also that the boat did not swing back into the bank as it tends to do, either to crush her or knock her unconscious. We haven't had too many boating holidays since.

After we were wed Elsie came to London where she found a job as a state registered nurse at St Stephens. We were reminded of those days recently when we went to see the brilliant West End show *Letter of Resignation* at the Comedy Theatre with Edward Fox and John Warnabe, recalling the days of Harold Macmillan and the 1963 Profumo scandal. Elsie had gone back to work at St Stephens after my 1962 move to Fulham for a second spell there, and Dr Stephen Ward, a leading player in the affair, died at the hospital while Elsie was there.

When I moved to West Bromwich Albion in 1956 Elsie, of

course, had to hand in her own letter of resignation and find a job for herself in the Midlands. She eventually took a post at the Deritend Stamping Company as an industrial nurse, although it was a little time before she was able to join me. There was no question of Elsie stopping work altogether as a footballer's salary was still capped in those days at a very low level: twenty pounds during the season and eighteen in the summer as I remember, and that only after a recent increase from fourteen and twelve pounds.

I moved down to the Black Country initially to digs on my own where, I was told, I would be breathing in pure iron filings and would wake up to hear the birds coughing out the dawn chorus. Indeed, our training ground was surrounded by heavy industry on three sides and the cut, or canal, on the other, the canal where Jimmy Hagan took an unscheduled dip in his car on his way home from training. The Albion players saved their rather abrasive manager from a watery grave that day. I discount the theory that there was some debate first! The manager when I was at the Hawthorns was that astute tactician Vic Buckingham, a manager who learned the art under push-and-run expert Arthur Rowe of Tottenham Hotspur repute. Buckingham was vastly experienced – he had also had a spell in Holland at Ajax – and was not afraid to take on board the harsh lessons learned from the Hungarians and to experiment with our style of play. He turned the Baggies, as West Brom were known locally, into an impressive side until he lost his job after being named in a divorce action.

I quickly became used to the Midlands once Elsie moved down – in fact I loved it. I liked the friendliness of the area and especially the wit and the humour of the Black Country folk with their Enoch and Eli jokes and their own particular language, not that far removed from our own Geordie dialect.

While I was waiting for my wife to join me I made friends with the cultured West Brom full-back Don Howe who turned out to be a confidant for life and my strong right arm during my eight years as England manager. Don was a quality player, but the Baggies were full of top-notch players like Ronnie Allen, Jimmy Dugdale, Derek Kevan, Barlow, Joe Kennedy, Frank Griffin, George Lee, Jimmy Dudley and Maurice Setters.

We played lovely football and that provided me with the platform to gain recognition and earn my England spurs. It was in the days when the International Committee was in full power; they picked the team and then passed the names on to the coach Walter Winterbottom. It was a crazy system nurtured in football's Stone Age as chairmen of various clubs fought with each other to select their own players, leaving Walter to pick up the pieces. I made my debut in November 1957 against France and went on to win twenty caps, scoring four goals. But I was quickly taught to take nothing for granted and when the new year rolled around I found myself dropped from the next game. I was involved in both the 1958 and 1962 World Cups, but England made little impact – certainly we were not as productive as the quality of our players would suggest.

My first game was memorable in every sense, for not only did we win 4–0, I managed to score a couple of goals myself. The other two goals were scored by a tremendous centre-forward called Tommy Taylor and he, along with Duncan Edwards and Roger Byrne, was one of the fabulous Busby Babes of the time. Poignantly my first game proved to be their last: in February, fewer than three months later, they were taken from us in the 1958 Munich disaster. It was a terrible loss to English football and the national game's immediate future. I was particularly grateful that I had the opportunity of playing with Duncan Edwards, a young man with the world at his feet. He was a truly outstanding talent, capable of reaching God knows what heights. He seemed to be able to do anything and had an engaging personality to go with it. His loss was mourned even more in our area for although he was a star of Manchester United he was very much a local Dudley boy, worshipped by everyone.

My first taste of the World Cup Finals in 1958 threw up another example of the autocratic nature of the Football Association at the time, as they decided to cut the squad from twenty-two to twenty and the two players left at home, pre-sumably to the delight of our opponents, were Stanley Matthews and Nat Lofthouse. Both were still in their pomp with Nat having just put two goals past Manchester United to win the FA Cup for Bolton Wanderers; Stan, four years later, was one of the stars against Brazil at Wembley when he ran the outstanding full-back Nilton Santos ragged. Even so we were pretty sure that we would go through our group in Sweden as we were paired with the Soviet Union, Brazil and Austria, with two teams to qualify. But there were ominous signs when Tom Finney was injured in our first game against Russia in the Ullevi Stadium; there were no substitutes then and he finished the game but did not play again. I thought I had scored when a shot from my Albion colleague Derek Kevan came back off goal-keeper Lev Yashin and I stuck in the rebound. To this day I do not know why it was disallowed, and the result was that we drew 2–2 instead of recording a valuable win.

The next game was against Brazil and, to my eternal regret, a certain seventeen-year-old prodigy who went by the name of Pelé did not play. Nor, to my great disappointment, was Garrincha in the team. I would love to be able to say that I was once on the same park as the greatest ever footballer, but his time in the tournament was to come later and, in any case, I had my hands full with two other talented players, Didi and the balding Dino. We drew 0–0 and again luck was against us as we failed to win a penalty when Derek Kevan was brought down in the box. That left us needing to beat Austria in our third group game, but again we drew 2–2 and I had what I felt was a perfectly legitimate goal ruled out. The result meant that we finished with the same points and the same goals for and against as the Soviet Union, so we faced them in a play-off for a place in the quarter-finals. I was dropped in favour of Peter Broadbent, England went out to a single goal from Ilyin and we were on our way home. We lacked a little inspiration, the sort that might have come from the brilliant Tom Finney – or even Stanley Matthews and Nat Lofthouse.

Despite my sadness at being dropped and my frustration after England were edged out, I was in love with the competition. Unless you have played at that level it is impossible to appreciate the huge differences between club football, international football and the World Cup. Every player faced was of the highest quality and there were no apparent weaknesses; mistakes were punished and the standard was unflagging. I loved the challenge and wanted to be involved again.

The next World Cup in Chile four years later was even more of a calamity, both for me and for the country. I was injured, cracking an ankle bone in a warm-up match in Peru on the way out to Chile, and lost my place to a young whippersnapper called Bobby Moore – I was more of a defensive wing-half by then – and that proved to be the end of my international career. We had, on paper, a good team in Walter Winterbottom's fourth and last World Cup with Bobby Charlton, Bryan Douglas, Jimmy Greaves, Johnny Haynes, Ron Flowers, the aforementioned Moore, Ron Springett, Ray Wilson, Gerry Hitchens and Maurice Norman, and there was quiet confidence about our chances. I watched from the sidelines as we lost to the eventual group winners Hungary, beat Argentina 3–1 and then drew with Bulgaria to earn a quarter-final place against Brazil where two goals from the outstanding Garrincha sent us tumbling to a 3–1 defeat. The sadness for me was that I would have been fit for the semi-final had we made it – and, of course, had I been selected.

That defeat really sounded the death knell for me and my mentor Winterbottom. It was known Walter was going, and I was sharing a room on that trip with Jimmy Adamson of Burnley who was fully expected to take over when Walter stepped down. To everyone's surprise he refused the position and the FA turned instead to Alf Ramsey – and the rest, as they say, is history. I still felt good enough to have made the squad four years later when I was playing deep alongside the centre-half; I knew I was the best in London in the role and thought that I could do a decent job for England at Wembley. I guess there were a lot of us about who fancied our chances. Alf didn't agree with my conviction and, on reflection, he was probably right. In any case, England won the World Cup in 1966 without me.

My entire life was to change after that World Cup in Chile, but my time in the England squad and the influence of Walter Winterbottom shaped my future career. As at West Bromwich Albion, on the national stage I roomed and knocked around with Don Howe, and one day in 1958 Walter had approached us both and asked us what we planned to do when our playing days ended. We weren't sure at that stage but he urged Don and I to go to Lilleshall and take up coaching under his guidance. He could see how interested we both were in the game, its tactics and nuances. I owe Walter a lot for seeing that we had potential in that direction. He was a nice man who had a huge influence upon me and others of our generation. It was Walter, for instance, who showed me how to handle a difficult job with great dignity, coping with the egos on the International Committee and forming teams out of their selections. He didn't have the pressures that the job developed by the time I became manager, but his were pressures of a totally different kind and I doubt whether I could have managed to keep my composure under the circumstances in which he was forced to operate.

I returned from the World Cup in Chile looking forward to another season with West Bromwich Albion. I had settled well in the Midlands and I loved the place, and Elsie and I were very happy in our home. We had saved up £425 in cash and in 1957 had used it to put down a deposit on a house in Handsworth, borrowing £2,000 for the balance. West Bromwich Albion director Bert Millichip was also a solicitor and he completed the conveyancing for me on the property, the same Bert Millichip who was to become my boss at the Football Association when I was manager of England. He was a big help at the time and saved me a lot of money. Having been brought up in a fairly frugal manner I was almost paranoid about borrowing so much money – it worried me to death. I continually wondered what would happen if I broke my leg and how I would pay it off. It was a nightmare.

That didn't happen. I had already started to play for England by 1957, earning an extra twenty pounds when I played, and had been made captain of the Albion team. Although we didn't win anything we were always up there challenging with the best, who at that time were Manchester United's Busby Babes, Stan Cullis's great Wolves side, the Spurs team who were heading towards their great Double side, Burnley, local rivals Aston Villa and Arsenal.

The house we bought was close enough for me to be able to

walk to the Hawthorns. I couldn't afford a car and we weren't allowed to ride bikes, so team-mate and neighbour David Burnside and I would take the twenty minutes to half an hour walk together. He was a great ball juggler and always carried a tennis ball in his pocket and we used to play headers and pass the ball along the streets on the way to training. It must have looked somewhat strange, two grown men footballing their way from Handsworth to West Bromwich. We must have made an odd-looking couple. Can you imagine that happening now? Now they drive to the ground in a Mercedes or a Ferrari. We arrived belting the ball backwards and forwards against that long wall that runs behind the goal along the main Birmingham Road. After training some would go off to play snooker or have a bet, but Don, I and a few others would go to the local café for a bite to eat and talk football, football and more football. It was a great learning experience.

Yes, I enjoyed my time at the Hawthorns, but it all fell apart over the abolition of the maximum wage. I was captain of the side at the time and the players had asked for the top salary to be raised from twenty to twenty-five pounds. It was refused, so we all threatened to go on strike. Jimmy Hill and Cliff Lloyd, the chairman and secretary of the Professional Footballers' Association, had fought for an end to the maximum wage, finally winning and creating the first hundred-pound-a-week salary, the lucky recipient of such untold wealth none other than my old team-mate and former Fulham office boy Johnny Haynes. It was the breakthrough we had all been waiting for and I thought that I would be on a good salary as captain and a current England international, but chairman Jim Gaunt offered me just twenty-five pounds a week and a fiver a match in appearance money. The five pounds was not even guaranteed; if I was dropped or injured and then couldn't win back my place, I wouldn't receive it. I had just come back from the World Cup in Chile and was in the same team as Johnny Haynes, so I thought it unfair. We had fought a bitter battle over our rights and here I was back to where I had started. I was upset and promptly asked for a transfer. They took the captaincy off me and gave it to my mate Don Howe and put me on the transfer list in August 1962.

Within a very short time Fulham came in with a bid of £20,000 and, after six years, I was on my way back to Craven Cottage. They had since been promoted back to the top division, but were pulling up no trees. The season before I arrived was typical: Fulham just missed out on a glamorous FA Cup Final appearance against Spurs when they lost 2–1 to 'Double'-chasing Burnley in a semi-final replay, at the same time avoiding relegation by one point in twentieth place. Nothing, it seemed, had changed since I was last at the club in 1956.

My old inside-forward partner Bedford Jezzard was now manager and he joined the traditional roller-coaster ride, guiding us to a ten-goal victory over Ipswich who then put four past us a couple of days later on our own ground. But the signs were good, particularly with the development of a brilliant young Londoner named Alan Mullery. With his youth and my experience we fancied our chances, but suddenly the board pulled the rug from under our feet when they sold him to Spurs for £72,500 to help pay for a new stand that was being built. It was a potty thing to do, especially as it was done behind Jezzard's back. He was so upset that eventually he resigned, and who should take over in 1965 but my old Albion manager Vic Buckingham. But the impetus had been lost, and Fulham's prospects were further impaired when another bright young kid, Rodney Marsh, was sold to Queens Park Rangers, although Buckingham did pick up one nugget when he signed goalscorer

Allan Clarke from Walsall, who was later to move to Leeds United for a record-breaking fee.

Fulham certainly had some excellent players when I returned in 1962. In addition to Johnny Haynes and Alan Mullery there was George Cohen, who went on to grab fame as a member of the England team that won the 1966 World Cup, the Scot Graham Leggat, who scored some fine individual goals for the club, and Eddie Lowe. The problem was that despite all this talent we were still, as in the 1950s, two or three players short of a team capable of scaling the heights, and that is why we didn't go on to win any silverware. Had the club dared to invest a bit of money, then who knows what might have happened at Craven Cottage? But it was the opposite case, and when Mullery was allowed to leave to go to Spurs it was clear the board didn't have the ambition to go that extra mile. Fulham was a great club and we played lovely entertaining football, but the killer instinct, the necessary motivation for top-flight sport, was lacking.

Although I felt I still had several decent years left in me as a player, I needed, indeed, wanted, to start mapping out a future for myself in terms of coaching.

3

The First Stumbling Steps

I had, of course, already begun my journey down this road. Under the guidance of Walter Winterbottom I began the FA coaching course with Don Howe in 1958, qualifying for a full badge before travelling out to Chile with England for the 1962 World Cup. I remember very clearly my first day in front of a class. I was asked to talk for three minutes on the subject of football boots, and I was generously given a whole minute to prepare a speech about studs, shape, protection, lacing and anything else I could think of that was relevant. A student could be thrown any subject at any time, and the experience certainly stood me in good stead later in life in terms of speech-making duties. The course also helped me as a player, giving me a greater insight into what was going on around me, and I would recommend any player to attend such a course because it can only help in every respect. I am eternally grateful to Walter for the way in which he helped me; he was my mentor and I an FA disciple.

The same goes for former FA coach Alan Wade who really was the man to launch me on my career. When I returned from Chile and rejoined Fulham, Alan was soon in touch with me, asking if I wanted some coaching work. I jumped at the chance, because although the maximum wage had been lifted by that time I was still on a smallish salary and I had three growing sons

and a house in Worcester Park to pay for. Alan knew I was looking for some coaching experience and he felt that a spell with
Oxford University's football team would be a good thing for
me. So did I. Vic Buckingham, himself at one time deeply
involved in the amateur game at Varsity level (Ron Greenwood
had also done the job) and having managed the club Pegasus
comprising old boys of the two major universities, not only
gave me leave from Craven Cottage to carry out the role, but
positively encouraged it. So I went on Tuesdays and Thursdays
to coach the Dark Blues at the standard rate of two guineas a
session. I was only too happy to travel the 240 miles per week at
their expense.

I probably learned a great deal more from it than the boys
learned from me. It taught me how to stand up in front of a
group and address it with confidence, how to put on practice
sessions, how to motivate and search for a player's qualities. It
was wonderful to coach intelligent boys who took in every word
you uttered and did their best to put into practice what I told
them, and although the standard, naturally, was amateurish
they were a decent bunch of footballers; in my two years there
we beat Cambridge both times in the Varsity match. It was very
satisfying because they hadn't beaten their rivals for several
years.

I managed to keep myself quite busy outside the Varsity
games. I was a staff coach and fully paid-up member of the
Surrey Football Coaches Association – I am now the president
– and on their behalf I oversaw local preliminary courses for
school teachers, youth club and boys' club leaders and anyone
else who wanted to improve their knowledge of the game. I also
worked out of Crystal Palace National Recreation Centre along
with the head coach, the late Bill Whitaker, lecturing to, practising with and assessing contenders for the diploma, again at

the standard fee: two pounds two shillings per session. In all I was coaching and teaching somewhere a couple of times a week throughout my second spell as a player at Fulham. I even did a bit of freelancing. A friend of mine wrote to me, knowing I was handily placed at Worcester Park, to ask if I would like to help the players for the Pearl Assurance company prepare themselves for the season. It was two evenings a week, Monday and Friday, which suited me perfectly, and the money was three shillings over the standard fee, so I said yes.

All this meant that by 1967, when Southend enquired after my services as a player-manager, I had logged up plenty of coaching miles. I drove from London to Brentwood in Essex to meet one of their directors, the outstanding ex-England cricketer Trevor Bailey, the furthest I had driven in my newly acquired Morris Minor, my very first car at the age of thirty-four! I still felt I had a good year or two in the old legs, but it wasn't in my mind to drop down two divisions, nor was the money good enough to tempt me to pack in what I had and take a gamble. In fact, the club offered considerably less than the £3,500 salary I was still earning at Fulham. It wasn't a sensible option at the time. I was, of course, seriously tempted by Arsenal, of whose interest I was informed, but that came to nothing too, and I can only suspect that Fulham wanted too much for a player nearing the end of his playing career. I don't know for sure, because in those days players had no agents and they weren't involved in any of the negotiations, and had I enquired I would have been told it was club business and to keep my nose out of it.

I was serious about wanting to take up a player-coach post, so that's why in 1967 I quit playing and set off for Canada when the newly formed Vancouver Royals asked me to put together a squad for the coming North American season. Canada looked to be a great challenge as it meant starting with a clean slate and putting together my own team, albeit with what they described as multinational bargain basement buys. The biggest problem was persuading Elsie to take our three sons – Paul Martin, Andrew Peter and Robert Mark – out of school, uproot the family and head off to the unknown. It must have been a massive wrench for my wife and it was certainly a foretaste of things to come in later years, but she agreed and we set sail on the good ship SS *Oriana* to start a new life.

That was an experience in itself. I had not had a break for years so I negotiated that we (myself, my wife and our three boys) should go the long, slow way rather than fly, travelling first class, sailing via the Panama Canal and visiting places like Los Angeles, San Francisco, Bermuda and Port Everglades. The voyage took three weeks. I felt very good about the whole thing for I had fallen in love with Vancouver on an end-of-season visit there with West Bromwich Albion, and the new club had generously doubled my Fulham wages and were paying me the Canadian-dollar equivalent of about £7,000 a year. The job also excited the adventurer within me and I felt like a pioneer going into this huge area where football was a minor sport. I was to be at the sharp end and it meant I could play a bit longer at a level I could cope with. Apart from raising a team I was also contracted to promote the game and the newly formed club in and around Vancouver, holding coaching clinics, speaking at dinners and generally selling the game to the public. It all sounded rather special and the first few weeks were extremely exciting.

Then reality set in. Four months before the start of the season we still had no team, and not only did I have no money to give players contracts, I was not being paid myself. I had been promised the dollar equivalent of a £6,000 salary per player and I had given assurances to a handful of English footballers including Johnny Green from Blackpool, Peter Dinsdale from Huddersfield, Henry Hill and Pat O'Connell from my old club Fulham, as well as the Cypriot national goalkeeper – recommended to me by the great Arsenal and Wales goalkeeper Jack Kelsey – and a couple of skilful Chinese brothers, Chung Si Doi and Chung Si Wai, who played up front for Hong Kong when Fulham visited the island at the end of the 1964/65 season. There was method in the apparent madness for there was a growing Chinese population in Vancouver, already in excess of 300,000, and a great many Cypriots. I was trying to use my brain instead of just my feet for the first time in my life.

The club was in serious financial turmoil long before a ball had been kicked. No one was being paid and the prospects were looking exceedingly grim. An urgent search began for new financial backing and it looked as though we had been saved when George Flaherty, the owner of San Francisco Gales, pledged his support and merged the two clubs. That was just a continuation of my problems though because Flaherty had already appointed Ferenc Puskas – who had been one of my heroes since the day I watched the outstanding Hungarian team of the 1950s shatter England's unbeaten Wembley record – as the new coach of the Gales, paid him half as much again as I was supposed to be paid and set him up with a training camp in Madrid where the Hungarian had finished his glittering playing career with Real Madrid. My strength lay in the fact that the team was still to be based as Vancouver Royals in Canada and my contract stated that I was the head coach of that team. Flaherty wanted me out but I stood my ground and waved the contract under his nose.

But there we were with two squads being formed on two continents and two managers to run the same team. I was promptly dispatched to Spain to work with the man with the magic left foot. It was chaos. Puskas may be one of the greatest players the world has ever seen but he was unable to translate that talent into coaching. He had advertised in the Spanish newspapers inviting anyone who wanted to come to turn up for trials. He had a mixture of his mates from Hungary and Spain around him and it was not looking good. There was a bad feeling about the place with some of the players claiming they were having to pay 10 per cent of their salaries to Puskas as agents' fees, and they came to see me as their only hope of having this anomaly changed. It put me in a difficult position; Puskas and I could not even see eye to eye on football matters, on the rare occasions when we understood what the other was talking about. When I approached Flaherty about the problems he wouldn't hear a word said against Puskas and I knew exactly where I stood – with my back firmly against the wall. Clearly the owner had promised the Hungarian that he and he alone would be running the club.

It was a depressing situation and I returned to Vancouver to spend Christmas with my family and to see solicitors to try to recover the considerable amount of money, some 42,000 Canadian dollars, I was owed. I had a cast-iron case with my contract for head coach and my legal advisers told me not to work but to fight for the compensation I was legally due. It sounded good in practice but I was anxious to set my managerial career in motion, and when my old club Fulham, via secretary Graham Hortop, enquired about my availability I decided I couldn't wait for compensation, albeit amid much tut-tutting from my legal eagles. It proved to be the right decision as the Royals inevitably went bust at the end of a very short season lasting four months and I would have been left holding solicitors' bills and nothing else.

Little did I know then, but I was jumping out of the frying

pan and into the fire. It all looked fine, especially after my experience in Canada, as I met Hortop, the chairman Tommy Trinder and the financial muscle of the club Sir Eric Miller. They say in football that you are not a real manager until you have been sacked. I qualified straight away, lasting just over nine months – and that included the close season!

Fulham were in some trouble when I arrived in January 1968 and there was little I could do at that late stage to help them avoid yet another relegation. With the limited squad at my disposal we did not start the next season brilliantly either, but it still came as a massive surprise when I read in the newspapers in November that I had been sacked. After the disaster in Canada it was a shattering experience, especially as I had signed a three-year contract and fully expected to turn things around.

I had already set the wheels in motion by raising for the club a £150,000 profit by selling striker Allan Clarke to Matt Gillies at Leicester, who Allan surprisingly chose over the more glamorous Manchester United and the legendary Matt Busby. The deal suited me because there was a player exchange involved with the much-travelled Frank Large coming to Craven Cottage together with the balance in cash. I also bought a rough and ready left full-back from non-league Tonbridge for just £1,000. Chief scout Harry Haslam and I thought we saw something in this kid with a dynamic left foot and a bustling style and that we could turn him into a damaging centre-forward. We were not far off the mark, as was proved when Harry Haslam eventually took the kid to Luton and then watched his career take off with Newcastle United, Arsenal and England. His name? Oh yes, Malcolm MacDonald!

We had already begun to make progress, sorting out the dead wood, but the board panicked when we started the 1968/9

41

season moderately. In my place they installed my old mate Johnny Haynes, one of the great players and a wonderful servant to Fulham but never, ever cut out to be a manager. He lasted exactly a month before he realized it was not for him. Bill Dodgin junior, another good buddy of mine, was promptly brought in but still Fulham were relegated to the Third Division. I didn't envy Bill his job because even in the short time I had been back at Craven Cottage I had suffered interference from Eric Miller, who wanted to have his say in the buying and selling of players and, incredibly, in team selection. He was a strong, powerful man and although still not the chairman he was in control as the money behind the throne. That certainly was not my scene. I wasn't having that and I fought back.

I was on my way home from the ground when I saw the *Evening Standard* billboards proclaiming 'Robson Sacked'. I couldn't believe it, but when I read that the story was by Bernard Joy, an ex-Arsenal centre-half turned journalist, two and two suddenly became four. Bernard had telephoned me at the ground earlier in the day to ask if everything was all right. I was baffled and asked him why it shouldn't be. He didn't elucidate other than to say that something was up and my position could be in doubt, but he had stirred my interest enough to ask Graham Hortop what was going on. He claimed he knew nothing at that stage. I called Hortop back after reading the story and he was clearly embarrassed at the situation and told me I was to be at a meeting with the directors in the morning. I rang Chappie D'Amato, one of the directors I knew and liked, and he was even more embarrassed than Hortop and simply didn't want to talk about it.It was clearly nothing to do with him. The decision was out of his hands.

I attended the meeting with the Dean family, really nice people who owned a large slice of the club, but it was not them or anyone else making the decision – it was Miller. He sacked me that morning without a thought. He was curt and direct and told me that results were not good enough. I remember going out on to the pitch at Craven Cottage, looking around at the ground that had meant so much to me over the years and crying like a baby. I had had two wonderful spells as a player and another as a manager. They were happy years and it was heart-rending that it should end like this. I decided then that I would never go back to the club in any capacity.

It was to raise money to build the Eric Miller Stand that Alan Mullery had been sold to Spurs a few years earlier and history proves that Miller was not good for the club. That he eventually committed suicide by shooting himself gave me no satisfaction, for I have never been vindictive or bitter. But cross, yes! I had bought a house in the Surrey stockbroker belt, installed my family there and here I was out of work and wondering what the heck I was going to do to pay the mortgage and keep the boys at their fee-paying school. Walking our retriever on the local golf course was the highlight of my day as I waited for something to turn up, but in the end I was forced to eat humble pie and join the dole queue. I had been putting off going to the local job centre for weeks and my savings drained away. I had hoped something would come up quickly but nothing did. I had written away for a couple of jobs and had no reply, and in the end I was left with no choice but to join what I thought would be a bunch of scroungers and idlers. But any embarrassment soon disappeared when I realized that those in the Labour Exchange with me were businessmen, bank managers and even a retired army major. We were all in the same boat.

But the situation was increasingly depressing, particularly with the winter holidays on the doorstep. We didn't even have a television at the time and I thought we should have one for the boys to enjoy during their long break. I called *Radio Rentals* to hire a set and almost didn't get one when the engineer asked me what work I did and I told him I didn't have a job. I had to pay up front to make sure we had what we wanted.

I was down but not out. After two serious disappointments my resolve was greater than ever that I was going to make it as a coach or a manager. It toughened me up and I vowed that I was going to stand up to people and be determined about my future. The problem was that I had nothing to fall back on. I hadn't managed a single game in Canada and I'd had fewer than ten months at Fulham, some of which had been close season.

The Robsons looked to be heading for a bleak end to the decade when Chelsea manager Dave Sexton called me and kindly asked me to do some scouting for him. I jumped at the chance, but imagine my discomfiture when my first assignment was to watch Ipswich play Nottingham Forest at Portman Road. Both teams were without managers and I felt that everyone would think I had gone to the game touting for a job. Oh well, I thought, I might as well be hung for a sheep as a lamb, and the next day I wrote off to Ipswich Town and Nottingham Forest applying for the vacancy. There was nothing from Forest, but Ipswich came back to me to talk about the job created when Bill McGarry had left after four years. Although a small club, Ipswich had enjoyed incredible success under Alf Ramsey, winning the title in 1962, and had a reputation for looking after their managers. In fact since 1936 they had employed only five, and of those managers Scott Duncan continued as secretary after eighteen years in the job and Ramsey left after eight years to take over at England. I was, however, a long way down the pecking order with Frank O'Farrell and Billy Bingham the bookmakers' favourites. But fate decreed that

Frank opted to stay with Torquay, saying he would only leave for a club with greater potential, while Billy preferred to stay with Plymouth. No one could argue with their decisions as Frank went on to manage Manchester United and Billy, Everton and Northern Ireland.

In January 1969, two days after I had submitted my application, I was summoned to meet the affable chairman John Cobbold, Harold Smith and Ken Brightwell at the Great Western Hotel in London. I liked Mr John, as he was always known, straightaway but he could see my concern when he told me that they would prefer to dispense with the formality of a contract. 'Don't worry,' he promised, 'that means at least two years at this club.' I was in no position to turn the offer down, whatever the conditions laid upon me – I needed a job and I needed it badly. We asked each other a few questions and they offered me the job at around £5,000 a year. I asked to be excused for a short while to think about it, but soon returned to shake hands on the deal. I was in work again and determined to make it succeed.

I still had my doubts though. A guaranteed two years! Oh yes, I thought, struggle for results and see how well that promise holds. But it did. It was watertight. Everyone remembers my successful years at Ipswich but few recall those first two years when we did indeed struggle. I clashed with players and heard the crowd chant for my head, upsetting Elsie as she sat in the stand listening to them screaming 'Robson out, Robson out' as a little Irishman named George Best took my defence to pieces at Portman Road during the 1970/1 season. The supporters were not fair on that occasion because Best was in a different class that night, showing his full range of skills and scoring a classic hat trick – one with his right foot, one with his left and a wonderful back-post header. I remember turning to Frank

O'Farrell, by then at the helm at Old Trafford, afterwards and saying that had we been lucky enough to have Best on our side that night the result would have been reversed. He didn't disagree.

The chairman Mr John called a board meeting the next day and I feared the worst. He brought the board to attention and said: 'Gentlemen, the first business of the day is to officially record in the minutes the apologies of this board to the manager for the behaviour of the fans last night. Agreed? If it ever occurs in this ground again, I will resign as chairman. Right, on to the next business.' He then gave me permission to go out and spend £70,000 on central defender Allan Hunter, and myself and Ron Gray, my chief scout, set off to Blackburn Rovers to watch him play. I was fully expecting him to be the star of the show but he was bloody awful. I bought him on the basis of that poor performance, thinking he couldn't ever play that badly again. Ron Gray confirmed that he had never seen him as bad as that and we took a calculated gamble knowing that we would never get a better footballer for that sort of money.

The behaviour of Mr John and his board was the norm at Portman Road and when the team slumped to the bottom of the division in 1971 I was given a new, improved contract. John Cobbold was quoted as saying, 'Our manager's name is not written in chalk on his door with a wet sponge nailed by the side.' The precedent for the longevity of Ipswich managers was probably set by John's father, Captain Cobbold, who, as the story goes, appointed Scott Duncan as manager before leaving on a prolonged business appointment abroad. While he was away not all went to plan and Captain Cobbold responded by cabling the manager with instructions to 'Buy Rimmer of Sheffield Wednesday.' Duncan responded with his own cable declaring: 'Will not buy Rimmer of Sheffield Wednesday.' The irate chairman came back: 'I insist you buy Rimmer of Sheffield Wednesday', only to be trumped again with the reply: 'I insist I won't buy Rimmer of Sheffield Wednesday.' Exasperated beyond belief Captain Cobbold instantly cabled: 'Consider yourself sacked.' The correspondence ended with the final retort: 'Will not accept the sack.' The chairman knew then he had a manager strong of mind and will, and not only did he keep Duncan on, he set a trend for the future of the club, one I was certainly very happy to benefit from.

Mr John and his brother Patrick, who later had his spell as chairman, took everything in their stride and were never flustered or angry. The only time they ever recognized a crisis was one day when they discovered that the boardroom was short of Sancerre. When the club clinched a big sponsorship deal John Cobbold addressed the gathered media: 'It has been suggested that we will squander the sponsors' money on wine, women and song. That is absolute nonsense. We do not do a lot of singing at Portman Road.' He liked a drink and a cigarette did John, and he often claimed that was why he enjoyed our qualifying for Europe year after year because he could buy his duty free on our trips. He loved those away-leg nights, and when he set off to taste the delights of another new city he would carefully write the name of the hotel on his shirt cuff so that he could find his way home.

One day he walked into a board meeting at Portman Road and spotted brother Patrick sitting at the table wearing a tweed jacket, plus-fours and an old checked shirt with frayed cuffs and bones sticking out of the collars. I thought he was looking even scruffier than usual, but I was staggered when John exploded, 'Patrick you s—, you're wearing papa's shirt! I've been looking everywhere for that.' Papa – Captain Cobbold – had been killed by a German buzz bomb that had scored a direct hit on the

Guards Chapel in 1941. Personally I wouldn't have worn that shirt to do the gardening. Patrick did not care. He had a black retriever which he regularly brought with him to games. He was forever asking me to keep it in my office during the match but I wouldn't have any of it because I'd've had to clean up the mess, so I asked him to keep it in the boardroom. When I arrived to join the directors after one game there was this dog of his drinking water out of a beautiful crystal dish we had been awarded for winning a five-a-side tournament after beating Glasgow Rangers in the final.

John was the more charismatic of the two brothers and was a popular figure in the game. It was no surprise when the South East Counties League invited him to become their president. He accepted before realizing it would mean a speech at a dinner in a fashionable London hotel. He wanted me for moral support and we travelled down together by train, avoiding the traffic and arriving early, so early that the bar was still shut. John knew the barman and asked if we could have a drink. The barman replied that the bar was closed. 'That's alright,' responded Johnny, 'we will have a drink while we wait.' John, against my advice, took his Dutch courage and then continued drinking through the meal and the other, elongated speeches, including one by Lawrie McMenemy. Eventually it was his turn but when he stood up he swayed, closed his eyes and sank grace-fully to the floor. He disappeared under the table and never said a word. He was carried out to a standing ovation; the applause was prolonged and thunderous. What an inaugural speech! What style! What class! Whoever said that the best speeches are the shortest speeches clearly did not have this in mind. The chairman of Spurs, Sidney Wale, loaned us his chauffeur-driven limousine to take us to Liverpool Street Station where we poured Mr John onto the train and took him home.

No one was surprised because they knew about Mr John's little failings and how much he liked the odd glass or two. He and the Arsenal board had a particularly good relationship as the two dominant families, the Cobbolds and the Hill-Woods, had long been friends, and there was always a great spirit between the two clubs with each board entertaining the other to lunch at their ground whenever the two teams met. John brought the house down one Saturday when, as the buzzer went for them to take their seats for the start of the game, Arsenal director and official club chaplain the Reverend Bone said, 'Best of luck, may the best team win,' to which John replied, 'F—— good luck – we *want* to win.'

People rarely took umbrage against him even though he had the habit of using bad language, often just for effect. Sometimes he overdid it, though, and he actually cost me a player once with his wicked sense of the ridiculous. I was entertaining a Portsmouth player who I was quite keen to sign, keen enough to take him and his wife on a guided tour of the ground and the city and finish up at the chairman's house. John had a beautiful home set in 2,000 gloriously landscaped acres with two black swans floating on a lake. On his back lawn he kept two donkeys, mother and son called Alka and Seltzer, who enjoyed an illicit relationship and spawned a foal aptly named Calamity. As we took tea on the lawn with the player and his wife, John turned casually to the player and said: 'You don't f— donkeys, do you?' The player and his wife were staggered and promptly turned on their heels and walked out. Needless to say the Portsmouth player never came to Ipswich, but John thought the entire episode hilarious.

On another occasion we were at a banquet to celebrate one of our two FA Youth Cup victories in the mid-1970s. We invited the mothers and fathers, the landladies, the players –

everyone. It was a marvellous do at the Copdock Hotel with a band and magnificent food, and as it came to an end I persuaded Mr John that he should make a speech and thank everyone for coming. He made me accompany him to the centre of the stage, the band gave him a drum roll and Mr John thanked everyone for coming, praised the brilliant young players and finally turned to me and said: 'The manager here wants to win the competition again in eighteen years' time so I want you all to go home and have a jolly good f— and produce another team.' I couldn't believe what I was hearing – I just wanted a big hole to open up and swallow me. I need not have worried. The reception was sensational: they stood on their chairs, laughed, stamped and shouted their approval. No one else could have got away with it. Not one person took offence; Mr John was their hero.

He had a great sense of humour did John, and when we opened the new indoor training centre, heavily backed by our sponsors Pioneer, he insisted no one went near the new facility until the official opening. We found out why when he finally allowed in all the dignitaries and the players and there, in one half of the artificial grass pitch, was a crop of mushrooms. Everyone was flabbergasted as he collapsed laughing. He had popped out to the greengrocer's earlier in the day and sneaked in to plant them ready for our arrival.

John, to be honest, did not know a great deal about football, as he showed when we visited Leicester City's Filbert Street ground early on in my reign. We quickly went a goal down, then conceded another just before the break, and Mr John came up to me and congratulated me on how well the team was play- ing. As I looked at him in astonishment he carried on to ask me what changes I had made as he did not recognize all of our players. No wonder: Leicester were playing in blue and we were in our away change strip of yellow. He hadn't noticed and thought we were two goals up.

He was always particularly keen to win at Wolves because he felt that Bill McGarry, my predecessor, had walked out on him, and when we went one up early on in one match against them he asked me if we could leave there and then. Bill McGarry had been a strong disciplinarian and one of my first jobs when I arrived at Ipswich was to repair the doors and skirting boards where he used to kick out in his anger at defeats, and there were quite a few dents because when I joined the club was fighting against relegation. Bill had become disenchanted at this 'small town club' and had moved on to Wolverhampton Wanderers where he thought there was much better potential.

In those early days at Portman Road I was a young and inexperienced manager with no money to spend. I knew I would have to wheel and deal to get anywhere and, even more importantly, develop a strong youth policy to ensure the future of the club. In those days we would have 16,000 for our top games with just 2,500 seated in the stand they called the cow shed, which I eventually sold to the local speedway club. I not only built three good teams at Ipswich – winning the FA Cup in 1978, the UEFA Cup in 1981 and two successive FA Youth Cups in 1973/4 and 1974/5 – I also left them with an excellent stadium and a good youth system. There were no grants then from organizations like the Football Trust and any money for ground improvement had to be raised by the club, after paying capital gains tax. Other clubs preferred to spend their money on buying players before the tax kicked in, and who could blame them with that sort of disincentive?

But at the beginning of the 1970s there was little to indicate those dream days ahead. It only takes one bad apple, as they say, and there were one or two wise old boys in the dressing room during the 1970/1 season who clearly decided to test me and, if possible, take control of the situation. There were several spats and matters were clearly heading for an explosion – and what an explosion it was!

It began when right-back Tommy Carroll walked out after a minor row and returned to his home in Dublin, forcing me to suspend him and leave him out of the next game against Leeds United. I also dropped his friend, Scot Bill Baxter, another who had been making the dressing room an uncomfortable place while testing me to the limits of my endurance. We lost that game 4–2 and they revelled in our misery, laughing and joking and ordering a bottle of champagne to celebrate the defeat. It was despicable behaviour and there was no way they were going to get back into the team after that, so I left them out again. When Carroll realized he and Baxter were being continually omitted from the team sheet, he tore it off the notice-board and thrust it into my face telling me to stuff my 'effing' team. That was the last straw. He made an aggressive move at me and I felt justified in defending myself, so I took a swing at him. Bill Baxter immediately joined the fray and we stood toe to toe until my number two Cyril Lea came and stood by my shoulder, joining in the escalating fight. It was like a bad bar-room joke: an Englishman, an Irishman, a Scotsman and a Welshman swinging at each other. No one was knocked down but it certainly was not handbags at ten paces; punches were thrown, and it is not an incident I recall with any pride at all.

It required big full-back Geoff Hammond and the other players to break it up. I was furious that they had stopped me for it had come to the point where the two players had challenged my authority, and the act of ripping up the team sheet was unforgivable. That team sheet was sacrosanct, and all the players knew it. It was not to be touched, defaced or removed. Had I backed down after such a violation I was finished at Ipswich and, perhaps, finished as a manager after my two previous disasters. I had to stand my ground, and I believe that was a turning point for me, the team and the club. The other players, particularly the youngsters, backed me up and even requested that the two troublemakers be made to change elsewhere for training. That was not the way to do it; segregation would have led only to further disputes, probably with the Professional Footballers' Association. They were contrite, but as far as I was concerned their days were numbered. They had played their last game for the club.

The board backed me and Mr John's instructions were to get rid of the offending players immediately, and even to give them away for nothing to expedite the matter. We weren't rich enough to take such a moral stand, especially with two quality players who, had they been with me instead of against me, would certainly have played their part. Neither played for the first team again; Carroll went to Birmingham and Baxter to Hull for a grand total of £31,000.

It took me a good three years to learn my trade and sort out that club. I was fortunate to have a top-class chief scout in Ray Tyrell who had unearthed local talent like Brian Talbot, Trevor Whymark, Mick Lambert, Clive Woods, Laurie Sivell, Roger Osborne, Colin Harper and, of course, Mick Mills who I made my club captain at the age of twenty-one. Gradually I moved the old guard out and began to replace them with my own players. When Ray Tyrell left we were again lucky to have a great back-up team in Ron Gray, John Carruthers and George Finlay. George worked from Glasgow and brought me players like John Wark, Alan Brazil and George Burley; Carruthers was even more successful with Kevin Beattie, Eric Gates, David

Geddes, Robin Turner, Tommy Parkin and, of course, Paul Gascoigne.

Yes, that Paul Gascoigne, the same Geordie I was to give his head in international football and who proved to be the best young player in the 1990 World Cup in Italy. But then this little fourteen-year-old was the original Milky Bar Kid. He was a real Billy Bunter, as broad as he was tall and so roly-poly that his natural talent rippled through rolls of fat. There was no way you could gamble on a player of his stature on our budget, so we sent him back north again. It goes to show that youngsters should never give in, should keep working at their game and their ambitions even when all looks to be lost. Denis Law was turned away by Birmingham City because he was too skinny while Coventry City decided that the young Kevin Keegan was never going to be tall enough to be a professional footballer.

I also had some good luck. My brother Tom telephoned me after watching a schoolboy game in Derby near the pit where he worked to tell me that he had spotted another Kevin Beattie. He gave me the name and telephone number of this centre-half who had impressed him. The player turned out to be a future England international and one of the rocks of Ipswich Town – Russell Osman. Two-footed, great in the air, he and Terry Butcher were unpassable in the heart of our defence.

We worked hard at the scouting and Ron Gray had a brilliant little team. We used to target areas like Newcastle and Glasgow, pinching talented youngsters from under the noses of the local clubs. I was determined not to overspend and kept all my signings within the £40,000 to £70,000 price range, but still managed to bring in players of the quality of Allan Hunter, goalkeeper Paul Cooper who was an absolute bargain for £20,000, Kevin O'Callaghan from Millwall, Frank Clark, David Johnson and Jimmy Robertson. I couldn't afford mistakes; the players not only had to be of the right quality but also of the right character. That was critical as we were very disciplined with the young players coming through the system and they needed the right role models.

I had no previous experience and there was no one in the offices or the boardroom to help or advise me. I had to be judicious in my choices and I gradually earned the reputation of being a prolific dealer. I not only brought in good-value players but also managed to sell others like David Geddes to Aston Villa for £300,000 and Brian Talbot to Arsenal for £450,000. These were the deals which not only kept the club ticking over but made it flourish.

It was a matter of personal pride to keep the club in the black and we were always looking to balance those books, like the day early on when Cyril Lea, my assistant, and I wanted to watch two different matches on the same night. One game was in Leeds and the other in Manchester, and to save money we decided to travel north in the same car. Cyril's motor was a clapped-out job which I didn't fancy at all on such a long round trip, so we took my club car and drove to the junction of the M1 and M62 where I gave Cyril the car keys to drive on to Leeds and I hitchhiked to Old Trafford, thumbing a ride on a big lorry, arranging for Cyril to leave Elland Road early and pick me up at Old Trafford.

My 'disguise' of a flat cap and muffler was not necessary because the driver was no football fan. I told him where I was going and he responded that, as luck would have it, he was driving past the ground and he would drop me off on the doorstep. It wouldn't have looked good for one of the First Division's managers to be seen arriving at Old Trafford in a big wagon, and I felt I couldn't risk being seen jumping out of a lorry, so I told him I would be grateful if he dropped me off a few hundred yards away as, I pretended, I always went to the same café to meet my mates and have a cup of coffee before we went on to cheer 'our' team.

It was a good job I took the precaution for the first person I bumped into as I walked into the ground was Sheffield United manager John Harris. Without describing the last leg of the journey I told him of our odd arrangement and he promptly offered to drive me to Sheffield where it would be easier and quicker for Cyril to collect me. A secretary at Old Trafford promptly rang Leeds and managed to pass on the message to Cyril, and the night ended well with the connection made and the return journey to Ipswich completed without mishap. But I never told Mr John. He would have died a thousand deaths to think of his manager hitching a ride while on club duty.

Gradually it all began to come together with our youth system working hand in glove with the powerful scouting set-up; the players began to work their way through to the first team and results began to come. The club appreciated it too and my salary rose accordingly. In fact, when England came in for me and asked what I earned at Ipswich, Secretary Ted Croker was so surprised that he asked for the figure to be verified. At that time I was on £72,000 and I had to accept a cut in wages from the FA to take the job. England was about the only job which could have prised me away from Ipswich. I not only had an excellent wage, my choice of car and a winning team but I also had a great quality of life that few clubs anywhere in the world could match.

4

On a Roll at Portman Road

There is nothing more attractive to football clubs than the successful manager of another club. Top teams from around the country and Europe must have thought I was gasping to escape the claustrophobic confines of little Ipswich Town. But they could not have been more wrong.

Ipswich's achievements naturally caught the attentions of clubs looking to replace a departing manager or simply looking for a change of fortune. Illness had forced Harry Catterick to retire at Everton and they came looking in my direction in 1973, the first of several attempts over the years. They knew I wasn't under contract at the time and it was all very tempting, but the Cobbold brothers stepped in with a staggering offer amounting to a ten-year contract which offered me the sort of security my family and I craved since the fiascos at Vancouver and Fulham. Derby County also came knocking on the door when Brian Clough and Peter Taylor left in October 1973. The colourful Derby chairman Sam Longson told me that money was no object as long as I made a quick decision. Derby had become a leading club under Clough and the offer was worth more than a passing nod, but I wasn't sure of the set-up at the Baseball Ground because previously everything had revolved around the larger-than-life manager. I took the opportunity of a game against Arsenal to have a quiet word with Bertie Mee about them and he had no hesitation in warning me that I would be walking into a minefield if I took up Sam on his offer.

On the international front, Bilbao came in from Spain during the 1973/4 season, and Saudi Arabia offered me their national coaching job in October 1977 at a silly salary of £70,000. I secretly popped out to Bilbao to have a look at what this great Basque club was offering. A former West Bromwich Albion team-mate, Ronnie Allen, had managed them with great success and the club, founded and named by British migrants, was steeped in English traditions. Unfortunately I was caught out and had to go cap in hand to the chairman to tell him that I had only gone to look and that I had promised them nothing and didn't intend to leave Ipswich. Earlier on in my career at Ipswich, during the 1976 season, Barcelona came in with buckets and buckets of money, guaranteeing me a minimum of £115,000, three times my already very good salary, but they were not prepared to pay £200,000 to Ipswich in compensation for my not completing ten-year contract.

By far the strangest and most mysterious of approaches came in 1974 when our Portman Road switchboard received a call from the West Riding Referees Association. I took the call expecting it to be another invitation to speak at a dinner or to address a working party, but the caller turned out to be Tony Collins, one of the Leeds United assistants, who told me he had Don Revie sitting next to him and that he wanted to speak to me. Don, who was leaving Elland Road to take on the England job, came straight to the point. 'We want you here,' he said. 'It is the best club in the country with the best players and the best training facilities. It's made for you.' He went on, 'You are my recommendation to the board,' and he even told me how much they would offer and how much I was to ask for. It was very tempting, and Don was very persuasive. It was a good job: Leeds had just won the Championship in spectacular style to see Don off to his England job, and they had amassed an unbeaten run of twenty-nine games, in many of which they simply toyed with the opposition. They were already being installed as favourites for the European Cup the next season, and that was another temptation.

I had just forty-eight hours to make up my mind but, again, decided against it. Revie was a hard act to follow as most of his players had come through the ranks and had played for no one else, and in any case I felt that Ipswich were on the brink of challenging the likes of Leeds United and Liverpool for the top honours.

Sunderland were another club to come knocking on my door and they were prepared to top the Leeds bid and everyone else, according to Tom Cowie their chairman. He said he would double my salary if I agreed to go, making me the highest-paid manager in the land. Now that was tempting too, because my wife Elsie was educated up there at St Anthony's Convent, was a state registered nurse at Sunderland Infirmary and was quite keen on going home. I liked Tom Cowie and his board and I liked what they were trying to do at this famous north-east club. Tom came to see me and explained that they wanted me to do with Sunderland what I had done at Ipswich. Again it meant going back to scratch and starting all over when I still had an unfinished job on my hands with ambitions to fulfil, and after much thought I declined.

Then, of course, there was Manchester United. There was some gossip about the prospect of my going to Old Trafford, but it was quickly dismissed as a rumour devised by the club to 'gee up' the Ipswich players before the start of the 1981/2 season after the euphoria of winning the UEFA Cup and going so close to the 'Treble'. I can reveal, however, that an approach was made in May 1981 and that I was asked to take over at Manchester United just before Ron Atkinson was chosen to replace Dave Sexton.

The initial contact came out of the blue, immediately after we had clinched the UEFA Cup against AZ 67 Alkmaar in Amsterdam, via a telephone call from United chairman Martin Edwards. I was quietly celebrating with some friends when I took the call which I assumed was to be a polite word of congratulations. Martin was, as ever, terribly nice and correct, indeed congratulating me on the success of winning the UEFA Cup and telling me how good it was not only for my club but for the country as well. He apologized for what was probably a bad time to call but then posed the question of when there *was* a good time or a bad time in football, and said that following our victory in Holland he would like to talk to me about the prospect of managing Manchester United. Had I been holding the UEFA Cup at the time I would have dropped it. I have to confess that my heart skipped a few beats; after all, this was Manchester United we were talking about, one of *the* clubs in the world. He wanted to know my feelings on the subject before pursuing the matter through the proper club channels. He did not want to embarrass me if I was not interested nor to cause unrest at a club he respected. He pointed out that it was the end of the season and that maybe I would like to think about it and give him my opinions.

My mind was in turmoil. I was still on an emotional high after winning a top European trophy and here was Manchester United, of all teams, asking me if I wanted to coach their great club. The immediate feeling is to bite the hand off, but I had to think rationally about my future and what I wanted to achieve. We had a stunning team at Ipswich and had just been voted the best team in Europe by a top football magazine. More than anything I wanted that English Championship with the team I had built at Ipswich. I still had four years left of my contract at Portman Road and I had to consider whether there was, indeed, a better job in English football.

I gave it due thought and called Martin Edwards back and told him that I couldn't give up what I had and that I had decided to stay. Martin was as good as his word so far as discretion was concerned. There were whispers in the game but nothing concrete came out. Throughout Manchester United acted quite properly and with honour, and to say that I was flattered would be an understatement.

After our dodgy early years together, we were on a roll at Ipswich throughout the time most of these offers were coming in, and I wanted to see just how far we could go. My decision not to take the Leeds job, for instance, was quickly vindicated when in the next season, 1974/5, we finished third in the First Division, the highest position since Alf Ramsey took Ipswich to the title in 1961/2; not only that, we also knocked out the holders Liverpool in the FA Cup. If we were going to do the Double we were going to have to do it the hard way because after Liverpool we faced another top team in Aston Villa and then, of all teams, drew Leeds United. Now I would see whether I was justified in turning down the champions!

It took four muscle-sapping, heart-stopping games to decide the tie before we emerged as 3–2 winners at neutral Filbert Street. Maybe that was our undoing, a case of a game or three too far, because we lost in the semi-final in a replay against West Ham United after having two goals dubiously wiped out by the referee, Clive Thomas. What a mistake he made in that match! Two diabolical decisions robbed us of our place at Wembley. I remain convinced to this day that he was wrong, not once but twice. The television film proves it beyond doubt. Clive Thomas was a good referee but he had a head as big as Birkenhead. He wanted to be the most important person on the pitch, he wanted people to see him rather than be invisible and seemed to be deliberately controversial. He ruled out one goal from twenty yards away for offside when the linesman, who was in a perfect position, was running back to the halfway line having given the goal. He didn't even consult his second official.

Even worse was to follow because we lost the title to Derby County by a miserable two points, finishing in third place level on points with Liverpool who had a marginally better goal difference. In retrospect we simply didn't have enough depth to cope with the injuries that a season like that brings. Had we been a club with a fairy godfather who could have given us an extra £200,000 we would probably have won the title I yearned for, but we didn't and I was never going to put the club in hock by buying back-up players to sit on the bench just in case we had injuries and suspensions. I just had to throw the kids in, whereas Manchester United, Leeds or Liverpool would simply have gone out and bought the players they needed. It was sickening because we were the best team in the League that season, just as we were in 1981 and 1982 when we followed up a third place to finish second, first behind Aston Villa and then Liverpool. I built three good teams at Ipswich – in 1975, 1978 and 1981 - and it remains my one regret that I did not win the First Division title having come so close so often.

But there were compensations, and even during our worst season in the First Division during that spell, 1977/8, we finished three points clear of the relegation zone but battled our way through to a Wembley Cup Final against favourites Arsenal. We were not given much of a chance after our injury-racked season and just before the final we had lost 6–1 to Aston Villa in a dreadful display.

The problem that day revolved around our talented South African-born England international midfield player Colin Viljoen. He was an outstanding footballer – quicksilver over the ground, smart brain, intelligent first touch and he could score goals – but he was not the most popular person in the dressing room. He had that arrogant, self-confident bearing that is so often found in top South African sportsmen and it rubbed people up the wrong way in our down-to-earth dressing room. A classic example of his manner was the way he treated defender Derek Jefferson. The two shared digs and would breakfast together before Colin set off in his car leaving Derek to travel to the ground by bus! Derek, an affable guy with a slow-burning fuse, didn't worry about it but it used to upset others.

Viljoen had suffered some injuries that season along with so many of our players and when he came back he was in and out of the side as I shuffled the pack trying to gather enough points to keep us up. It seemed that I only had a full-strength side to pick from when the FA Cup came around and we were heavily reliant during our bread and butter games on the solid professionals like Roger Osborne who had played a lot during the course of that season. He was a popular player who pulled his weight and did his job quietly and efficiently. The players liked the good local professional but still appreciated Colin enough to call him 'ace'. His skills and ability to change the course of a match were undeniable.

With the Cup Final fast approaching I felt I had to be fair to Colin Viljoen and give him his chance against Aston Villa. I wanted to see whether he was in good enough form to be considered for a place against Arsenal, and the man he displaced was Osborne. Colin didn't play so bad but the rest of the out-field players were truly awful. The best player we had by far was an eighteen-year-old rookie goalkeeper, Paul Overton from Ely, who saved us from total humiliation.

I was furious and told the team the following Monday what a lousy lot they were and asked them how they could perform like that a week before an FA Cup final with their best player a novice goalkeeper. They all looked at the floor and said nothing. They were wrong and they were out of order and, in particular, they were not fair to Viljoen on that day. It was a case of poor ambition, poor motivation and a lack of professional-ism. They clearly did not like the fact that Osborne's place was in doubt. I was not going to discuss team selection with them, it was none of their business, but I did talk about it with my staff and afterwards I decided that I would leave out Viljoen and play Osborne in the final. The players had clearly discussed it between themselves and maybe to the press, but had any one of them come to me and made that request or demand for a player to be picked or not they would have been left on the sidelines themselves. It was never a case of player power, although the players had spoken through their performance at Villa Park and I couldn't risk that happening at Wembley.

I was almost forced into a late change as it was when our key central defender Allan Hunter faced a ten o'clock fitness test after breakfast on the morning of the final. At 8.45 a.m. there was a knock on my door; Cyril Lea burst in and said. 'It's Allan Hunter.' At that instant my thoughts were that our big centre-half had woken up ill, but Cyril said the player had demanded his fitness test there and then and wanted to declare himself ready before breakfast, not after it. Within minutes he was run-ning up and down the lawns at Sopwell House Hotel showing that he was ready to play the biggest game of his life.

The die was cast and the team was picked, and as fate would have it Roger Osborne played a massive part in one of the Cup's great upsets, scoring the only goal of the game with just thirteen minutes remaining. Such were the congratulations and the emotion of the moment I had to take Roger off even before the game restarted as he was suffering from emotional exhaustion mixed with a bit of sunstroke. He must be the only player in FA Cup history to score the winning goal and not touch the ball again. I had to take him off because he was completely overcome. The victory was no more than our team had deserved. They had worked desperately hard to nullify the threat of the favourites, and if you had asked them who they would most like to have scored the winning goal to cap a hard, grafting performance like that they would have said Roger Osborne in unison.

I will never forget that day in May 1978. The FA Cup is special, unlike any other domestic cup competition in the world, watched by the entire globe these days and always chock-full of romance and upsets. Of the five finals I have won in my career it is, without doubt, the most cherished and momentous. Year after year I used to make my pilgrimage to Wembley for the final, always using my players' ticket and not once being tempted to give it away or sell it. I used to stand or sit and desperately wish it was me running out there for this classy occasion so steeped in history. When I finally made it as a manager rather than as a player it meant a great deal to me as I led my team up that golden path and into the sunshine to be greeted by that shattering crescendo of noise with the massed citizens of Ipswich garlanded in blue and white packed behind us. We could have sold those tickets ten times over.

Getting there was not enough – we were always there to win it and not to make up the numbers. The odds of 5–2 against were ridiculous, but it helped in many ways to be cast in the role of underdogs, with nothing to lose and everything to win. Consequently the players were relaxed and happy, laughing and joking in the dressing room before the game. The goal was late but it was no more than we deserved for our performance that day, and if anyone was looking for a little romance to go with the gritty, professional performance it came when substitute Micky Lambert replaced the goal-scoring hero Osborne. Loyal servant Lambert was scheduled for his testimonial match at Portman Road three days later, and such was the euphoria that 20,000 people turned up to salute a great club servant. It was some night, and a Suffolk Punch, part of the design on the Ipswich Town badge, paraded around the pitch with the cup. The partying went on and on, with the cup always the guest of honour; every person at the winning banquet wanted to be pictured posing next to or holding it. Next morning the entire population of Suffolk turned out to see it as we travelled back to Ipswich by coach.

That cup hardly left our possession for the next eleven months as the FA turned a blind eye and let us keep it.Their trust was honoured for the famous trophy could never have been looked after better as it went from school to school and country show to country show, village fêtes, shop windows and, of course, the Portman Road boardroom every other Saturday. Each night it was locked up in the local police station. It was looked after better than the crown jewels; whenever we took it out of the police station it had to be signed for and then returned that night. Only once were we too late to return it and that night I slept with it under my bed. Every so often it paid a visit to the local jeweller for a proper buffing and shining, and the FA could have had no complaints for it was returned to Lancaster Gate a month before the 1979 final in better condition than when Mick Mills walked up the steps at Wembley to receive it. It was a very sad day when we had to return it, like seeing one of the family emigrating to Australia, not knowing if you would ever see them again.

Winning the FA Cup did not disguise the fact that we had suffered a grim season in the League and this was emphasized when Nottingham Forest began the next season, 1978/9, by humiliating us 5–0 in the Charity Shield at Wembley. With Hunter and Beattie struggling with dreadful knee injuries we were short of a little craft, despite the emergence from the youth ranks of the mighty Terry Butcher, Russell Osman and Alan Brazil, all three destined to become full internationals. I had seen exactly what I needed to strengthen the squad on a pre-season tour of Holland, a young man named Arnold Muhren playing for Twente Enschede, and I couldn't believe my luck when the asking price was only £150,000, a figure that can be put into perspective by the fact that I sold Brian Talbot to Arsenal in July 1978 for three times that amount. I signed Muhren in August 1978 and had enough spare cash to go back to Enschede the following February to buy Frans Thijssen for £220,000.

I could get to Holland quicker than Sheffield and I had spotted these two outstanding players on one of my frequent trips over there. When they came up for sale at that price I jumped at them. They were both great professionals and loved the English style of training. They had no problems with the endurance work and quickly became popular with the other players. They loved the work and loved the ball. Arnold had every pass in the book, long or short, while Frans was a dribbler, left or right, able to take people out of the game. He was also a good competitor and a good tackler. The other players appreciated that they were top professionals and could play the game a bit.

They were cheap to buy but it was still a fortune to me as my previous highest outlay was £150,000 for Paul Mariner (Mr John thought I was buying a sailor when I told him I was going to Plymouth for Mariner), but having both Dutchmen not only enhanced the quality of my team but also meant each of them had some good company, alleviating any homesickness. It was a successful manoeuvre also used by Spurs when they bought the Argentinian pair Ossie Ardiles and Ricardo Villa, and since then by many other clubs at home and abroad. They gave us the impetus we needed to regain our place among the contenders, and come the 1980/1 season we were back on top form.

That we were the best team that season no one could deny – we beat the eventual champions, Aston Villa, three times – and at one stage we looked a good bet for the Treble, but the heavy workload allied to injuries took its toll as the season progressed and a change in the rules for the FA Cup conspired against us. For the first time it was decreed that there should be extra time after the first semi-final before a replay. We played Manchester City, going in as favourites but suffering as we lost the unlucky Kevin Beattie with a broken arm, while the half-time interval was spent patching up the walking wounded. I am convinced that had we walked away from Villa Park after ninety minutes with a 0–0 scoreline we would have come back three days later and beaten them. It is not being boastful to say that we had a better team than John Bond's Manchester City at that time, but we finally succumbed to a Paul Power goal in extra time.

Ironically we were back at Villa Park three days later and, as if to prove my point, we beat our closest rivals for the second time that season with goals from Brazil and Gates. The title race looked all over at that stage in our favour, but in our final run-in we contrived to snatch defeat from the jaws of victory as we lost to Arsenal, Norwich, Middlesbrough and Southampton. The only game we won in that spell was against, would you believe, Manchester City whom we defeated 1–0 at Portman Road with a Terry Butcher goal.

But the UEFA Cup was a different matter. Although we were regulars in Europe every season because of our consistency in the League and our FA Cup success in 1978, few gave us a chance in a competition featuring Juventus, Manchester United, Barcelona, Porto, St Etienne and Dynamo Moscow not to mention the powerful German contingent of Hamburg, Cologne, Stuttgart and Eintracht Frankfurt. We put out Aris Salonika (6–4 on aggregate) and Bohemians Prague (3–2)in the early rounds, and then faced Widzew Lodz of Poland, who had put out Manchester United in the previous round. This was clearly going to be a tough tie and before the home leg I was surprised to get a message that the Polish coach wanted to speak to me. I was even more surprised when I found out why: he wanted to have a bet with me! In all my years in football I had never heard anything like it. The interpreter said, 'The coach wants to have a bet with you.'

'Pardon,' I replied, thinking I had misheard.

'The coach wants to bet that Widzew beat Ipswich tonight,' he repeated.

'What does he want to bet in? In English or Polish money?' I asked, stalling for time.

'He only has Polish money,' answered the interpreter.

'First let me say I don't want his money whatever it is,' I said, 'and secondly I don't bet in circumstances like this. I am not interested.'

I saved his money for him as we stuffed them 5–0 with a John Wark hat trick. There were no wagers offered for the return in Poland in December when the temperatures plummeted way below zero. It was so bad that the UEFA representative told me that the pitch was unplayable and that if we didn't want to play we did not need to. The problem was that Polish football was about to shut down for the winter and if we didn't play it then we would not be able to go back until March. I took a chance and we lost 1–0 on ice in front of 9,000 fans. It was a fine overall victory for us against a side which boasted top internationals like Boniek, Smolarek and Zmuda.

Our performances in the quarter-final against the classy French side St Etienne were, perhaps, the highlight of our season. Here was a quality team full of stars like Battiston, Platini, Rep, Janvion, Larios and Castenada. I'll never forget that 4–1 win in France when two goals from Paul Mariner and others from John Wark and Arnold Muhren stunned and silenced the 40,000 fans who thought their talented team only had to turn up to beat these 'unknowns' from England. I have rarely seen scenes like those in our dressing room after that game and the St Etienne president walked in right in the middle of them. He came across to me and congratulated me and my team on the best performance he had seen against his team in Europe. He added that he had never seen a side take apart his team the way Ipswich had that night. It was, indeed, the first time that St Etienne had lost a European tie at home for twenty-six years.

The semi-final was against Cologne, and after beating them 1–0 at home with another Wark goal we were caught in the backlogged fixtures trap when we played the return in Germany. We were forced to play Arsenal at home on the Saturday, losing a critical League game 2–0, local rivals Norwich City on the Monday at Carrow Road, losing 1–0, Cologne on the Wednesday and Manchester City on the Saturday. No wonder the Germans were laughing at us and writing off our chances. They were convinced their team of internationals like Schumacher, Konopka, Zimmermann, Bonhof, Littbarski, Muller, Engels and England's Tony Woodcock would slaughter us in front of a 55,000 packed house. We added to their amusement when I decided to cancel training on the Tuesday in favour of going to a local fairground for two hours to try to get the players relaxed and unwound after two defeats which had thrown open the League Championship door to Aston Villa. The Germans couldn't believe their eyes when they saw newspaper and television pictures of our players enjoying the rides and sliding down the water chutes. They weren't laughing at us at the end of the ninety minutes for we played professionally in an aggressive game and not only held onto our one-goal advantage but added to it with a headed goal by Terry Butcher from a free kick. It was another outstanding performance.

Not everyone saw it like that. We flew into Norwich Airport after our great triumph only to be stopped by customs officials and made to show them the contents of every skip and every case. They took everything out and had us there for an hour and a half. Of course they found nothing and their only comment was that they were just doing their job. I had a suspicion it had something to do with football rivalry and more than a bit of jealousy, and it did take the edge off an otherwise wonderful trip.

Our opponents in the two-legged final were another of the outsiders, Dutch team AZ 67 Alkmaar, and what a carnival night it was at Portman Road for that first leg. Just when it looked as though our promising season might yield nothing, we turned it on and won 3−0 with goals from John Wark, Frans Thijssen and Paul Mariner to give us a great cushion for the second leg in Amsterdam a fortnight later. This was another top-quality night against top-quality opposition. They were not short of stars with the little midfielder Peters, who had recently scored twice against England, Metgod, Spelbos, Hovenkamp, Nygard, Jonker and Kist.

We needed the safety of those goals as, on another amazing night, the Dutch beat us 4–2, leaving us 5–4 winners on aggregate. We were always the favourites, however, as Thijssen scored first against his countrymen, but that doesn't tell half the story. The Dutch threw caution to the wind, played two at the back and hurled the kitchen sink at us. They should have been easy to counter with Mariner and Brazil up front but we couldn't get the ball or get out of our half. When we did they stepped up and played our two strikers offside. It was clever tactical stuff and they made a tremendous game of it. (Years later I was to try the same tactics myself when Atlético Madrid led us 3–0 in a Spanish Cup quarter-final, and Barcelona came back to win a sensational game 5–4. I had learned that once on the slippery slope it is hard to get off.) Every now and again Alkmaar notched a goal to pull us back and we were more than relieved when John Wark scored. That gave us a little breathing space because our two goals away from home meant they needed another two to beat us. No one could complain about the entertainment level of our cup run as we played attractive, attacking football, scoring twenty-nine goals and conceding fourteen.

Our challenge for the major domestic honours in 1981/2 was severely hit by injuries to our small squad with Paul Cooper, Frans Thijssen, Russell Osman, Terry Butcher, Paul Mariner and Alan Brazil all missing for varying lengths of time – and, of course, we had lost the beleaguered Kevin Beattie altogether.

It was the injury to Terry Butcher which remains etched in my memory. He missed fifteen League games in succession through what was on the face of it a nose bleed; in fact my big England central defender had to battle for his life. Butcher was stretchered off after a clash in a cup tie at Luton Town where David Pleat's team was quite fancied to give us a run for our money. As it transpired we played well and won a place in the fifth round with a comfortable three-goal victory. We had to take Terry off because we couldn't stop the bleeding from his nose. The doctor continued to work on him but as we boarded the bus home it began to bleed again, and instead of coming with us he remained in the Kenilworth Road physiotherapist's room before his father rushed him straight to the Luton and Dunstable Hospital for emergency treatment as he became weak with the loss of blood.

He eventually went home that night but after a long liquid lunch at the Centre Spot restaurant at the ground the bleeding started again. This time it was clear that it was really bad and after going into the Ipswich Hospital such were the complications that they transferred him to the London Hospital, and still they couldn't find out why the flow of blood could not be stopped. Eventually they discovered a ruptured nerve behind the nose. By that time it was a serious situation and he nearly died; he had to have nineteen units of plasma pumped through his veins, almost three times the normal content of blood. It was all very frightening. I visited him on a regular basis and he looked truly dreadful. He underwent a massive weight loss and just a cough or a sneeze could set the bleeding off again. Seeing him then, thin and gaunt, it was hard to imagine him returning to the team that season, but in typical Butcher fashion he did just that, playing in our last nine games as we vainly chased the title.

Paul Mariner was off at the same time with an Achilles' tendon injury while Frans Thijssen missed a total of thirty games,

73

too many for us to cope with. By our own high standards it was a disappointing season as we lamely surrendered our UEFA Cup after bowing out to Alex Ferguson's Aberdeen side in the very first round, losing 3–1 away after drawing 1–1 at home. Winners one year, out in the first round the next. That's so typical of football.

The FA Cup was even worse: after beating Birmingham and Luton we blew it in grand fashion by losing to underdogs Shrewsbury Town on one of those days made for a Cup upset. It was a heavy, small pitch with the ground packed to capacity. In the League Cup we beat Bradford, Everton and Watford only to lose to Liverpool in the two-leg semi-final, drawing 2–2 away after a disappointing 2–0 home defeat. To a large degree we had been hoisted by our own petard, for while we could go to grounds in the early years and spring surprises, now we were the team to beat and the opposition were always up and ready to face us.

At least it meant we could concentrate on the League, and despite our problems we lost only once at home to Swansea City, who that year also showed that small clubs could achieve big things, finishing in sixth place. Ipswich suffered notable defeats that in retrospect could have changed the course of the League Championship, none more so than a four-goal thumping at Liverpool when we were without both centre-halves Osman and Butcher and our leading goalscorer Alan Brazil, while both Paul Mariner and Frans Thijssen were injured and played their last games for a long period. There was also a critical 4–3 defeat by Southampton at the Dell when we had been coasting to victory with a 3–1 lead. Terry Butcher was sent off and our players claimed that Southampton captain Kevin Keegan had influenced the referee. Mick Mills, in particular, was furious that one England player should get another sent off and it was thought in our dressing room that Kevin was trying to run the game as well as play in it. Mr Keegan was not my favourite person that day.

We had a great run-in to the end of the season losing just twice in sixteen games, crucially to Spurs on 10 April and Nottingham Forest on 15 May. Liverpool, the eventual champions, also lost only two games in their last twenty-five, a sensational run which saw them crush Manchester City 5–0 as we lost to Spurs and beat Spurs 3–1 as we went down to Forest. Pivotal moments.

We played quality football throughout the season and performed creditably. If Paul Mariner had been available he would undoubtedly have scored goals which would have made the difference, but in his absence both Alan Brazil and John Wark were absolutely outstanding with fifty-one goals between them, Brazil scoring twenty-eight of them. Alan Brazil came good that year. He was tremendous in a one against one with the goalkeeper – you would always back him to score in that situation. He had a lot of confidence and a good left foot, and was a bit of a Jimmy Greaves in the way he could shimmy and shake to send the goalkeeper the wrong way, something he could do to the very best, whether in the form of Peter Shilton or Ray Clemence. John Wark was also prolific. He had the same qualities as my England captain Bryan Robson, always arriving late in the box to steal a march on defenders and score important goals. He was an instinctive player who knew where the ball was going to drop with his perfectly timed runs, rarely running offside. He could score with his left or right, on the volley or half-volley, and he was brilliant in the air. He was quite an extraordinary player. He had a good engine and was very brave, in fact very much like Bryan Robson in every respect.

I had a foretaste of things to come in May 1982 when I was

asked to take an England B side to Reykjavik to play Iceland while Ron Greenwood was away with the seniors in Finland. I enjoyed the experience at the time, even though it finished in a 1–1 draw, but there was a nasty taste left in the mouth by a player I had previously respected, Steve Perryman. The uncapped Perryman had been a terrific servant for Tottenham Hotspur and it was Ron's choice to reward him with a trip to Iceland, and he specifically asked us to give him a cap by bringing him on at some stage, something I was only too delighted to do. He returned the favour in his book, which made him a nice few bob from serialization in a national newspaper, where he criticized me for the way the team was run and the lack of organization since the days of Alf Ramsey. How he knew that on the strength of twelve minutes of international football is only known to him and his ghost-writer. We didn't meet until the Monday so he didn't have a great deal of time to observe the England structure. It was, sadly, something I was to experience later when Terry Fenwick earned his thirty pieces of silver by having a go at me. That was even sadder because I liked Terry; I had brought him into the side and appreciated what he did for England. Shame he didn't reciprocate. All too often the lure of an open cheque-book can induce young men to say things they may regret later, particularly when their own managerial careers hit the inevitable problems.

Although Brian Clough had been strongly backed by a sensationalizing press as the people's choice for England manager, it was clear that I was in the frame as the FA had already approached Ipswich for permission to speak to me. The club agreed that if the country wanted me they would not stand in the way, and there was no question of asking for compensation. Ipswich did, however, float the idea that I should do both jobs. It was a crazy scheme that had been occasionally aired by writers such as Brian Glanville who had little conception of what either job entailed. Club management is a seven-day-a-week effort at the best of times, and a look through my diaries for the eight years in charge of England will show that the national job is not a great deal different. Even if it was possible it would not be practicable to split your loyalties. In a word, it was impossible. It was a nice thought from the club, who were showing that they did not want to lose me, but the FA naturally wanted a full-time appointment.

I, in the meantime, recommended that my assistant Bobby Ferguson should be the choice to replace me at Portman Road. He had been with me for some time and I thought it only right for the club to give him a chance. He was to claim later that he deserved the job as he was behind much of our success, which raised my eyebrows more than a little and made me wonder who had been coaching the first team when he was looking after the reserves. I gave him bits and pieces to do to bring him along, but he was daydreaming if he thought he could take the credit for Ipswich's success. I gave his observations the attention they deserved – I ignored them. I suppose he felt that he had to be seen to be standing on his own two feet, not in my shadow. Perhaps he needed to build himself up. Whatever his reasons his actions did not impress me.

I had left him a good legacy with capable players, a smashing ground and no debts. I know that some critics said that if we had gone out and spent money on players in those last two seasons we would have emulated Alf Ramsey and won the League, but we had to balance the books. It is all very well taking Caribbean holidays and buying a Rolls-Royce if you can afford to do it but it is pretty stupid if you cannot. We simply did not have the money or the gates to support the sort of financial outlay that was being recommended. At that time there were any number of clubs in serious financial difficulties; there were no sugar daddies around or millions of pounds coming in from television. We had to operate on the proceeds of gates of around 18,000.

I tried to take the broad view and made sure that the ground improved along with the team. That was building for the future. One of the things I was attacked for by Bobby Ferguson when I left Portman Road was that it was me who gave the go-ahead to spend money on the new stand. It was absolutely true. Three directors said yes and three said no, leaving me with the casting vote. It would have been easy for me to keep the money to buy players, but I was looking to the future. Had we not done that at the time and left the stadium as it was we would have been in trouble when the Lord Justice Taylor Report came in and forced clubs to upgrade their grounds.

My one regret in all my career is that I didn't win the Championship in England, but what we built and what we achieved at Ipswich was enormous. It was sad that in my last season we finished empty-handed, but I knew that unless some-one came in with five million pounds and told me to spend at least three million of it on players we would always be a bit short. I thoroughly enjoyed my time at the club – I was loyal to them and they were loyal to me, the sort of relationship that transcended the usual employer–employee set-up. During all my years away from the club I didn't once contemplate selling the home which is just a stroll away from Portman Road.

Ipswich had been doing it against the odds for ten seasons, so maybe when England knocked on my door it was the right time for me to move on. Even so, I was still a little surprised when they came for me. Although I was an FA man and had done all the coaching courses and they knew all about me, the wise betting money was still on Brian Clough.

The first I knew of it was when Patrick Cobbold told me he had received a call from Ted Croker asking if the FA could approach me. Patrick left it up to me and put no pressure on me either way. He told me that, if I wanted it, I was at the club for ever and he offered me a new ten-year contract at a great deal more than England were prepared to pay me. But when the offer came I knew I had to take it. I consulted my wife Elsie and my family, and while they knew that the pressure would be immense, they also knew I would regret it for the rest of my life if I didn't accept. I didn't know exactly what lay ahead. Nor did they.

5

England, My England

Let me say right away that being the England manager is no easy job and I freely admit that from the moment I was appointed in June 1982 it took me fully two years to settle in and bed down. It is so different from running a club where you have the day-to-day business, the nine a.m. until whatever time commitment, the contact with the same group of players and a couple of games a week – all this disappears. You are largely isolated and on your own with few people to talk to. Of my close friends and assistants, Don Howe was busy with Arsenal and Dave Sexton was with the youngsters at the FA's residential school, but they were always available to me. My main point of contact and discussion was Charles Hughes, the director of coaching. Now most people in the game thought that we were constantly at odds because of our differing views on how the beautiful game should be played, but in truth we got on famously and spent hour upon hour talking and arguing our respective views.

I found Charles a very able person. He had a certain way of thinking and I had mine. I remember saying to him one day that I had grown up and worked with managers like Don Howe, Terry Venables, Jackie Charlton, David Pleat, Howard Wilkinson, Dave Sexton and others at coaching courses at Lilleshall where we used to talk about passing, possession and control for hours on end and stage training sessions to put those ideals into practice. Now, I said to him, it is all about direct football. What, I asked, had happened? The answer was that he had watched thousands of videotapes, analysed them and discovered that most goals were scored with one or two passes and that, therefore, was the way to play. I argued that that was the way to lose the ball, a crime in international or any other sort of football. If you don't have possession you cannot score. I put it to him that it was because of all the other things that happened in between that one- and two-pass goals were produced; he countered that the Brazilians were doing it the wrong way because they were all pass, pass, pass.

We battled away with our own principles but never fell out over it. Charles could debate and talk and put over his ideas. Of course he had a point, but in practice if the game were played the way he preached, and he was correct in his assumptions, the scorelines would be in the twenties. Football is not like that. Two-nil is a good win, but to score two goals teams have to do other things properly in order to create the chances. He did have his strong points, though. Charles emphasized the importance of free kicks and other set plays because more than 40 per cent of all goals come from those situations. He was right. It is important to work on free kicks, corners and, these days, penalty kicks. They do win and lose teams matches and a season could turn on a poor shot in a penalty shoot-out.

I got on with Charles and stood up for him in front of his critics. Unfortunately he didn't have a good relationship with the public or the press, but if they had known him as I did they would have liked him. He had no public persona and suffered because of it. Of course he was not always right, but then who is? Certainly not me.

I was lucky at the FA for I had good people all round me.

The FA Secretary, the late Ted Croker, was a good man and very knowledgeable, while the chairman, Bert Millichip, was top-class and the late Dick Wragg, chairman of the International Committee, backed me throughout. I offered my resignation from the national job twice in eight years and each time they would not consider it. The first time was after the World Cup Finals in Mexico in 1986. After we had lost to the infamous 'Hand of God' goal I went to Bert Millichip and told him that if they were thinking of replacing me then that was the ideal time to do it to give a new man time to build his own side for the European Championships and the next World Cup. When they said they did not intend to replace me I suggested that the time was therefore ripe to change the system at Lancaster Gate and appoint an assistant in much the same way as the Germans and other continental countries operated. It would mean I could groom a younger manager for four years so that when he did take over he would not struggle as I had done for the first two years. They could certainly afford it financially, but the response from the then Manchester City chairman Peter Swales was that there was not enough work for one, never mind two. I was flabbergasted; he must have been reading the self-important Brian Glanville who always wrote that he thought the England manager's job should be part time. I know what every England manager would have said to that.

There were plenty of bright managers and coaches about at the time, people like Terry Venables, Steve Coppell, Howard Wilkinson, David Pleat, that type of guy. I didn't have Graham Taylor in my list of contenders in 1986 because he had not emerged as any sort of candidate by then. It wasn't for a Brian Clough or a Jack Charlton, they wouldn't have accepted the number two role in any case, but for a younger man who was prepared to wait and work for the top job. It would have provided greater continuity, and I believe my point was proved when Graham Taylor struggled to settle and then, when Terry Venables left, so many of the youngsters wouldn't touch the job with a bargepole. Anyone with the slightest suggestion of a skeleton in the cupboard stayed a million miles away from it. Think how much easier it would have been for Glenn Hoddle had he worked under Terry for a couple of years before stepping up. It is just common sense.

The FA were short-sighted over that, just as they were when I wanted Don Howe to be brought into the system full time. Far from being a one-man job it would have been a handful for two. Don would have been a great asset both to England and to me, but the wise heads of Lancaster Gate couldn't see it. He was a good judge, a great coach and was the perfect devil's advocate. Don Howe would have made my job easier and England a better team.

The next time I offered my resignation was two years later in 1988 after we lost all three group games – to the Republic of Ireland, Holland and Russia - in the European Championship Finals in Germany. I fully expected Mr Millichip to accept it this time; instead he turned round and asked, 'Why?'

'Well,' I replied, a little taken aback, 'we did lose all three games and the media are screaming for my blood. It would be better, perhaps, if I moved out and someone came in to take the pressure off you a little.'

'If you can take the pressure we can,' he said. 'It's two years to the World Cup and no one knows more about it all than you do. So we will back you. If you are happy to face the media and the public then so are we.'

I didn't need any persuading. I didn't really want to go but had felt that offering my resignation was the honourable thing to do. We were awful in Germany. We outplayed Jack

Charlton's Irish team and lost 1–0 despite having a ratio of eighteen–five chances on goal. In the second match we stood at 1–1 with fifteen minutes left, hit the post twice and then saw a mishit shot from Ruud Gullit fly straight to Marco van Basten, who scored with a screaming volley and then scored his third with his head when we had thrown everyone forward looking for an equalizer. We had lost two games we deserved to win, but in the third, against Russia, we deserved and got nothing. I talked about pride and prestige and told the players that even though we could not progress we needed to salvage something and finish with a win. Instead we got off to a dismal start and got worse. It was the poorest performance in my eight years and one of the saddest defeats, even though it was a dead game, perhaps second only in terms of disappointment to the defeat by Germany in the World Cup semi-finals two years later. Heads dropped, we lost our spirit and the team died.

I was shattered. I volunteered to take the blame but it should have been shared by some of my leading, senior players, not least of all current England coach Glenn Hoddle who had an absolute nightmare. But he was not alone. Players were ill, tired and injured after a long season, but there are no excuses once you cross the white line.

There were plenty of good times to offset the bad, of course. Winning any game at Wembley was always a great feeling; winning qualifying matches against top players who had as much to play for as we did was even better, particularly when it happened at Wembley. Even now it still means so much for a team to beat England under the Twin Towers. Just look at their reaction when they do. There was the 1–0 win against Russia in Tbilisi in March 1986, although it was only a friendly; the 4–1 victory over Yugoslavia in Belgrade in November 1987 when we had to draw to qualify for the 1988 European Championships;

the goalless World Cup qualifier in May 1985 in Romania – three really difficult places to go to and come out with a result. There was Poland in Mexico in 1986 when everyone thought we were down and out and Gary Lineker proved them wrong with a hat trick; the friendly with Brazil in Rio when I was down and nearly out; and the 8–0 win over Turkey in November 1984.

That last match was a World Cup qualifier and the Turks were the up-and-coming European nation and fancied that they could not only score their first ever goal against us but beat us as well. Our hotel virtually overlooked the stadium, and by eight in the morning we could see that the ground was full – I had to check to make sure they hadn't changed the kick-off time. If anyone was to ask me where you find the most hostile atmosphere in the world for a football match, I would have to say in my experience that it is Turkey. I remember going out on to the pitch before the game and turning to Bryan Robson and saying, 'Is it my imagination or is the ground shaking?' Bryan confirmed that the singing, chanting, dancing fans were making the earth move. The atmosphere was extremely volatile. Lineker scored three and John Barnes two as we turned that crowd into a mourning mass. Many teams have found out since that Turkey is not a great place to go, and when we went back we were taken not to Istanbul but to Izmir where the atmosphere was quite sinister. Manchester United and other teams have since had problems as the expectations of the Turkish fans rose higher as football continued to improve in their country.

At least these days the Football Association is aware of how football everywhere has moved on, and Glenn Hoddle has considerably more help in his preparations than I had. I can only remember two Saturdays cleared of fixtures before important qualifying matches in my entire eight years, spanning four major championships. I couldn't help smiling when I heard

Glenn complaining in March 1998 about the number of players he had lost before a friendly against Switzerland. Every England manager, me included, has complained that we have been worse hit than anyone before us. I used to wait for players like Mark Hateley, Ray Wilkins and Trevor Francis to return from their Sunday games in Italy, desperately hoping they would all be injury-free because I was down to eight or nine fit players. I can remember asking Don Howe what the heck we were going to do with eight active players for training one Monday morning. We didn't have enough for a single team, never mind a practice match.

The same applied to Ron Greenwood when he was manager of the national side. In April 1978 he called me, begging me to release my skipper Mick Mills for a friendly against Brazil. Ron opened the conversation by saying that he had a big favour to ask – he wasn't wrong there for we were due to play Liverpool away and we were, that particular season, playing for our First Division lives. Ron explained that he had no one left to call on to play right-back so I sent Mick off to Wembley and he played in a 1–1 draw against the Brazilians while we scrambled to a tremendous point with a 2–2 draw at Anfield.

Our physiotherapist Fred Street knew the score. He could tell me who would be fit to train before they even arrived! He knew all of them and their little foibles, players like Trevor Francis and later Gary Lineker who preferred a massage and hot baths the day after playing rather than training. But more often than not they were ready to play for their country come the day. It was just difficult working on tactics and systems when half the team was back at the hotel having treatment.

It was the same with the managers. You knew those who would help and those who would not. Alex Ferguson, a Scot, was one of the very best. He had managed Scotland himself and knew the problems I faced and he could not have done more. He never left it to a secretary or an assistant to telephone me, he would always give me a rundown on his players and their fitness himself. Brian Clough was alright – when it suited him! While I was trying to bring the squad together on a Sunday to have that important extra day with them, he would be fighting to let them have the day off with their families. He would tell me they would be fit to join us on Monday night. Do that for one and you would have to do it for the lot. He would try it on now and again, but on the whole he was fine if you compromised with him.

All the same, I thought I was entitled to a little more help from an Englishman, especially one of the three top managers at the time. Apart from Alex, the Scottish managerial contingent also included George Graham and Kenny Dalglish. Why should they help? They were running big clubs and it was not easy for them, consequently they only gave what they had to give. The minimum. No more, no less. I understood and sympathized; they were with high-pressure clubs and they needed their results and didn't want players coming back from internationals tired and injured. Their allegiance was not to England, which made Alex's generosity all the more appreciated. I got on well enough with George and he couldn't have been more polite or helpful whenever I visited Highbury to watch a game. He always made a point of seeking me out beforehand to have a chat and bring me up to date with his English players, their form and their fitness.

Personally I got on with all of them, but I still felt I could have been given an easier ride by the likes of Dalglish and Graham when it came to releasing players for international duty. They had enjoyed their international careers, with Kenny winning over 100 caps and clearly not having any problems with his managers and George making a dozen appearances. They maybe should have appreciated the position a little more, having been given the freedom themselves to play for their country. Now the England manager doesn't have the same fight on his hands because the Saturday games are cancelled and the FIFA regulations are there to be adhered to. It means that there isn't the frustration, the little bit of needle which may come in because of mixed loyalties. It can still happen though, as Glenn discovered when he lost the players from Manchester United, Arsenal and Chelsea, the three top clubs in the Championship race, just before a friendly against the Swiss.

It is always going to be difficult to compromise in football. While that situation has improved, another has replaced it with the foreign players being released for all sorts of FIFA-sanctioned tournaments. Players like the South African Mark Fish at Bolton Wanderers and Australian Harry Kewell at Leeds United sometimes disappeared from the Premiership for weeks on end. Therein lies the danger of signing one of the top Brazilian players, because the first thing they do when they sign for a club is to get a written guarantee for their release for all games, as I was to discover to my cost when I lost Ronaldo at Barcelona for the run-in to a domestic and European season.

I suppose the biggest problem I ever had with a shortage of players was at the end of the 1983/4 season. It had not been a great winter for me. We had lost the one and only unsuccessful qualifying match in my eight years, 1–0 at home to Denmark, costing us our place in the European Championship Finals, and we were also beaten by France, defeated by Wales and had fallen to Russia 2–0 at Wembley. I was without nineteen possible internationals for the trip to play, of all teams, Brazil, Uruguay and Chile. My only senior players were Peter Shilton, Kenny Sansom, Ray Wilkins and Bryan Robson, and as far as everyone at home was concerned we were heading for humiliation in South America.

The English crowd at Wembley for the Russian game left me in no doubt as to what they thought of me as I walked round the touchline to the dressing room at full time. They not only chanted 'Robson out, Robson out' but spat at me and threw beer over me. I was nearly in tears, not for myself but for my eighty-one-year-old father Philip who had travelled down for the game, as he often did. I just hoped he had left early to beat the crowds to the tube station and hadn't seen or heard the abuse piled upon me. Jimmy Hill, my old Fulham team-mate, went so far as to suggest that we should pull out of the tour to avoid embarrassment. He asked me live on television why we were going, as if I could suddenly cancel a tour of that magnitude. The pressure was on and the media were turning the screw. There was no doubt at all that my job was on the line and that another defeat in Rio de Janeiro could tip me over the edge. What a place and what a match to overcome massive pressure.

I started the tour with two young wingers, Mark Chamberlain and John Barnes, gave Dave Watson and Terry Fenwick the central defensive roles after Graham Roberts had been taken ill with appendicitis, and I played Mark Hateley from Portsmouth in Division Two through the middle. He looked so much like his footballing father Tony, whom I knew well, that I often called him by his dad's name for fun, adding weight to the saucy stories that I didn't know my players' names. I brought him in because I didn't have Trevor Francis, Luther Blissett, Paul Mariner, Peter Withe, Gary Lineker and Paul Walsh, and at that time there was a massive question mark against Tony Woodcock's fitness. The Brazilian journalists laughed when I told them I was going to attack their team with a 4–2–4 formation; some openly thought we were trying to con them while others walked away tapping their foreheads in derision.

The result is history. John Barnes scored a sensational solo goal which was to make his name worldwide while young what's-his-name Hateley launched himself at the far post to score a bullet header from a Barnes cross which was to rocket him from the relative obscurity of Fratton Park to the dizzy heights of AC Milan. I often thought that the Pompey chairman should have sent the FA a slice of that fee . . . or me!

I am not exaggerating when I say that everyone expected us to lose, but I put my faith and my fate in the hands of four experienced players and seven greenhorns. They say that fortune favours the brave, and it certainly did that day. The three youngsters took the headlines, but it was the work of those four seniors – Peter Shilton unpassable in goal, Kenny Sansom having his best ever game for England at left-back and Ray Wilkins and Bryan Robson commanding the midfield – which gave us the springboard for a remarkable and rare victory in the famous old Maracana Stadium.

The newspaper campaign to oust me was at its height at the time and had I returned from South America with three bad results I have little doubt I would have gone. Twelve months later I was almost out of a job again, but this time it had nothing to do with results as we were well down the road to qualifying for the 1986 World Cup Finals in Mexico. In preparation for that we undertook a close-season trip to Mexico where we were to play Italy, the hosts and West Germany in a real test of our character. But before a ball was kicked I genuinely believed that England would be banned from international football and that there would be no job for me to keep.

We were on our first full day in Mexico and the highlight was to be the European Cup Final between Juventus and

Liverpool at the old Heysel Stadium in Brussels. We sat in our luxurious hotel, the Camino Real, waiting expectantly for the kick-off but, oddly, the screen remained blank with no explanation for ninety minutes after the final should have kicked off. News began to filter through of fighting between the fans, but we dismissed as exaggeration reports of deaths. Our reaction seemed to be justified when the game finally started, surely confirming that the reports we had heard were rubbish.

It was only when the players began ringing home at half-time that the awful truth emerged: thirty-eight people had lost their lives, bringing shame on everyone connected with the English game. The ramifications hit me quickly; for a start, we were due to face the Italians in the Aztec Stadium days later with players from both teams due to join us. A ban on all English clubs in Europe looked inevitable and our own place in the international arena was instantly questioned.

We felt that the game should be played otherwise there would be an unbridgeable gap between the two football-loving countries; fortunately the Italian coach Enzo Bearzot was in agreement and also wanted the game to take place. Both teams attended a memorial service for the dead and there was enough time between the tragedy and our game for us to show our respect for the dead and still play the game without being considered callous. The foreign journalists did not share this view and their attitude was, why didn't we just pack our bags and go home? We didn't, we stayed and we played in a surreal atmosphere with the English players under orders to behave immaculately whatever the provocation with the penalty for falling out of line an instant plane ticket home and eternal disgrace.

There were only 13,000 in the huge stadium with a handful of fans from the two countries, the remainder Mexicans who, of course, were on the side of the Italians. We walked out with the teams mixed, standing alternately as we stood for a two-minute silence as a mark of respect. We played against the reigning world champions without a friend in the world, particularly among the three Mexican officials who gave us nothing. The players were brilliant and it looked as though we would walk away with what would have been the ideal result in every respect, a 1–1 draw. We were waiting for the final whistle when Gary Stevens passed the ball back to Peter Shilton only for Vierchowod to throw himself across Stevens's outstretched leg. No one could say a word as the Mexican referee pointed to the spot and Altobelli scored to give the Italians a 2–1 win. There was still time for us to have one last throw of the dice and we swept forward and looked to have righted the wrong when Gary Lineker was blatantly fouled in the penalty area. Play was waved on and we still kept our lips buttoned and our emotions to ourselves.

It was the same story against the Mexicans in the second game when the respected German referee Volker Roth denied us an equalizer with another appalling decision. We were getting exactly what we anticipated – nothing. Strangely our stiff upper lip attitude and our impeccable behaviour gradually won us sympathy, not just from the locals but from around the world, but we were set up to play the Germans in what promised to be our third successive defeat, the first time it would have happened since 1959. It didn't. This time the Mexican referee was all we could have asked for and we went on to win 3–0, our biggest win over our old rivals for fifty years. Their manager Franz Beckenbauer had gambled on beating the high altitude by flying in at the last moment whereas we were well and truly acclimatized.

There was still considerable doubt, however, as to whether we would be allowed to return the next year and whether

England would have an international team. There was a threat of complete isolation and the FA had to do a great deal of lobbying to keep us alive. I could understand the revulsion of the world against us. A section of our so-called supporters was hated and rightly so. They were the scum of the earth and many of them who travelled with us were so-called National Front. They had even refused to acknowledge John Barnes's goal against Brazil the previous summer because he was black, and on our flight to Argentina made racist remarks and chants aimed at John and Mark Chamberlain until the English press took the matter into their own hands and shut them up. They were there again in Mexico that summer and I pondered on just how they could afford to undertake such expensive trips and whether they were, in fact, subsidized by some politically motivated group. Of course they were only a small minority, but the few can often shout louder than the many and with a tribal beast like football the herd syndrome applies and the group finds itself swept along. In the lovely little country of Luxembourg the hooligans turned over cars in the streets and attacked ordinary people going about their business. It was all quite unbelievable and sickened me to my heart to feel that they were being connected with the England team. They were the last people we wanted.

We were allowed to stay in world football, but the consequences were that I had to pick an England side who hadn't experienced any European football for years. There were only a handful playing abroad so that only made a small difference, so our players were trying to live with the best in the world having competed only in domestic football. If five of your best teams are playing in Europe with seven or eight Englishmen in each team, then up to forty players are gathering that crucial experience. We didn't even have the foreign players in our League to offer us the difference.

The memories of Heysel were still vivid a year later when we travelled to Mexico for the World Cup Finals, and there were major concerns over crowd behaviour when we faced Argentina in Mexico City so soon after our conflict with them over the Falkland Islands. Happily the fears proved to be unfounded and we were able to concentrate on the difficult preparations rather than spend our time apologizing for the animals.

Make no mistake, this was a difficult World Cup. It wasn't popping over the Channel to France, but playing in a country that offered a major test with the heat, altitude and health hazards which had brought England down under Sir Alf Ramsey in 1970 when he lost Gordon Banks with a stomach bug before the critical game with West Germany. One of the biggest hurdles to overcome was that while everyone else played at high altitude we were drawn in a group which played their games in Monterrey at sea level, but if we qualified from that group we would be playing our games at altitude without the opportunity to acclimatize properly. To live at 6,000 feet, where ultimately we would have to play, would have been too far away from our preliminary games. No such place existed within reach, and the nearest we could find was a little town up in the mountains called Saltillo which sat at a little over 4,000 feet. It meant an hour and a half ride through bandit country for training and games at the stadium, but even that was something special as we were escorted by an armed convoy of helicopters, police cars, motorcycles and armed guards which travelled at great speed with our coach and the journalists' transport sandwiched in between.

It didn't solve our problems completely and the doctor, Vernon Edwards, and myself went higher up into the mountains and found somewhere at 10,000 feet. What I didn't realize at the time was that while we were up there panting and gasping for air, Vernon suffered a heart attack which knocked him out of the World Cup and was later to cost him his life. No one realized at the time, but the doc was eventually whisked into hospital before being taken home. Our discovery solved the problem of acclimatization. We would travel up after training, have picnics, stroll around or play cricket. We didn't need to train or work at that level, just to get used to it so that we would be able to cope later on in the competition. The other problem, of course, was the heat. Training often took place in temperatures hovering around the hundred-degree mark. That signalled the danger of dehydration and terrific weight loss, which had to be continually monitored.

The team eventually did so well, and a lot of the credit must go to the backroom squad of Norman Medhurst, Fred Street, Mike Kelly and Don Howe who made it all possible. We had a massively experienced staff, prepared brilliantly in Colorado Springs, and before that, used the USAF facilities to help us acclimatize before we left. No stone was unturned and there was nothing I regretted after we had been put out other than the fact that we lost Bryan Robson with injury, something over which we had no control at all. The only tummy upset we had on the entire trip was when one of the players overdosed on orange juice! Not a lot else went our way during the tournament and we were eventually defeated by that famous combination of rule-bending and sheer genius that tended to characterize the life and times of Mr Diego Maradona, but he was the best player in the competition by some distance and he was *certainly* the difference between the two sides in that quarter-final. That result aside, it was my first World Cup as manager and I enjoyed every minute of it. I had scouted for Ron Greenwood in 1982 in Spain and got the taste for the competition, but that was just watching games and submitting team reports.

This was the full monty, total involvement, and I loved it.

When we qualified for Mexico I had invited Ron Greenwood to the Football Association and unashamedly picked his brains to learn as much as I could. I liked Ron a lot, he was a really nice man, very helpful and supportive. He didn't hold a thing back, all the good and the bad. The man I could really have had serious help from was Sir Alf as he had actually experienced the problems we were about to face, but such was our relationship because of his vitriolic attacks in the *Daily Mirror* that it was never possible. I felt totally betrayed by the man who lived just a few streets away from me and who had managed Ipswich Town and England so successfully. When he was sacked as England manager in April 1974 after a goalless friendly with Portugal in Lisbon, I wrote to him and sent two directors' tickets for himself and his wife with an invitation to come to Portman Road whenever he wanted. He came a couple of times but never once looked me out to say hello or thanks. I could understand that he should be upset at the FA, but why me? What had I done to deserve such scurrilous attacks? Goodness knows I tried, but even when I offered him a lift back from a Chelsea match he refused, saying, 'I came by train, I shall return by train.' We never did discuss Mexico, which I found sad.

I stayed on after the team had departed to discharge my duties with ITV for the remainder of the competition, and just before the World Cup Final a group of us – Bob Harris, Jim Rosenthal and the ITV crew – had a short break in a beautiful resort called Ixtapa where the sun and the sea air proved to be a big contrast to Mexico City's choking smog. It was all very relaxing with a little beach football and, of course, plenty of swimming in the inviting blue seas among the swell of the Pacific rollers.

We splashed about happily, gradually moving out to deeper

waters until a commotion on the beach caught our eye and we spotted a woman running up and down, frantically waving her arms and shouting in our direction. It made no sense at all until she shouted, 'Big fish! Big fish!' That needed no interpretation; we had a pretty good idea what she was on about and suddenly we were all swimming faster than we had ever done in our lives. We scrambled ashore and looked back to see a sinister black fin weaving among the waves. We immediately turned to the lifeguard in his high chair and asked him why he hadn't warned us.

'Oh,' he replied, 'we get a lot of dolphins around here.'

'Was that a dolphin, then?' we asked, feeling rather silly.

'No,' he said, 'that was a shark.'

At the end of the Mexico World Cup I wouldn't have put England any higher than eighth in the world rankings, exactly where we finished in the tournament. We were top ten, but nothing more. Two years later when we went to Germany for the 1988 European Championships I believed we had moved up the pecking order considerably because I had one of the best attacking forces in the world in Gary Lineker, John Barnes, Peter Beardsley and Chris Waddle. As it transpired Lineker was suffering from hepatitis, Waddle hadn't recovered as much as we had hoped from a hernia operation and both Barnes and Beardsley were suffering from exhaustion after giving so much in their first successful year at Liverpool.

By the time we went to Italy two years later I felt that we had a team ready to challenge the best. We improved and developed as the tournament progressed: David Platt and Paul Gascoigne came to the boil; Des Walker, Mark Wright and Terry Butcher were outstanding; Paul Parker was at his best; Stuart Pearce was a strong competitor; we were commanding in midfield with good back-up; Waddle, Beardsley, Barnes and Lineker were match-winners; and Peter Shilton was just about the best goalkeeper in the world. It was a quite remarkable performance considering the long club ban from Europe. We went into the tournament with very good players, great spirit and a lot of heart; we came out with prestige and our reputation enhanced. We won the Fair Play Award which, considering the troubles the game had suffered, was of great importance to us.

What we did not realize during our run was exactly what was happening back at home. We had left as no hopers, derided by our many critics, but had turned into heroes in the eyes of the public, forcing the newspapers to change their script. It was only when we were preparing for our quarter-final game against Cameroon in Naples and I took a telephone call from Bryan Robson, who had returned home injured, that we learned of the full impact and how the entire nation was behind our bid. He told me: 'I cannot believe it. The whole nation is jumping. I am experiencing it for the first time having been away with the team on the two previous occasions and I cannot believe what is happening. The atmosphere is incredible. I have never seen anything like it in my life. The whole country is behind you and the team. That is why I am ringing because I had to let you know.'

They might have been keen back home, but in the stadium we were second favourites by a long way as Italy and the rest of the world got behind the attractive underdogs from Africa, and for a long time it looked as though our World Cup would end there and then until those two Gary Lineker penalties saved our bacon. In all my eight years as England manager we had been awarded just two penalties – and now we got two in twenty-three minutes. Perhaps our luck had turned at last. At the time we were struggling at 2–1 down against the biggest team I have ever seen. They were very physical and they could play. To make matters worse Mark Wright was injured and had to shuffle the pack, but we turned the game around and that was one of my best moments of the entire World Cup.

On to Turin and the Hasta Hotel in Asti where England had stayed ten years earlier under Ron Greenwood during the 1980 European Championships. We were welcomed with open arms by the management who had just seen off the Brazilians. The South Americans had been a nightmare with their behaviour and indiscipline, ordering steak and chips at two a.m. with families and children running around at all hours to the background of the inevitable samba music. It was chaotic. The manager told me his staff were on the point of a collective nervous breakdown, and had they suffered another team like the Brazilians they would have closed the hotel until the World Cup was over. I was not surprised that the Brazilians had such a poor competition.

They loved us because we were exactly the opposite. We were totally dedicated and focused on our semi-final against West Germany. Throughout the tournament we had become like a club side in terms of spirit, never more so than in the sweaty last few seconds against Belgium in the last sixteen, and against Cameroon when we trailed. Both those games went to extra time, as did our semi-final against West Germany – and all that in ninety-degree heat. It was a serious disadvantage, just like playing an extra game. It says an awful lot not only for our spirit and skill but also for our preparation that we looked the side most likely to win in extra time against the Germans, and it was only the lottery of penalties that defeated us. A game like that has to be decided some way, but it was an awful way to go out of the competition.

The country was moved and when the team returned home – I stayed on in Italy to receive the Fair Play Award – they were greeted by thousands of people at Luton Airport. Imagine what it would have been like had we gone all the way. Personally I had gone from zero to hero and I couldn't help smiling to myself as I thought back over all the aggravation I had suffered in the course of managing England. I had been used as a pawn between the two biggest-selling newspapers in Britain, the *Sun* and the *Mirror*; I was seen as fair game. I was old enough to take that, but what really hurt was when others who should have known better joined Sir Alf Ramsey's tirade against me and my players. Former skippers like Kevin Keegan and Emlyn Hughes and established internationals like Alan Ball and Malcolm MacDonald took their money and ran off at the mouth. There were others, like Steve Perryman, who based his thoughts on international football on one appearance; Terry Fenwick, who I had brought into the England team; and even a veteran Rugby League player, Alex Murphy, jumped on the bandwagon.

I never really fell out with the football journalists, who had their jobs to do, but I despised those who tried to bring down me and my team when they had enough experience in the game to have known better. They helped turn the public against me. I was spat at in my beloved St James's Park over the Keegan affair and again at Wembley when we lost to Russia. Fruits of the job. There is nothing nastier than that. We were also dogged by the news reporters in Italy, a totally different breed to their colleagues from the back pages. They were there with their cheque-books, sniffing at empty glasses to see if the players had been drinking and offering money to anyone who could give them a yarn. Inadvertently they helped pull us together in Italy when they claimed that the team had been involved in some sort of orgy with an Italian World Cup hostess at our team headquarters in Sardinia.

There were some wretched headlines over the eight years, probing into my past and private life to the constant cry for me to be sacked from my job. I was told to go in the name of God and the name of Allah and I was described as everything from a plonker to a prat. Nigel Clark, then working for the *Daily Mirror* and ghosting the worst excesses of Sir Alf Ramsey, stood up in front of the television cameras on one away trip and with his courage helped and his tongue loosened by the free champagne on the FA flight he announced to the world: 'We are here to fry Robson.' Yet for all the persecution and the vilification I would have come back at any time had I been required to help out my country, and I would have done it for nothing. I am, above all, a patriot.

As a proud Englishman it was the greatest of honours to be made a CBE for my contributions to the national game by the Queen herself in the magnificent surrounds of Buckingham Palace. What a place! It lived up to every expectation with the deep carpets, crystal chandeliers, the opulent decor and the dazzling ballroom. It was without doubt a day to remember, especially as the Queen graciously, and clearly well briefed, said to me: 'I understand you are in a very tough game.'

'Yes I am, ma'am, but it is most enjoyable,' I responded.

She added, 'I am sure it is, but you have done very well.'

Although it was very formal and proper, everyone was at pains to put me at my ease and I was backed up by my wife Elsie and two of my three sons, Mark and Paul. It was particularly nice to have alongside me that day my goalkeeper over those eight eventful years in charge of England, Peter Shilton, former cricketer and official Raman Subba Row, Dame Mary Gow, television personality Esther Rantzen and the then editor of the *Daily Star*, Brian Hitchen.

No one ever works with an end product of that nature in his or her mind and I hadn't even thought of the prospect after returning home from our exploits in Italia 90 until I received a telephone call to inform me and ask me if I would accept a CBE. These honours are not handed out lightly and invariably they are given in recognition of years of hard work, a large chunk of the recipient's life. Over the course of my career I have been lucky enough to pick up awards ranging from Fair Play trophies to a fabulous gold and crystal cup sculpted by Nevio De Zolt and given to me during a grand ceremony in Frisinone, just outside Rome. But this one beat them all.

I would happily have stayed after Italia 90 for I honestly believed that with what I had left and with what was coming through, the next four years could be prolific. My vision was that Graham Taylor was walking into a very good job. It prompts the question – what went wrong? It just didn't go for Graham. He was a thoroughly decent man who knew football and loved England every bit as much as I did. He, like me, went to watch England games, even standing on the terraces in the Nep Stadium in Budapest with his wife when genuine England fans were attacked by the locals. He had my sympathy for the way he was harangued by the press and I know only too well how his family suffered. I, like only a handful of others, know the job he had, the frustrations and pressures that come when you don't win games. He was a nice, intelligent man and I felt sorry for him. He never came to me for help and had he done so I would have offered advice gladly. I spoke to him a couple of times, but there was nothing substantial. That was fair enough; he wanted to do things his own way and he had the experienced Lawrie McMenemy to help him.

He eventually seemed to come unstuck when he took Gary Lineker off during the 1992 European Championships in Sweden. I have to confess that I wouldn't have done it. He needed a goal and Gary is one of those players who can be out of the game, seemingly ineffective, and suddenly, like Jimmy

Greaves or Denis Law, be capable of doing something instinctive at the right time and score the goal the team needs. He had already done it once for Graham in Poland to help him qualify, and he had done it often for me in the past. Graham Taylor took off Gary Lineker because he felt he had a point to make, and if England had won Graham Taylor would have been a hero. Maybe, in hindsight, Graham feels he would have done it differently given a second chance. Let's face it, we are all guilty at one time or another.

Bad decisions? I have made a few. Overestimating the Danes at Wembley in September 1983 was one, playing too many inexperienced youngsters against France in Paris in February 1984 was another (we lost 2–0). I certainly overemphasized the Danes' qualities before the game. They were to prove to be an outstanding side and in that respect I was right, but I pushed it too hard at the time and it became a negative. Equally I was wrong to play Stein and Walsh together against Platini's team in Paris, along with other youngsters, and I vowed after that that I would never play more than two new players at a time unless circumstances dictated.

Tactically I got it wrong against Holland in the 1988 European Championships when I had two versus two against Ruud Gullit and Marco van Basten. I vowed then that it would never happen again, and that I would in future play a sweeper to cover myself against teams like the Dutch or the Germans, who had a dangerous front two in Voller and Klinsmann, if we met them in the World Cup in Italy. That is why I waited for Mark Wright to prove his fitness before I named my squad and why I picked him to play against the Dutch in Cagliari, not because I had a deputation of senior players as some of the press continue to suggest. I never had that happen in my eight years and would never have tolerated it. I also made a mistake when

I tried to play my three best midfield players – Bryan Robson, Ray Wilkins and Glenn Hoddle – in the same side and it simply didn't work. It was not right. I picked them because I felt that I had to try to get them into the same team. It never gave us quite the right balance; I saw it and eventually had to discard it.

Graham Taylor had the same problems. He got it wrong tactically in June 1993 against Norway in Oslo, losing 2–0 in a vital World Cup qualifier, and again when he brought back veteran Gordon Cowans to replace the young and exciting Paul Gascoigne against Ireland in Dublin in February 1995, that night of shame when the match was abandoned after twenty-seven minutes due to crowd trouble, with England a goal down at the time. Cowans could make the game function but he was not a match-winner like Gascoigne.

We all do it. Don Revie took five centre-halves to Italy in November 1976 and regretted it afterwards when England failed to qualify for Argentina; I doubt whether Glenn Hoddle would use again the same tactics as he did against Italy at Wembley in 1997 or pick the same sort of team he fielded against Chile in February 1998. The important thing is whether or not you learn from these mistakes. Certainly you are always going to be found out because you are in a goldfish bowl in every game you play. If you screw up in one of them then everyone knows, that's part of the job.

I enjoyed Terry Venables's couple of years at the helm, especially during the 1996 European Championships in England. I have always liked Terry without knowing him that well. I always saw him as a bright young coach, a thinking coach, bubbly with a good footballing mind, and wherever he went he had been popular because of his attitude and his personality. That is why I recommended him to Barcelona. He was a good choice to follow Graham Taylor because he was so different, just as Ron

Greenwood, with his freedom of expression, was the right man after the strict regime of Don Revie. Terry was a popular choice for the public and the press, as well as for his professional colleagues who reckoned his good experience of every level of football in this country would stand him in good stead. He had enjoyed the big jobs at places like Barcelona and Spurs. They didn't frighten him and neither did England.

The lovely thing for Terry was that he didn't have the pressures of qualifying. He could experiment, there was no scrabbling around for points or difficult trips to make to eastern Europe. Everyone, or almost everyone – even the media – said get on with it, you have two years to get it right. He was bright enough to take full advantage. He came out with the 'Christmas Tree' formation and everyone said it was a brilliant concept. If Graham Taylor had tried that a year earlier he would have been branded a lunatic, he would have been buried. I rang Don Howe and asked him what the heck it was and he was as amused as I was. It was a great story rather than a great tactical plan, and a good example of the predictable relationship between type of personality and press reaction. When Charles Hughes came out with POMO – Position Of Maximum Opportunity – everyone scratched their heads or laughed, but had Terry introduced it he would have been hailed a genius.

It was party time and England had the right man in the right place. He did a great job, even though the Christmas Tree went up the chimney with Santa Claus as we knew it would. By the time Euro 96 came along he had a lovely system working with Alan Shearer and Teddy Sheringham in tandem, playing international football with a good defence and an attacking theme. They played wonderful stuff at times and thrilled the crowd with their performances against the Scots and, particularly, the Dutch. He was, perhaps, a little lucky to overcome Spain in the quarter-final – the Spaniards were a better team on the day – but was then very unlucky to lose *again* to Germany on penalties when he had the better team. It raised some old memories on my part. We were the better team on the day in 1990 too, and had we overcome them I have no doubt we would have been champions.

Terry gave England two great years of good, exciting football, a bit of fun and almost a major championship for the first time in thirty years. I imagine most were sorry to see him go. I certainly was, because he had done a good job for England. It was a great pity he did not go all the way at Euro 96, and instead of finishing the tournament as the happiest man in the world he was the saddest.

Three days after the German game I went to a dinner party at the Hilton Hotel in London on the night of the final with friends from around the world and I spotted Terry sitting at the bar on his own, head bowed. I went up to him, slapped him on the back and said, 'Hi.' He turned round slowly and was clearly in great distress. My immediate reaction was that he had been to the final, seen Germany win it and came away thinking that it should have been England. Naturally I asked what the matter was. He looked up at me and said, 'Bobby, I have some terrible news for you. Something awful has happened.'

I knew that he shared my liking of Paul Gascoigne and instantly I put two and two together and got five.

'Gascoigne?' I asked.

'No. Bobby Keetch is dead.'

Suddenly I was as stunned as he was. My old Fulham team-mate, the larger than life Bobby Keetch who had recently opened a restaurant in London. Poor Terry had been out with him for dinner only the night before, and at moments like that football is put in its true perspective.

6

Three Lions on their Shirts

Kevin Keegan has made it clear many times in the past that I am not his favourite person after I left him out of my first ever England squad, but he remains one of the players I admire most, and as a manager he is definitely international class. Should Glenn Hoddle tire of his position as England coach I would have no fears about Keegan fulfilling his ambition by taking over and leading his country with the same boundless energy and imagination that made him a Messiah on my native north-east soil with my home club Newcastle United.

It is one of the few areas of regret from my eight years of England management that Keegan and I fell out in such a public manner and were unable to reconcile the row which led to the Newcastle public spitting at me and verbally abusing me for ignoring the England captain of the previous season in my opening squad for the European qualifier in Denmark on 22 September 1982. There are a good many theories and reasons put forward as to what exactly happened, not least of all by Kevin himself who, I am told, felt that it was my assistant Don Howe who had some sort of vendetta against him and persuaded me to omit him. That was simply not true. I did my homework and I alone made the decision not to pick Kevin Keegan. Of course when I took over I talked to various members of the England management team who had been in Spain the previous summer and I made up my mind on what they told me and the fact that Kevin had decided to sacrifice his position in the top division to play for Newcastle. There are not too many players who can move into the lower divisions at that sort of age and pursue an international career.

It was certainly a very tough decision for my first match as Kevin Keegan had been one of my personal favourites for a long time. In fact I used to go back to Ipswich after watching him play, sit my players down in the dressing room and tell them about this little bundle of dynamite, his enthusiasm and his motivation despite being one of the richest and most successful players in the game. He not only made the most of his considerable ability but played with the enthusiasm of a youngster just breaking into the big time. I was more than happy to hold him up as an example and a role model for all my players. But in Spain during the 1982 World Cup he was suffering with a bad back and he upset some of the England staff with his decision to return to Germany for treatment, a trip which meant a long, long drive in a tiny car. In the end Kevin played for just a few minutes in the second-round, Group B game against Spain and it was felt that his presence as an injured player for virtually the entire World Cup campaign was more than a little disruptive.

That fact, allied to the bad back which caused him the trouble, his increasing years and his choice to drop a division, convinced me that I should leave him out. It was a clinical decision made by my head rather than my heart, the sort of resolution of difficulties Kevin himself had to start making when he returned to the game as a manager with Newcastle United. Selling Andy Cole was one of those decisions, and I remember Kevin going onto the steps at St James's Park to try to explain his reasons to annoyed and exasperated fans, a brave thing for any manager to do and particularly to a public who idolized Cole for his goalscoring talents. He has had to make many a decision like that since, both with Newcastle and now with Fulham, and I hope that he would now have more of an understanding of my situation in 1982.

As my appointment to the national job was only recent, I was also full of ambition and looking to the long term. Did I play Kevin in a squad I wanted to develop for the next World Cup in four years or look at what other talent I had in the country? I thought that if I left Kevin out for the start I could always bring him back at a later date. I had no idea he would react the way he did. His main gripe with me was that I did not have the courtesy to tell him of my decision before news of the squad was released to the press. He felt that he deserved more than that for what he had done for England and the Football Association. That, I have to say, was nothing to do with me. It was my first game and I was picking a squad from scratch. I felt then that I didn't owe Kevin or anyone else an explanation. I was wrong. In hindsight I should have realized that Kevin Keegan was an exception to the rule. A telephone call or a letter to him before the announcement of the squad would have been in order, and if I had thought of it at the time maybe we would be friends now. Perhaps a word in my ear from someone in the FA might have helped, but I have to take the responsibility.

What confused the issue, according to Kevin later, was that I had met with him in August after watching his opening game for Newcastle at St James's Park and spoken to him privately afterwards, enthusing about his performance and giving him the impression that he was in my plans. He contends that should have been the moment to tell him face to face that I didn't intend to use him, but I couldn't do that because at that stage I had not come to a final verdict. It was an emotional day at Newcastle for the game against Queens Park Rangers. The ground which had stood half empty was thronged with people, the atmosphere was electric and all it needed was for Keegan to score a goal to bring the house down. He did, and as a Newcastle supporter it provided me with one of the most pleasurable days of my football life. He became a Messiah in one day and has remained so ever since. But I also saw other things. I saw in him a player who had slightly passed his peak, one playing a more mature role, far deeper and not getting into the box so often. It was still very effective, but not really what I was looking for.

I was really upset when he launched into me through the pages of the *Sun* newspaper. If I was wrong in not giving him a call then he was equally wrong in not confronting me personally before he went to the media. I tried to put things right at a later date when I wrote a letter to him and sent it via his manager Arthur Cox to ensure that it was handed to him personally. I felt I owed him that and I told him how keen I was to bury the hatchet. I also told him that the row was the last thing I wanted and I tried to explain my thinking and that he was not ruled out of my plans for the future, but it brought no response. Kevin would certainly have added to his sixty-three caps had he not turned his back and slammed the door shut in my face. There were times later on when Kevin could have done a job for me both on and off the field with his effervescent style.

We have bumped into each other occasionally since then and, happily, time seems to have healed the rift a little each time and I am hoping that soon we will be able to look at each other face to face and eye to eye. We are grown-up men and shouldn't go through life like that, bearing grudges. The game needs Kevin Keegan. I was delighted when he came back from his eight-year retirement. I honestly thought he would struggle after such a long time away but he had forgotten nothing, and what he had forgotten he made up for with the same enthusiasm he had as a player. English football needs the best it can get and he showed himself to be one of the best and one of the most inspirational managers in the game. I loved the style of football Newcastle played under him. He had a go and wasn't afraid to play wingers and attack. England supporters would respond to that type of football if Kevin ever gets the chance at international level, but he might have to wait a long time for I have the feeling that Glenn Hoddle might just fall in love with the job and could be there for many years.

I remember the late Jock Stein talking to me about the Scotland job at a senior coaches course in Split (then in Yugoslavia) and he was telling me how much he loved the job and that he wouldn't want to go back to the daily grind of club management. I feel that Glenn could be the same type of person. He is a laid-back character and a dozen games a year would appear to be a better bet for him than fifty or sixty in the hurly burly of the domestic fixture list.

It was often said that I did not rate Glenn and underplayed him. That is something I dispute. When I was made England manager I fully intended to build my side around this elegant player and, indeed, I gave him more of his caps than any other manager and at one stage had him involved in the team in all but one or two of a run of thirty games. It has to be remembered that Glenn was not always fit and available for selection because of the battering he took in the domestic game. He was a special, gifted player with high technical qualities, but like a lot of players of his style and temperament there were other qualities that were lacking. He wasn't a Nobby Stiles any more than Nobby was a Glenn Hoddle. You had to take Glenn as he was and accept that he wasn't going to put his foot in, track back or tackle. He had to be played in a situation where the best could be obtained from him and be satisfied with what he had to offer, not look for things he couldn't provide. He had to be put in a situation where his natural ability would be brought out to the full. There were many things he could only wonder at. His choice of pass and the delivery of it were exquisite; his long and short game was exemplary; so was his guile on the ball; his talent at getting through impossibly narrow spaces was unique; his shooting from either foot, dipping or swerving from almost any distance, was lethal; but you couldn't ask Glenn to mark someone and you wouldn't want to.

He was a bit like an American quarterback who you had to protect with other players and to whom you had to give a platform to do the special things. The problem with that scenario is that when you lost him through injury or any other reason you had to rewrite the team's tactics because you couldn't replace him. I had hoped that I could blend him in with two other great midfield players I had available to me, Bryan Robson and Ray Wilkins, but sadly it didn't gel. I thought I could get away with it because they were three such good players and three such good characters, but it didn't work out at all.

Glenn was a beautiful trainer and lovely to work with. Peter Reid, who I know will forgive me for saying he was a totally different type of midfield player to Glenn, far happier winning a tackle and giving a quick short pass, walked off the training pitch with me after one World Cup session shaking his head at what he had seen. Glenn had not missed a shot or a cross all day, and Peter said, 'I never knew that he was so good. I didn't know we had a player of that quality in our league. It makes me feel just like a journeyman.' Peter was right, but he was also wrong because his sort are just as important as Glenn's type. One needs the other.

One thing that has pleasantly surprised me is the strength of character Glenn has shown as England manager. When he was on form as a player he was a joy to watch, particularly when he and his mate Chris Waddle were on song at the same time. But there were other days when he was completely ineffective and the game was a battle which sometimes passed him by, such as the June 1988 3–1 defeat by Russia in Frankfurt during a disastrous European Championships. Any weakness he showed then is not reflected in his work as a manager.

Happily there were few of those games. Glenn was a gifted player with a great eye and a good brain, always knowing what he wanted to do with the ball before he received it. All the great midfield players have that quality, with Michel Platini a striking example, a player very similar to Glenn. I got on well with Glenn on a one-to-one basis and enjoyed talking to him about the game, but I honestly never felt that he would stay on once his playing career had finished. He had some good ideas on the game but I didn't for a minute think that he would relish the man management and the aggression that you sometimes need to be a manager. Sometimes you have to be a bit crude and rude to players and I couldn't see him doing that.

What I really admired about him was the way he grasped the nettle and took the England job when so many others were turning it down even before they were officially approached. They had seen what had happened to me, to Graham Taylor and to Terry Venables and decided that that sort of hassle and hounding was not for them. He wasn't afraid of the job or the baggage that went with it. He had the guts and the courage to take it even though he is the youngest ever England manager with only a modicum of experience.

Of course he has made mistakes, particularly against Italy at Wembley in February 1997 and Chile at Wembley a year later,

113

but the important thing is that he learned from them and became a better manager. He quickly found the way he wanted to play and sorted out the players to fit into that system. He has used what he learned from playing at home and abroad, not playing rigid 4–4–2 but always ready to revert to it if he feels it is necessary. He likes finding his width from the wing-backs and using the three central defenders, and against Italy in Rome he didn't panic when the pressure was on. He is not afraid, either, of bringing on young players like Paul Scholes, Michael Owen, Nicky Butt and the Neville brothers where others may have hesitated and waited for them to prove themselves. He talks sensibly with the media and the players and is straight with both, except when he feels that he can use a bit of gamesmanship to fox the opposition, as he did in Italy when he was writing off players as injured when he knew they would be fit to play. That is fine with me. I have done it in the past and if it gains an advantage then all is fair in love and war.

If there is an area where he can improve it is in the use of substitutes. The international game these days is about fourteen-man squads, not eleven-man teams. I remember in Italy I kept saying to myself that he must make changes. I desperately wanted him to bring off Paul Gascoigne and bring on a strong midfield defender to hold the position for which they had worked so tirelessly. Paul had given the team and his country a good hour but it was obvious he was tiring and I knew that a tired Paul Gascoigne could make mistakes in important areas. I was muttering to myself for Glenn to be loyal to himself and the country and not over-loyal to the player. That, I hope, is something that will come with experience – learning to read a game and the situation and where and when to make changes. All the great managers know how to make the alterations that can switch a game and win it. It was a great advantage for him

114

in the World Cup in France to have all eleven reserves stripped and on the bench so that he could replace like with like without altering his game plan.

Who knows what the right ingredients are to make a manager? Brian Clough, Bill Shankly, Alex Ferguson, Matt Busby, Alf Ramsey, Joe Fagan – all of them different with varying characteristics and styles. I often looked around at my England squad and wondered who would be the future managers. Some I was right with, others I was not. In Hoddle's case I would have said no; Gary Lineker was another I didn't think would want the daily hassle and grind of the job. For various reasons I found it hard to imagine Kenny Sansom, Trevor Steven, Tony Adams, Ian Wright, Sammy Lee, John Barnes, Phil Neal or Phil Thompson in the role, but I always thought that Bryan Robson, Ray Wilkins, Chris Waddle, Peter Reid and Peter Shilton might have a chance.

The other one I cannot in any way see as a manager or a coach is Paul Gascoigne. No chance. It bothers and worries me what will happen to Paul when his playing days are finished. I just hope that he has invested some of that money he has earned through the game and doesn't end up on the scrap heap, because he'll find many of his 'friends' will disappear when the light goes out. It is hard to see him doing anything other than play football – that was what he was born for. He is certainly a player I will never forget. He left a lasting imprint on my career and was undoubtedly one of the most talented players I ever handled.

I remember him as the fat little boy at Ipswich, and then as the international-class player with the cockiness and arrogance on the pitch and the dizziness off it. I meant it when I called him daft as a brush, because he is. The big question then was whether we could get that dizziness out of him and get the best from him because there was no doubt he had what it took. He wanted the ball the whole time, he was never afraid to try things. He had a marvellous touch and feel for the ball and he was strong, very strong, hard to knock off the ball, and I always felt that if only he would take a stone off he would have that extra yard of pace which would make him even more devastating. Sometimes he would try things in the wrong areas and he also lacked discipline in those early years, but the more I studied his faults the more qualities I could see as well: his powerful running, his spot-on passing, the ease with which he could beat an opponent on the edge of the box and shoot, his sureness in the air and his sometimes brilliant ability to win the ball.

He was right up there with Bryan Robson, even a bit quicker through the space and furnished with a little more trickery, but where Robson scored over Gascoigne was in his discipline. He never did daft things or risked the ball in an attempt to please the crowd.

I took a lot of criticism for not picking Paul earlier, but that was deliberate on my part. I could see his qualities and I could see his faults. I brought him into the squad, I used him and watched him in training. He was instantly popular with the other players, making them laugh with his antics and relaxing everybody. He was a good trainer and he loved to work, particularly when it involved the ball. There were no problems over that side of his game, but I was keen to hold him back because I knew how desperate he was to play, so much so that when I did unleash him in the World Cup finals he would be a tiger. I frustrated him on purpose. I wanted to be sure that he was ready and that I was ready, and when his name was finally on the sheet I hoped that the relief and happiness would make him an even better, more responsible player. I wanted him to value that England place and not to believe that it came easy or that it was just there for the asking. And he wasn't afraid to ask! He used to come up to me at training camp and tell me, 'I can do it you know, boss.' But I would smile and reply, 'I'll tell you when.'

One thing was sure: he wouldn't lack confidence when he did finally run out for me. Paul made his debut in November 1988 as a substitute for Neil Webb against Saudi Arabia in a 1–1 draw in Riyadh. Rather than welcome the player they had been screaming for, the press largely ignored him as they went again for my throat. I was greeted after that game with the head-line 'Go, For the Love of Allah', a change on the usual theme of 'Go, For the Love of God.' He then came on as a sub against Albania at Wembley and scored his first international goal before making his full debut in an undistinguished goalless draw against Chile at Wembley in May 1989.

But it was not until the World Cup in Italy that I really threw him into the fray – and how he responded! He was always up to something and always the centre of attention. He had so much energy to burn and whatever seemed to be going on within the squad he was in the middle of it. I once had to stop him playing a full-blooded game of tennis the day before a World Cup game. He was hyperactive and even struggled to sleep properly at night, such was his energy. He would often wander off on midnight walks. How his room-mate Chris Waddle ever managed to play World Cup football was amazing because Paul hardly let his fellow Geordie sleep at night.

He was also inclined to put on weight because of the sort of food he ate, and while I was very keen on my players having a proper diet with plenty of carbohydrates and protein I was always ready to listen to Paul. When he did tilt the scales too far he was conscientious about losing weight and would ask me and the doctor if he could miss out on a main meal. Provided the doctor gave his okay I would go along with it and I assumed he would sit in his room watching television while the rest of us gathered as a group in the dining room of the hotel. We met sharp at seven and on one occasion I was rushing down to dinner a fraction late after taking a telephone call when I bumped into Paul in his England tracksuit going through the revolving doors on his way out. I was somewhat non-plussed and asked him where he was going. 'I'm off down the pub to meet me dad,' he replied, as if it was the most natural thing in the world to do. I was stunned. I told him, 'You cannot do that, man, especially in an England tracksuit. Even if you had an orange juice there would be stories in the papers of boozing before a game.' He still couldn't see any harm in it. He thought it was all right.

He was a funny guy, always up to tricks. I will never forget the day he suddenly staggered round the corner of the hotel where Don Howe and I were discussing our increasingly critical injury problems. He was swathed in bandages from head to toe with an apparently blood-stained head and broken limbs. He was whimpering and moaning for help and my immediate thought was that he had tumbled from the balcony outside his hotel bedroom. 'Where's the doctor? Where's the doctor?' he moaned, and it was only then that Don and I twigged that it was another of his pranks. He was aware that every day had brought with it a new injury problem and this was his way of taking the mickey and lightening the atmosphere. He had gone into physiotherapist Fred Street's room and pinched the bandages and improvised with hotel serviettes and liberal splashes of tomato ketchup. Once the game was up he raced away and dived straight into the pool, bandages and all.

For all his daftness I still loved the lad and liked to talk football with him. I would tell him about the need for discipline,

With my wife, Elsie, and our three sons, Mark, Andrew and Paul.
(Ken Coton)

As manager of Ipswich Town, UEFA cup winners May 1981 with
Arnold Muhren (hidden) and Frans Thijssen.

With staff of Ipswich Town Football Club, August 1978 with the FA Cup.
Left to right: Cyril Lea (First Team Coach), me, Charlie Woods (Youth Team
Coach), Bobby Ferguson (Reserve Team Coach) and Ron Gray (Chief Scout).
(Owen Hines)

Directing the traffic while managing Ipswich Town.
(*Sporting Pictures*)

At home in Suffolk in the early 80s with my father Philip, and mother Lilian.

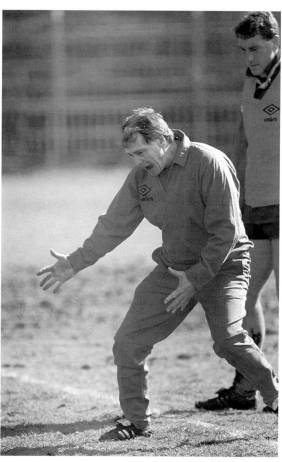

Above: In my eight years as England manager I saw more of the press than I did my players!
(Sporting Pictures)

Left: Never happier than when coaching. Here showing Terry Butcher how it should be done.
(Sporting Pictures)

Tense moments in my first spell with PSV Eindhoven. *(Allsport)*

Training session at Sporting Lisbon with Figo.

Above: Grabbing the few moments available during extra time in the Portuguese Cup Final for Porto against my old club Sporting Lisbon in 1994. *(Manuel Lopes)*

Left: Obviously my tactical changes worked – we won! Also in the picture is my assistant Josë Mourinho. *(Manuel Lopes)*

The fabulous Nou Camp Stadium, Barcelona. *(Ben Radford/Allsport)*

With my highly expensive, highly talented squad at Barcelona in 1996.
We went on to win three trophies and finished second in the league.
(Shaun Botterill/Allsport)

My second European trophy for Barcelona – the Cup Winners' Cup – won with a goal by Ronaldo against Paris St. Germain in Rotterdam, May 1997. *(Ben Radford/Allsport)*

Away from the madding crowds on the beach in Sitges near Barcelona which was home during my two year stay in Spain. *(Ben Radford/Allsport)*

talk to him about his attitude, try to get him to be himself but to keep things in check. I became more and more certain that he could make it and I went so far as to predict in an interview the December before the 1990 World Cup Finals that he could be our version of Roberto Baggio, the darling of the Italians and the football critics around the world. I forecast that if he handled himself properly he could be the star of the finals in Italy. I wasn't far wrong.

The competition for midfield places at the time was fierce with other contenders like Steve Hodge, David Platt, Trevor Steven, David Rocastle, Neil Webb, Bryan Robson and Steve McMahon all jostling with Gascoigne for places in the final squad, not to mention the team. The turning point for Gascoigne came in a friendly at Wembley in April 1990 against Czechoslovakia who, against all the odds, decided to play an attacking game against us. It suited Gascoigne down to the ground and he really turned it on in a game which was more like a testimonial than a serious World Cup warm-up. There was hardly a tackle in sight and Gascoigne had a hand in every goal as we won 5–2, scoring a spectacular goal himself at a time when I thought he was knackered and ready to come off. He maintained his Wembley form against Denmark on 15 May and Uruguay a week later. He had proved to me his fitness and all that concerned me was his temperament, but by then I had seen enough and I had decided to go with him.

The bigger the stage the better he liked it, and in Italy he was a sensation. He was the finest young player in the tournament without a doubt and he installed himself as a household name not only in England but around the globe, particularly when he burst into tears in the semi-final against Germany. He had already been booked once and his world collapsed when he was cautioned eight minutes into extra time when he tackled full-back Berthold right in front of the German dugout. It was nothing more than a mistimed challenge but the entire German bench leapt to their feet and, I am sure, influenced referee José Ramiz Wright in his decision to give Paul the caution that would keep him out of the World Cup Final if we went on to win. Gascoigne was aware of the implications immediately as he pleaded with the referee. He was distraught and tears began to wash down his face with the cameras showing every moment to a captivated world audience. It was heartbreaking. His Spurs team-mate Gary Lineker wanted me to take off Gascoigne there and then. Lineker had quickly spotted that Paul was now shrouded in a purple mist and likely to do anything. I watched the situation carefully, not wanting to upset the balance of the team, and gambled that he would not get himself sent off in the few minutes remaining.

I reached him at the changeover and told him to get his country to the final even if he couldn't play in it himself. 'I can do it,' he said, 'Nay problem.' He tried his best but it finished with a penalty shoot-out and the rest is history. What is not widely known, however, is that despite the trauma he had gone through Gascoigne put himself on the line and would have taken our sixth penalty had it been necessary.

There was nobody better than him in Italia 90. He was dominant, he was confident. He did great things on the ball, ran the ball through midfield, he passed it, supported the front players and defended well. He linked defence with attack and was inexhaustible. He was marvellous against both Holland and Belgium, but in the first half against Cameroon he played very poorly, losing his discipline and his common sense. The composure went and he chased the ball around the field like a cat after a bird in the back garden. The obvious thing was to take him off, but by this time I had a lot of confidence in the boy and I took hold of him at the break and told him he couldn't play like that in an international match and not be destroyed. I told him, instead, to play off his opponent and not to get himself out of position, letting them play the ball in behind him. He listened and he acted upon it. He played well in the second half and helped to pull us around with two slide-rule passes which brought penalties for Gary Lineker.

The world was at his feet. Italy was the place to be in those days with big, big money and a pop-star lifestyle. It was inevitable that Gascoigne would be going there as Rome club Lazio came in with an offer of £8.5 million which made him an instant millionaire. By this time he was up to every commercial ticket available. He was in great demand everywhere and the stage was set for his final domestic game in England – and what better stage than the FA Cup Final at Wembley against Nottingham Forest?

I can still picture it now. He was so hyped up, so desperately keen to show everyone he was worth every penny, wanting to run the show and be the star of the final. He wanted to be clever, score the winning goal and be the tough guy as well. I knew what was going through his head as if he had told me. He had wound himself up like a coiled spring, but instead of providing power it snapped. It was self-induced, a moment of sheer madness which all but ended his career and could have ended the career of the unfortunate Gary Charles who was on the end of it. It was the old Paul Gascoigne self-destruct button which he was prone to press now and again, both on and off the pitch. No one knew how serious the injury was as he was stretchered off the field but it was quite obvious that this was nothing minor, and as the news gradually seeped through it appeared that his glorious career may have been halted prematurely.

I kept in touch with the lad for a while and I was frequently linked with him when at my various clubs around Europe. I kept an eye on him but never once asked about him. The injury undoubtedly took its toll and then there was always the nagging fear that he may do something stupid again. Had he avoided that long-term injury then I might well have tried to take him with me. At his best he would have fitted in with any of the teams I coached, including that very fine Barcelona side. He was never really fit enough to do himself justice at Lazio and he was not the same influential player until Walter Smith took a gamble on him and carried him off to Scotland. I feel that Scotland was a good choice for him. The knee injury settled down and he matured a little. The Scottish scene suited him because there was not the intensity of the English or the Italian game with only a handful of matches each season to test the nerve and press him into overdrive. I am sure it prolonged his career, particularly his international career.

He is still apt to do the crazy thing but more often off the pitch than on it. But despite his knowledge and understanding of the game I do not believe that he would have the application to be a coach or a manager, working out training schedules, travelling the country watching players, talking to the chairman, placating irate fans, acting as a psychologist to players and knuckling down to hard work when the results go wrong. Somehow I just cannot see a marriage between Gascoigne and football when the playing days are over.

Bryan Robson was different in every way to his fellow Geordie, and while he is already establishing himself as a deep-thinking and innovative manager he is also, I understand, financially independent from the game, thus reducing some of the incredible pressure exerted on the modern-day manager. Perhaps the only similarity is that they both admitted publicly to liking a drink!

Robson was a warrior, a great player with remarkable application. He bestrode the pitch like a Colossus but suffered terribly with injuries at crucial moments in his career. I suffered with him, because he missed thirty games under me and didn't complete either World Cup in Mexico or Italy, each time playing just the first two games before succumbing to problems, leaving me to ponder what might have been for both of us.

Great is a word too lightly used in football parlance, but I have no hesitation in describing Bryan Robson as a 'great player', a fighter with a desire to be perfect and to do things the right way on the pitch. He never dodged a tackle in his career and frequently his injuries were as a result of his bravery. Take away that courage and he would not have been the same player. It was that quality which lifted him out of the ranks of the good and made him exceptional. There were those who said that his bravery bordered on the stupid, but this was his extra dimension. I wanted him just as he was and England certainly suffered during the times when he wasn't there.

My heart bled for him in Mexico when a dislocated shoulder ruled him out. I knew it was always going to be a risk but it need not have been had Manchester United manager Ron Atkinson listened to my plea to allow Robson to have an operation mid-season which would have ensured his fitness for the summer. But Bryan was as important to United as he was to England and Ron refused on the grounds that he could not do without him for two months. I begged, but Ron insisted that they would win nothing without his skipper. They still won nothing with him and we had him for barely two games before the problem flared up again.

By the time Italia 90 came around Alex Ferguson was his boss at Old Trafford and I couldn't have asked for greater co-operation from any manager, but the end product was the same and he returned home for more surgery on a troublesome Achilles' tendon. We were only a whisker away from going through to the World Cup Final after losing to Germany in that penalty shoot-out and I am convinced that Bryan could have made the difference; after all, he was three players in one: a tough tackling defender, a midfield player of vision and a phenomenal goalscorer.

He must have been a fierce and daunting opponent to face. He was as brave in the air as he was on the ground and didn't mind going through a tackle or two when in possession. He would hunt a rival down and get in the tackle, face to face. He challenged fairly, powerfully, correctly. He was certainly physical and played football as a man's game, but rarely overstepped the mark unless severely provoked. He respected the opposition and I never saw him try to put an opponent out of the game. Maybe he didn't quite have the vision or the range of passing of Hoddle but he still had the eye for a good pass and a wide peripheral vision that allowed him to make the smart pass instead of just the good pass. Put the best qualities of the two together and you might just have the perfect midfield player.

Bryan Robson was also one of the boys. He led by example on the pitch and was first to the bar to buy his team-mates a drink afterwards. He made the papers now and again with his exploits but I can honestly say that it never bothered me. I always respected him and his relationship with the team and trusted him to do the right thing at the right time. He was always able to rally the troops either on the pitch or socially.

He was an unrelenting player who never admitted a game or a cause was lost. It was a great pity that he had his problems with his fitness. He missed thirty-five caps under me alone and had he had a normal, relatively trouble-free career he would have broken the all-time British record with something to spare. As a manager he has stuck at it just as he did as a player, displaying the same sort of spirit and passion after suffering the humiliation of relegation and the disappointment of two losing cup finals within weeks of each other. But he bounced back, changed his team, showed bravery in buying players like Paul Merson and took his team to a third Wembley game in three seasons. How far he goes as a manager is entirely up to him and the commitment he will need to show. He needs to be able to cope with these sorts of pressure season after season without it affecting him either on or off the pitch.

If there was one player in the England squad who matched Robson for dedication in training and performance on the pitch it was my goalkeeper Peter Shilton, certainly one of the best in the world and a man who probably kept me in the England job more than once when he stood up to everything a rival team could throw at him. The man was a fantastic trainer and a marvellous example on the training ground although he could be moody and problematic off it with his well-documented incidents. He was another who publicly confessed to liking a drink or several, and it is an affliction which blighted the English game severely to the amazement and amusement of continental players who knew how to look after their bodies much better.

But I never had any personal difficulties with Peter Shilton. When I took over from Ron Greenwood, who was alternating him with England's other outstanding goalkeeper Ray Clemence, he came straight to me and laid all his cards on the table. He told me he didn't like the alternative game system and wanted to know who I thought was the best number one and to make a choice. He was straight and blunt with me and I could sympathize with his point of view. As it happened, Ray

Clemence made the job easy for me as he chose gently to fade into the background. In fact throughout my time as international manager I selected Ray only twice, both times against Luxembourg where he was in semi-retirement anyway, and then gradually introduced others like Gary Bailey, Chris Woods and eventually current goalkeeper David Seaman, who I picked for his debut, along with Paul Gascoigne, against Saudi Arabia in November 1988, as a substitute for Shilton. But in the main it was the immovable figure of Shilts who was first on my list.

I could understand the problems Ron Greenwood had had in separating the two goalkeepers because, although different in style, they were both world-class and deserving of international careers. Bryan Robson was robbed of a record number of caps by injury, and Shilton was certainly denied world records because of the presence of his rival who won sixty-one caps. Clemence was certainly not the same sort of worker as Shilton. He preferred to play centre-forward during training. I am not sure he would ever have made an outfield player but there was no doubting his qualities between the sticks: he was a total natural, tall with quick reflexes, great hands and a superb command of the box. Make no mistake, Clemence was a great goalkeeper.

But Shilton was phenomenal. He was something of a character, never afraid to have his say if he thought something was wrong whether it was on the pitch or off it, sometimes making one or two enemies on the way. He was a dour man at times who often went into deep moods for days on end, and there was never any doubt that he was a gambler who loved his cards and his horses. There was also a lot of speculation about his home life but it never interfered with his international duties and for me he was in a different class. He applied himself, was totally professional and wanted to play in every game and take part in every training session.

He had some crucial games for me. He once made a vital save in a World Cup qualifying match against Poland to keep us in contention, the goalless game in Katowice at the tail end of 1989 when, in the dying seconds, he watched a shot hit the top of the crossbar. I thought at the time that it was either incredibly cool or very foolhardy, but afterwards he was adamant that he had watched it on to the woodwork because he did not want to touch it over the top and give away what would have been a very dangerous corner. He was quite relaxed about it afterwards, shrugging his shoulders and saying, 'I knew it was going to hit the bar and wouldn't have gone in.'

We always felt that it was going to take some special sort of shot to beat him, and our opponents must have felt the same way. When you have a goalkeeper of that quality, forwards tend to try that much harder in front of goal and often lose their natural instincts. In fact it was two totally freak goals which sent England home from the World Cup Finals of 1986 and 1990. Against Argentina in Mexico City, Diego Maradona clearly punched the ball into the net with everyone, with the exception of the referee and linesman, seeing the incident. I have never needed to see the replay because it is etched into my mind's eye. There are no bitter feelings directed toward the man himself. Maradona cheated and he got away with it; let it be on his conscience, not mine. If there is any anger at all it is directed at the FIFA referees committee which appointed relatively inexperienced international officials from Costa Rica (the linesman) and Tunisia (the referee). I am not being clever after the event for I voiced my fears before the game. It was a potentially explosive situation for the two countries had been at war only four years earlier; clearly it was a game which needed strong officials.

There were many supporters from both countries present in the magnificent Azteca Stadium and the dangers were obvious.

Little went in our favour during that game as Maradona scored one of the great goals of that or any World Cup, dummying Shilton at the end of a mazy dribble which, incidentally, started in the centre circle with a foul on Glenn Hoddle – neither seen nor given – which gave the Argentines possession. The illegal goal gave Argentina a tremendous lift, but even so we came back and almost forced it into extra time. I have no doubt that had we beaten Argentina we would have gone on to win the World Cup that year. Shilton was distraught at the decision. He chased the referee up the pitch. He knew it was his ball. He was deeply hurt by the decision. It shattered all of us, but I had to put on my brave face and not use the decision as an excuse for defeat.

If that wasn't enough it happened again to poor Peter four years later in Turin when he conceded a goal which was in no way his fault in the semi-final against Germany. It began with a doubtful foul conceded by Stuart Pearce against the already limping Thomas Hassler. Brehme stepped up to take the free kick which hit the boot of the advancing Paul Parker, looping high into the air and spinning over the head of the helpless Shilton, squeezing in at the angle, probably touching the crossbar on the way down. If the German had taken it a hundred times again it would never have been repeated.

Shilton might not have been in Italy in 1990 for I almost left him out after the fiasco of the European Championship Finals in Germany two summers earlier. He was thirty-eight then and I had to decide whether he could sustain his form as a forty-year-old. He was certainly one of those written off by the press. If he had been at all out of sorts in the September 1988 game against Denmark at the start of the next season I would have thanked him and said farewell. As it was he announced that he had cut alcohol from his diet and his form, if anything, improved and I decided to keep with him. A decision he fully vindicated in Italy.

He was big in goal, had long arms and a good leap. He never lost his agility or his handling because of the work he put in, although his kicking began to fail him later on. I would place him not only alongside Lev Yashin of Russia, Gordon Banks of England, Dino Zoff of Italy and Gilmar of Brazil but would go further and say that they could consider themselves lucky to be classed in his company.

Another top-quality player was Gary Lineker who will be remembered not only for his goals and his sunny personality but also for an injury to a big toe which curtailed his training with me for England, restricted his performances and appearances when he went to Japan, eventually caused his retirement from the game and finally became the butt of a running joke on the panel game They Think It's All Over.

He was one of those footballers who could get by on a minimum amount of training. He was much more a player than a trainer as, after a game, he was always very stiff and could hardly move. My physiotherapist Fred Street and the team doctor used to talk to me about him. He would wake up the morning after a game and struggle to get out of bed. It would be a couple of days later before he could ease himself into the action. It was agreed among us that he was being genuine about the reaction of his muscles and such was the toll on his body that he would always only just be fit if there was a game three days later. As for the toe, that was genuine as well, as we saw when his career was brought to a full stop. It would be wrong to say he didn't train because he did, but he did prefer to play and he liked to rest the day before and have hot baths the day after.

The toe became quite a problem during the 1990 World Cup, hurting him when he kicked the ball and making it difficult for him to do up his boot.

During a World Cup you need to keep your players together, working and training in preparation for the big games ahead, but he couldn't join in. It was a problem for him but it was also a problem for me, and I had to explain to the other players that he wasn't skiving off. Even so his fellow professionals, as they are wont to do, gave him terrible stick, saying things like, 'You be careful how you walk Gary,' or 'Be careful how you tie your boot laces.' Fortunately they did it with a smile and Gary took it well and didn't throw the toys out of the pram as some might have done.

There was nothing wrong with his courage as he showed when he broke his arm in a pre-World Cup game against Canada in Vancouver on 24 May 1986. I thought we had lost him for the finals but he had a cast put on the arm and didn't miss a single game. I never saw him pull out of a challenge and once the ball was in the box that was all he saw – the ball. He went where the bullets fly, where some other players are afraid to go. He always seemed to play particularly well against the Poles, and for me his best match in an England shirt was not the 3–0 win in 1986 in Mexico but the 3–0 win at Wembley one Saturday afternoon in June 1989 in a World Cup qualifier. He not only scored his usual goal against the Poles but led the line really well and held the ball up brilliantly.

I could never see him going into management. He wouldn't be able to put up with all the hassle and the nasty side of things, and I don't blame him for that. He doesn't need that aggravation, especially as he has talents in other directions. In fact, I am told he might well have been a cricketer and I can well believe that after watching him score a century for us in a cricket match in Mexico before the World Cup Finals. He is a good presenter on television and radio and has established himself quickly. He and Michelle were a great couple to have around and I could not be more delighted for them that baby George came through his problems.

I liked Lineker a lot. He had a pleasing personality, was nice to work with and was very intelligent. He also had a bright mind on the field, but he was not a thrusting centre-forward, more touch, timing and technique. It was not a sophisticated technique but more one-touch, very instinctive, knowing when the ball was going to come in and where to be so that he was on the end of it. Sometimes it was first post and at other times the back post; he could always read it well and he never minded how he scored or which part of his anatomy he used to put the ball in the net.

His game was never about what he did for other people but what others did for him: he was the finisher at the end of the build-up; he was the end product as opposed to the initiator. He was very good at his job because you could always rely on Gary being in there. Quick on the ground, he would spin defenders and get in behind them. He could head the ball quite well for a shorter man and although he was never going to be another Tommy Lawton he developed his technique so that if a chance came to him in the air he could take it more often than not.

He and Peter Beardsley developed a good understanding, working together and reading each other very well. He knew he wasn't a George Best or a Ryan Giggs so he didn't try those things; he kept it simple and most of his goals were scored from inside the six-yard box. He was always looking for the space behind the defenders so that he could get in his shot. That was his game and he did it so successfully that he scored forty-nine times for his country, some of them very important for me, particularly the hat trick against Poland in Mexico in 1986.

Gary was very adaptable, adjusting to whatever company he was in whether it was other players, the media or businessmen, which is why he has been so successful in life after football. He didn't need to go into management because he had already mapped out his plan of campaign, with the media predominant. His direction didn't surprise me, nor did his success. But that was the joy of working with England. The players were all talented, mostly committed and all totally different. It is an experience I would never swap.

7

Dutch Treat

The hardest moment of my football career was walking away from the England job at Lancaster Gate, especially as I was labelled a 'traitor' by those who knew nothing about the manner of my departure. Despite all of the baggage that went with it – the abuse, the vilification, being spat upon by the fans, the assault on my past personal life, the stress on myself and the strain on my family – I would have gone back at any time to help out in any capacity.

People who saw what the job did to me will be mystified by this, but I hated it when I had to go after the highs and lows of Italia 90, and when I heard that my successor Graham Taylor may have been on the point of departing with three games still remaining for the qualifying competition for the 1994 World Cup in the USA I would have been prepared to drop everything to return and try to help out with results against two of my old adversaries, Holland and Poland, with little trepidation about the final game against San Marino. As it happened Graham stayed on, I remained in Portugal and England failed to make it to the United States.

Despite my anguish at our failure to join the élite again, I would not criticize Graham Taylor through the media at or for any price – and believe me, I was offered plenty as the wolves gathered on the England manager's doorstep. Such was the vitriolic criticism I received from former England players who should have known better, and especially from ex-Ipswich and England manager Sir Alf Ramsey, that I vowed when I left that I would never attack another England manager while he was trying to do his best for himself and his country. I never did and I never will, because I know just how much it can hurt.

Was it worth it, those eight long years? Clearly there are a lot of young managers around who do not think so, judging by those who turned down the job after Terry Venables had departed and before the inexperienced Glenn Hoddle bravely stepped into the breach with such success. He was right to do so because there is no doubt that for an Englishman managing your national team is the best, the greatest honour in the game bar none. I was made aware of the prestige of the job, if I needed to be, simply by the way people treated and greeted me. There is no doubt at all that being in possession of the job opened all sorts of doors and if I had wanted to cash in I could easily and quickly have made up the difference in the drop in salary I had to take when I left Ipswich. Being manager or coach of England is like being the Prime Minister of football. When I went to watch a club match I was, in most cases, treated with respect bordering on the point of deference, while the public gave me great respect almost all of the time.

Basically I am a simple, normal man and when I travelled in from my Ipswich home to Lancaster Gate I did so on British Rail and the London Underground. Why not? It was quicker and easier than by car, and what was the point of a taxi from Liverpool Street when I could get a Central Line tube direct? People were shy of saying much until they were about to get off the tube and then, on my short walk to the office, cabbies and others would shout, 'Keep it going Bobby!' 'Don't let it get you down, son!' It was nice; I wasn't looking for it, but it was a big boost. In the past it happened only in Ipswich, but now people voiced their support wherever I went around the country, and it quickly made me aware of the massive importance of the job and the success of the England football team.

When we won there was no better feeling and this was reflected by all the supporters I met up and down the land. It was much bigger than winning a club game because this was for the entire country and you only had a dozen or so games a year in which to make your mark. The enormity of the job, the pressure, the tension, the responsibility makes you realize that you are not just running a football team but one of the biggest 'clubs' in the world. You don't think about it like that when you take on the job, but it soon hits you and it was marvellous to have the public support. The negative pressure came not from the people but from newspapers like the *Sun* and *Mirror* who thought they were representing the public's feelings when what they were really doing was massaging the sports editors' egos in a vicious battle for circulation.

It may have looked to some as though my sudden flight and subsequent stay abroad was something of an exile, running away from the attention of the press and the pressure. It was purely and simply circumstances. England was a hard act to follow. What do you do after managing your country in two World Cup Finals? Where do you go? It is a serious problem, and I solved it in my own way.

I was still managing England when PSV first approached me. I was in Eindhoven to watch an important game involving a number of international players in preparation for the World Cup Finals in Italy when I met Tom van Dallen, the manager of FC Twente Enschede at the time I bought Frans Thijssen and Arnold Muhren for Ipswich. During our conversation he asked me what I was going to do after the World Cup. It was difficult to give him a proper answer, for although I still had a year of my contract to run, that extra year was usually given by the Football Association in case they wanted to reward the manager with a year's money upon his departure. In truth I did not know at that stage what was in the minds of the Football Association's top brass. I wanted to stay but I knew that they would be under pressure to bring in someone new as throughout my eight years I had been under pressure from certain sections of the media and even from within Lancaster Gate itself. Tom explained that the reason he was enquiring was because PSV were looking for a new coach for the next season and I fitted the bill. As he was a friend of the general manager Kees Ploegsma, I guessed he knew what he was talking about, but I was non-committal. I returned to England and put it out of my mind.

Then, as winter gave way to spring in 1990, signalling the approach of the end of the domestic season, PSV contacted me officially for the first time as they wanted to be sure of a coach in place for the start of their next campaign. Without losing my sense of commitment to the England job or my eagerness to retain the position, I went straight to the FA chairman Bert Millichip and the chief executive Graham Kelly to ask them where my future lay as I needed to make plans after the 1990 World Cup in Italy. They told me that if I had received a good offer they would not seek to stop me from taking it. I asked if this meant I could talk officially to any interested club and they gave their permission, but asked if we could keep it quiet until after the World Cup. That, of course, suited me although it did seem that their complicity was giving clear indications that they were not exactly fighting to retain my services.

On the surface of it I didn't foresee any problems; I had a good relationship with both of the men I had spoken to and with the chairman of the International Committee Dick Wragg and his assistant Peter Swales. Funny how wrong you can be sometimes. The Manchester City chairman, Swales, was clearly no friend of mine. He might have been nice to my face but when we went out of the World Cup he was reported as saying, 'It's a good job we didn't win the World Cup or we would have been stuck with him.'

All I was doing at that stage of my career was protecting my future in exactly the same way any international manager does. I was certainly not being a traitor. Even so, there was plenty of cloak and dagger action as all sides tried to shield the content of the discussions from the media. There was a top-secret meeting with all the trappings of an old James Bond movie when PSV officials – Kees Ploegsma and Jacques Ruts, the president – flew in from Holland on a Philips private jet – one of the perks of being sponsored by the giant electrical company based in Eindhoven – to a private airfield in Cambridge where we picked a quiet restaurant for our initial discussion. They told me about the club, the players they had and their ambitions. At that stage there was no talk about salary and no rush for a decision. I told them I would make up my mind one way or the other as soon as possible. I wanted to stay on as England manager, but did the FA want me? And if I did leave, what else could I do? It would be difficult to take an English club, even a top one, but I did have the urge to return to the day-to-day involvement of club management and PSV were offering to provide me with the opportunity. It would, I thought, be a new experience, a new adventure.

I knew a fair bit about Dutch football from my experiences with Thijssen and Muhren, as well as from scouting the Dutch team and playing them in European and World Cup competitions with England. I admired their approach to the game and the way they played their football. I knew it was a system to which I could adapt very quickly.

At the time I trusted the FA to keep the situation to themselves and asked my accountant John Hazell to go to Holland on my behalf to talk to PSV, rather than be seen over there myself. John came back with what was on offer – which, incidentally, was double my FA salary, which said a lot about their perception of value. I had taken a drop in salary from Ipswich to take on the England mantle in the first place. I started on £65,000 a year, and by the time I left eight years later I was on only £80,000. At that time the top club managers in England were earning between £200,000 and £250,000, and I believe that showed I was never driven by money and that my motivation was loyalty to my country. Despite the offer from Holland, if the FA had offered me another four years on the same salary I would have stayed on. I truly believed that England could win the World Cup in the USA.

At this stage of my career I liked the England job. I knew it back to front, I felt comfortable doing it, I was used to the problems and I was happy. I had overcome a lot of the obstacles and had even built up an excellent rapport with the majority of the number one football writers in England, many of whom had been at my throat at one stage or another. They left it to their number two football writers or the news reporters to have a go at me or to dish the dirt. It was all part of the game. Even as I told Millichip and Kelly that I had been offered the job and was seriously considering accepting it, I was quietly wishing they would try to dissuade me and offer me an extension. I even delayed the actual signing of my new deal with PSV until after the World Cup Finals, but at no stage were discussions forthcoming.

There was, however, plenty to attract me to PSV. I had been

there many times. I liked the Philips Stadium and I enjoyed the sort of football they played. They were ambitious, had money to back up that ambition and wanted their Dutch title back. It was also very convenient – only a fifty-five-minute flight away. In fact, I could reach Eindhoven quicker than I could get to Leicester!

Despite all the precautions taken, somehow the story leaked, and to this day I do not know whether it came from the FA or from Holland. The world of football is a small one where keeping secrets is next to impossible, but the way it came out in the newspapers was positively bizarre. I had been on a visit to the House of Commons to talk to the Sports Minister Colin Moynihan with Glen Kirton about the importance of behaviour and properly representing the country on the eve of our departure to Italy for the World Cup Finals. There was very little depth to it all; indeed, it was a waste of everyone's time. No team in the world knew better how to behave on the pitch than England. We had the best disciplinary record of any of the top teams and we knew that, because of our fans' awful behaviour at the time, we could not afford to be seen to provoke anyone. I felt the meeting was a bit of an insult.

Afterwards I went back to report to Bert Millichip and Graham Kelly at the Great Western Hotel in London where they were meeting for the FA's AGM. Someone saw me talking to Bert and, during the conversation, it was alleged that I proffered a brown envelope to him and then to every member of the International Committee present, offering my resignation in a handwritten letter. I volunteered a million pounds to be paid to a chosen charity if anyone could produce just one of those supposed handwritten letters, but of course no one could because there was no letter. It was pure invention from the fertile mind of a journalist.

To add to the problems there was a further assault on my personal life in the papers. Some tabloids had decided to take over my past, dangling huge fees in front of people's noses to encourage them to make all sorts of wild claims and accusations. Between the two stories that came out my departure to the World Cup was hardly the calm prelude I had hoped for to the announcement that I was to leave after the tournament. Indeed, my house in Ipswich was besieged by journalists and photographers as the papers claimed I was being greedy, unpatriotic, a cheat and a liar who was running out on England. I telephoned FA official Glen Kirton at Lancaster Gate to tell him it was like Custer's Last Stand in Ipswich and he told me it was even worse over there with television cameras, photographers and journalists clamouring for statements and pictures. I was, it seemed, the dish of the day.

The FA backed me as they had always done and Glen organized a hasty press conference to reveal the true facts. That was an experience in itself. The photographers and writers were literally fighting with each other to gain the best position. They ignored a request to stop and I told them to look at themselves and see how they were behaving while criticizing others. I had never seen anything like it in my life. I was so incensed that I took legal action against the *Today* newspaper for calling me a traitor and they settled out of court. I should have taken a few more of them to task but it was neither my style nor a wise course of action to take on the might of a newspaper empire – certainly not on my England wages. The only people who were happy about the story coming out was PSV Eindhoven who were delighted that they could tell their public who was going to coach their team next season.

I had hoped that I could tell the England players and, especially, my coach Don Howe personally, before the news became public. Don, who I first met when we both played for West Bromwich Albion in the 1950s, remains one of my best friends in football. As soon as I had finished with the marauding press at the FA headquarters in Lancaster Gate I drove straight to Luton to tell them. I had planned to tell Don first and then the players once we were settled in our World Cup headquarters in Sardinia. They took it a great deal more calmly than the media with Don, always a strong man for me, saying, 'You don't have to explain to me. What you have done is perfectly justified. In six weeks' time you could have been out of work. You have done the right thing.' The players' attitude was no different. 'So what,' they shrugged. That, to them, was the modern, transient world of football. In fact there were half a dozen World Cup managers negotiating or completing contracts with clubs at the time with a starting date after the World Cup.

To me it was more than just a change of post. After all, I had only had two jobs in twenty-one years, so leaving before I felt ready was a big wrench. But the die had been cast and despite our success in reaching the semi-finals and being knocked out on penalties by the eventual winners Germany, Graham Taylor was the new man at the helm and I was on my way.

I had one day back in England after the World Cup before Elsie and I caught the night boat from Harwich to the Hook of Holland and then drove to Eindhoven. As someone who had done little or no motoring abroad my first problem was to remind myself to keep to the correct side of the road; even so, I was at the superb PSV training ground in the leafy suburbs of Eindhoven by ten a.m., walking into a totally different way of club football to my rich and rewarding experiences at Ipswich.

Chairmen on the continent were far more involved in club business than those in England, although they seem to have more than caught up since. At Ipswich, John Cobbold was very much a figurehead, attending board meetings once a month and match days. He gave me his telephone number just in case, but I rarely used it. PSV president Jacques Ruts was very much involved in all that happened.

One of the big differences I had to get used to straight away was the way in which the club dealt with transfers. It was an area I had to come to grips with on my first day. My Dutch assistant Hans Dorjee told me that the team was desperately short of a quality 'libro' defender. While in Italy we had every team scouted and I had been impressed, both by watching and from the reports I had, with the Romanian Gica Popescu, a tall and elegant ball player. I telephoned Howard Wilkinson, one of the top managers I had used as a World Cup scout, who had watched him more than most, and he confirmed what a good player he was. That was enough for me, but instead of going out and signing him as I would have done at Ipswich, I simply informed Kees Ploegsma who I wanted and he went out and negotiated the fee and the contract before presenting me with the player.

There had been plenty of player movement at the club with Wim Kieft and Flemming Poulsen departing for other clubs while both Ivan Nielsen and Soren Lerby retired. We had brought in Johnny Bosman and Erwin Koeman and tried to sign a promising young goalkeeper, Ruud Hesp, from Fortuna Sittard, later to sign for Louis van Gaal at Barcelona. It is a system I have become used to in my eight years abroad, and there is no doubt that it works. I can say in all honesty that had the system been in operation in Britain, the game would not have been besmirched by the bung scandals.

Basically it was a very happy two-year stay in Holland. The players were brilliant and I made many good friends. The second year was inevitably much better than the first, especially as we once again pipped great rivals Ajax to the title. The biggest problem I had in the first year was with the English media. They still followed me and my first big match, which we lost 3–1 to Ajax after dominating much of the game, was covered by a huge segment of them, seeming to delight in my defeat and promptly asking Ploegsma about the security of my position! The Dutch press, without the sort of tabloids we had back at home, were amazed, but they soon became used to it as we went out of European competition and the Dutch Cup early on.

The Dutch press pack rarely instigated that sort of criticism or story, but they would often carry what the English papers were saying about me. Generally, though, they were far more interested in the tactical side and how I would handle that. English coaches did not have the greatest reputation at the time because of the proliferation of route one and the long-ball game. They thought that would be the football I would be taking to Holland with me. It has never been my style, but coaches are apt to be pigeon-holed. Even had I wanted I could hardly have played the long-ball game with my main striker, the Brazilian Romario, and with the quality of our midfield. It would have been criminal to bypass them.

As it happened we lost our ace in the pack, Romario, from September 1990 until January 1991 through injury and we missed him badly. His prolonged absence meant that our chase for the title was hampered and it wasn't until the final day of the season that we finally clinched it after a head-to-head struggle with the powerful Ajax team managed by Leo Beenhakker. I was quickly reminded that in my last two years at Ipswich I had lost the English title on the last day and I was hoping that I wasn't going to be jinxed and become a third-time loser. Dutch officials with walkie-talkies made sure that our game and Ajax's last fixture kicked off at exactly the same instant. We were level on points going into that last day and, after a 4–1 defeat by third-place Groningen the week before, we held only a two-goal advantage. Ajax were at home to Vitesse but had been forced to move out of their little stadium into the bigger national stadium, while we were playing Volendam at our own Philips Stadium. A year earlier Leo and I had pitted our wits against each other in Sardinia in the World Cup, sharing the honours in a goalless draw.

The link between the two deciding games were thousands and thousands of transistor radios, so everyone involved knew that when we were one up, Ajax had cut the deficit to a single goal because they were two up. The tension crackled across the Netherlands but it was going to take a mighty display from Ajax to score two more than us as we were thoroughly professional, restricting our opponents to a couple of shots while scoring three ourselves, retaining our two-goal advantage by the end of a very exciting afternoon.

In the end it came down to the results of the season's meetings between the two teams. We had been unlucky to lose the first game 3–1, our 4–1 home win over the defending champions gave us that vital edge in the tight run-in. My assistant Hans Dorjee was leaving at the end of the season to become coach at Feyenoord, and as a sort of farewell gift I asked him to take charge of the last training session. Shades of England and things to come at Barcelona, as this was interpreted by the watching media as the assistant being put in charge above me to ensure we clinched the title!

I will never forget the after-match celebrations. There was no waiting for the next day, not in Eindhoven – it was there and then. We paraded through the streets of the town led by the Philips band in an open-deck bus in a downpour straight after the game. It seemed that just about everyone had turned out to

144

congratulate us as we headed for a reception at the town hall with the players taking off their sodden jackets and throwing them to the cheering crowds. When I discovered that this was all planned *before* the game, I said to my assistant Hans Dorjee, 'What happens if we lose?' He shrugged his shoulders and replied, 'They cancel it.' Talk about adding to the pressure!

There was still no rest for us, and even during the midwinter break we were contracted for a tour to India. I was glad we went because it was one of the great experiences of my footballing life. The enthusiasm for the game over there is phenomenal and we played to packed houses for all three of our games, including 100,000 in the Salt Lake Stadium. Even without the injured Romario, controversially back in Brazil, we rattled up nineteen goals and conceded one. Clearly their ability did not match their enthusiasm.

For the second season, 1991/2, I had Frank Arnesen as my assistant and we brought Wim Kieft back to the club to replace Bosman, who had gone to Anderlecht. Otherwise things remained very much as they were. We retained our Dutch title, beating off a strong challenge from Hans Dorjee and his Feyenoord side, which faded in March, and eventually finished three points clear of Ajax, dropping only ten points and suffering one defeat on the way. It was another great domestic season but the big dilemma for me was that once again we failed in Europe.

I was desperate to do well in the European Champions Cup, but after putting out the Turkish side Besiktas in the first round we drew Belgian champions Anderlecht and went out after a goalless draw at home and a 1–0 defeat in Brussels. It was heartbreaking because we went into the key game without Vanenberg, Romario, Ellerman, Kieft and Gerets. We were just not equipped with the depth to cope with that sort of absenteeism – no club in the world would have been. But there are no excuses at the top level in football and that result was the direct reason why I was not offered an extension to my two-year contract. But it is no big deal on the continent. Even though I had won the League for two seasons running, my contract had come to an end and they were ready to move on and had already approached and secured the word of Groningen coach Hans Westerhof long before I made my exit. Not that it changed their fortunes: they still failed in Europe the next season and lost their title into the bargain.

I enjoyed my return to club football and with two Dutch championships under my belt there were certainly no regrets, even though it was all so different compared with managing in England. As a manager at Ipswich I did everything, but PSV had their own general manager in Kees Ploegsma, a strong man who worked hard to protect his own job. I quickly became used to it. No longer did I have to arrange our Friday night travel, the hotels where we were to stay; there were no more fights with players over contracts. That was his domain and he handled it very well. There were stories in the English press that we didn't get on. Not true. I never fell out with him once. Obviously he was as disappointed as I was about our lack of success in Europe because that was the cream, that was where he made the money for the club to reinvest in players, but throughout my two years there we had a good working relationship.

When I left the club at the end of that second campaign the folks back home in England assumed I had been sacked. I was neither embarrassed nor hurt by PSV's decision. They had employed me for two years and I had delivered two championships; they were happy with that and so was I. England is only just catching up in that respect, although I cannot imagine a scenario where a club here waves goodbye to a coach who has won two titles. But managers don't last for ever, unless you are as successful as Alex Ferguson had been at Manchester United. Italy, Holland, England, wherever you look coaches do well to last for their two years these days. It is about as safe and secure a job as hang-gliding off the north face of the Eiger.

I liked Eindhoven and it was a classy football club where the directors never interfered with the way I ran the team. Hans and then Frank were good assistants who helped me a great deal. They would brief me about our opponents when I lacked the local knowledge and were good in training. I could happily pass anything on to either of them in that sphere. Hans I respected both as a coach and as a person, always correct and very polite, while Frank, who I snapped up from his job coaching the ten to twelve age group, was much more of a friend, in fact one of my best friends. We would go to games together and he was always very bubbly. The only problem I had with Frank was that at the time he was not a qualified coach and if for some reason I couldn't take training, through sickness or other appointments, he was not allowed to go on the field to take the players until he had earned his diploma. It was a rule of the Dutch Federation, and a good one at that. It wouldn't hurt to have the same regulation apply in England where they seem to think that 300 games and ten years as a professional is enough to qualify someone as a coach or a manager, to handle lots of money and make big decisions.

There were periodic stories about player power but they were about as true as the rubbish written on the same subject with the England players in Italy. The players backed me and I liked them. I was especially fond of the big central defender Stan Valckx, who I was to take with me when I moved, while the veteran Belgian Eric Gerets was an excellent player and a very strong and respectful captain who went on to be a very good coach himself at FC Liege. Goalkeeper Hans van Breukelen was another great character who, at the moment it was predicted in the press that he was going to walk out on me, fooled them all and signed a new two-year contract. He always had plenty to say for himself but was always proper. Barry van Aerle provided the fun and light relief in the dressing room, as well as quality on the pitch, and Romario was the icing on the cake.

The Brazilian was an exciting player who was capable of turning a game in an instant with his skill around the penalty area, but he could also be frustrating, disappearing for long periods of the game, rarely shouldering any responsibility and sometimes socializing and dancing late into the night before important games. His goals made up for everything, though, and I could never stay cross with him for long because he had such an angelic face and such a nice temperament. If there was such a thing as player power at PSV, he was it. He did pretty much as he pleased, flying home to Brazil, refusing to make the trip to India with the team when he was supposed to be the star attraction, and not always pulling his weight. Fortunately the off-the-pitch problems were not my concern, and as he was on a six-year contract earning a lot more money than I was with my two-year contract I was not about to test my strength against him. Certainly not while he was winning me games and titles.

The previous manager Guus Hiddink had left me with a good legacy, PSV having finished as runners up in the League and winning the Dutch Cup the season before I came, and I built on that, particularly on the right side with Eric Gerets, Barry van Aerle and Gerald Vanenberg, who I called twinkle feet because he wore such small boots. When they got going they were unstoppable. They used to overlap and interchange and they had such a fine understanding that I didn't have to touch it. There was no way to improve it. As well as Popescu I also had Johnny Bosman in that first season and Erwin Koeman, a solid professional. I was delighted with them even though they were not my signings because they were both quality players.

The Dutch League maybe didn't boast the depth of the top English division, but the top half a dozen clubs were of an excellent quality and always provided difficult matches. There were, of course, easier games when you could take the foot off the accelerator and rest key players or bring on the youngsters. We, like Ajax and Feyenoord, had the advantage of being able to afford to bring in top-quality foreign players. I had Romario from Brazil, Popescu from Romania, Gerets from Belgium and Jan Heintze from Denmark, and this facility lifted the top clubs away from the lesser lights and maintained the gap. There were three levels in the division, just as there are in England, comprising a handful of clubs chasing the title, those who were happy with mid-table safety and a stab at the cup and those fighting to stave off relegation. The difference in England is that the clubs near the bottom are so much stronger and always likely to cause an upset. Spain is more like England, where you have a club like Seville being relegated with 60,000 gates. As I found out to my cost later, there are also strong teams in the lower divisions, teams like Gijon, Celta Vigo, Oviedo and Compostella. Holland did not have that same depth and in my last season the big clubs shared the pots with Eindhoven taking the title, Feyenoord the Cup and Ajax weighing in with the UEFA Cup.

I left the club and Eindhoven itself with a lot of new friends. Despite the ups and downs I had never, ever been put under pressure by the chairman Ruts who was more often than not embarrassed by the strength of negative publicity in England. By March 1992 it was evident that I wouldn't get an extension to my contract after the latest failure in Europe. Ruts let me know in a meeting, telling the players himself rather than announcing it through the press. Gerets stood up and thanked me, pledged the team's support and promised a big effort to retain the Championship the following season. He was a good, honest man who was never afraid to speak his mind, as he did one day in the dressing room when he took Romario to one side.

He told the little Brazilian that win bonuses were very important to the players and their families and that he expected the same effort from Romario as the team members made themselves. He was making a valid point because Romario was on a far higher salary – around £300,000 a year at the time – than everyone else and was not nearly as reliant on bonus money as players, like Gerets, who were on a comparatively low basic wage. Naturally there was some resentment towards the Brazilian, but always tempered with the knowledge that he was the one who could make things happen when he was on song. It impressed me that Gerets was careful to make the point that he didn't begrudge Romario his money because he was the better player, but he wanted that extra effort.

I fully expected to return home to England from Holland, but I admit I had rather become used to the continental lifestyle, and when Sporting Lisbon came in for me in the spring of 1992 I took the job. Maybe I was wrong to take it but it sounded good and immediately it became known the players at PSV came up and congratulated me without ever the slightest reduction in their efforts or commitment to me or the team. I had never been to Portugal other than to play, and I thought it would be a great experience to try yet another lifestyle, that maybe I would do another two years before calling it a day and retiring gracefully to Ipswich.

It was an attractive package. Sporting were and still are a big club. They offered a new challenge in a totally different environment and it would satisfy my curiosity as to what the football was like in that part of the world on the Iberian peninsula. I also fancied the sunshine after the cold of England and Holland and, once more, the tabled salary was considerably higher, offering me and my family security in later years.

Such was my relationship with PSV that they allowed me a couple of trips over to Lisbon to look at the team and see what they had to offer before I accepted the contract for the 1992/3 season. I liked what I saw. They had a good team, a nice stadium and those involved seemed to be very affable people as they wined and dined me.

Once I had agreed to start with them in the coming summer I concentrated on my job with PSV and retained the title. I knew that there would be sufficient time in the close season to prepare for the new season.

8

A Bitter-sweet Experience

It was a new world for me when I first went to take up my appointment at Sporting Lisbon: another new language, another new experience, another style of football. In other words, a new challenge. I had, of course, been there to play football, the first time as a player under Walter Winterbottom in a World Cup tie at the impressive home of Benfica, the Stadium of Light. Strangely, in ninety-five matches as England manager I played Portugal only once, and that was a 1–0 defeat in the Mexico World Cup.

My arrival certainly generated more interest than I expected and I was surprised when a big contingent of the Portuguese media arrived at my Ipswich home as I was packing to leave for Lisbon. They wanted pictures of my house, my garden and my paintings and to talk to me about everything, and then they followed me to the airport where they were booked on the same plane. There were even more waiting for us when we arrived at the airport with the media fighting for elbow room with the fans and the directors of the club.

Sporting had made a great fuss of me when they were wooing me to sign on, and that continued when I was met by their delegation at the airport: the new club president Sousa Cintra and a young man, José Mourinho, who was to follow me to Porto and Barcelona as my career moved on. José was a personable chap, nominated to look after me and help me because of his good English and his strong background in football. He was a school teacher and his father had been a professional goalkeeper with Vitoria Setúbal and was then general manager of the same club. José was to prove a marvellous asset, covering my back and looking after me while building up a good rapport with the players of each of the three clubs we have been to together. Whenever I needed him or his support he was there, even though it often meant putting himself in the firing line.

There was a distinct pro-British feeling around the club, not least of all because I was following in the footsteps of the likes of Malcolm Allison, John Toshack, Keith Burkinshaw and Jimmy Hagan. There has also always been a large British expatriate community in Lisbon and Portugal in general. The British are credited with inventing port when they added brandy to the rough red wine of the time.

Having seen the team twice I knew I needed a Portuguese coach to help me over the obstacles, someone who knew the scene. The club appointed Manuel Fernandes, a former Sporting player for twelve years and an ex-international who was coaching in the Second Division. He was an excellent choice, trustworthy and friendly with a little English. He was also a friend of José's which made life a whole lot simpler. I didn't stay in Lisbon long initially as I immediately took the team away to France to the national training headquarters. It meant I got to know the players, their ability and what they were like off the pitch very quickly, observing them not only in training but during their meals and relaxation hours.

My first managerial decision was to go back to PSV to buy central defender Stan Valckx for half a million pounds and left-sided midfielder Sergei Cherbakov from the Ukraine, an outstanding twenty-one-year-old player picked up for a give-away $600,000. Stan was a brilliant signing, playing for the club for two and a half years before returning to Holland for a million pounds. I also inherited some good players like Figo, Jorge Cadete, Krasimir Balakov and Fernando Nelson, who went to Aston Villa at a later date, while the club brought in Portuguese players Carlos Jorge from Maritimo and Barni from Boa Vista on the recommendation of my assistant.

The team had been going through a very indifferent period and had won nothing for a dozen years when I arrived, and clearly there was a lot of work to be done. I had seen this for myself when I travelled to Paris before the official end of my spell at PSV to watch Sporting play Aston Villa in a friendly in Paris. There is a big Portuguese population in the French capital and a large crowd turned out to see us beat Villa 2–0. Nominally in charge that night, I used all the players I had for a quick look at everyone. I brought in Andrzej Juskowiak, a Polish Olympic player who had performed well in the 1992 games in Barcelona and who we had looked at on trial at PSV, rejecting him only because of the number of foreign players we had on our books. I played the striker against Villa, he scored a goal and we promptly signed him.

To my great disappointment we won nothing in that first season, 1992/3, finishing third in the League behind Porto and Benfica and losing in the semi-final of the Portuguese Cup. We were not good enough and lacked a bit of quality. I didn't feel too much pressure but it was there lurking in the background, and my lack of Portuguese meant I couldn't read a lot of the criticism in the papers. What you don't know you don't worry about. Cintra was also disappointed that we had won nothing, but to balance that the players had responded well to my training methods, we had played decent football, attracted big crowds and finished close up to our two big rivals in the race for the title.

From a personal point of view Portugal was a lovely place to live. In the first year we found a tenth-floor apartment between Benfica's Stadium of Light and our Alvalade Stadium, a suggestion from my wife Elsie to persuade me to cut down on my travelling time. In the second year we moved out to St João in Estoril where we had a house, garden and swimming pool. Elsie admitted that she missed the grass, the air and the birds, but the move suited me as I could play golf at the superb Japanese-owned club nearby, close to the Formula One circuit.

In the second year English fitness coach Roger Spry joined me while the president brought in Antonio Pacheco and Paulo Sousa in the summer from Benfica. They were out of contract and Cintra just stepped in to snap them up; it was a terrific piece of business for us, a great blow to Benfica and a wonderful boost for our fans. I had nothing to do with the deal at all but, fortunately, they were two quality players with Sousa going on to play for both Juventus and Borussia Dortmund after leaving Sporting. What I would have done had they been two players I did not rate I am not sure. Certainly it would have thrown the president and myself into serious conflict.

The rivalry between the two Lisbon clubs was so acute that when Benfica beat Lisbon for the signature of Paulo Futre from Atlético Madrid our president severed all links with the club, and when Manuel Fernandes and I went to watch them play our other great rivals Porto, we had to buy our own tickets because he didn't want us to accept their hospitality – in fact he didn't even want us to go to their ground. That was how petty the so-called King of Mineral Water could be. Cintra also brought in a Portuguese goalkeeper, Paulo Costinha, an under-21 international from Boa Vista who was indirectly to cost me my job.

But with players like the Bulgarians Krasimir Balakov and Ivailo Yordanov, Emelio Peixe and Budimir Vujavic, we felt we were ready to have a real tilt at the title. We started the 1993/4 season really brilliantly and quickly went to the top of the table. The future looked very rosy for the average age of our team was only twenty-three and they were winning while they were still learning. I had settled in, the players were responding.

We received another boost when we knocked Celtic out of the second round of the UEFA Cup, pulling back a goal deficit from the first leg to beat them 2–0 in front of 70,000 fans. It was a really good European tie with Cadete scoring two outstanding goals to put us into a tie with the Austrian club Casino Salzburg, impressing the Scots enough at the same time for them eventually to come back and buy him. We beat Salzburg in early December by two clear goals at home but should have won by five, misses we were to regret and which had massive repercussions on me and my future. In the return match we were holding on comfortably at 0–0 at half-time, but mid-way through the second half our reserve goalkeeper Costinha, the man brought in by Cintra, let one in from thirty-five yards out to put the tie back in the melting pot.

We had chances to wrap it up after that but looked safe as the ninety came and went with the Dutch referee constantly looking at his watch. Both myself and my assistant Manuel Fernandes were making frantic signals to our players that there were seconds to play. Perhaps we should have kept quiet for one of their midfield players picked up the ball and, instead of passing it as he would have done at any other stage in the game, he let fly, again from thirty-five yards out. I was delighted as I knew it was their last chance, and he surely was chancing his arm from that distance. Wrong. The ball bounced in front of the nineteen-year-old goalkeeper who dived over it, and instead of being on the plane home and in the quarter-finals we were facing extra time and a team with their tails up.

The extra half hour was frantic as Figo hit the post and we did everything but score. The game was heading for penalties when, again in the last minute, we conceded a corner and they scored the winner with a header on the far post. We were out of a game we should have won three times over.

We were shattered as we boarded the plane home and I was aware that Cintra was talking over the intercom in Portuguese. Although I had been learning the language it was too soon for me to follow what he was saying. In any case, he was a president who could never keep his mouth shut. He was always on the television and radio, and if we won away from home he would drive back in his Mercedes in front of the coach to take the adulation from the 1,500 or so fans who would always be waiting at the gates. I ignored him and his latest diatribe until I noticed that the players' heads were dropping, prompting me to ask José Mourinho what was going on. He was embarrassed but explained to me that the president had told everyone that this performance was a disgrace to Sporting and how unhappy he was with it. I couldn't believe what I was hearing, especially when he followed it up by telling everyone on the aircraft – supporters, directors and players – that he was going to speak to Mr Robson about this disgrace as soon as we were home.

He was as good as his word. We travelled back late on the Wednesday night, and at our next training session on the Friday, 10 December, he asked to see me as I went out onto the pitch and told me he was dismissing me. I was stunned. I had expected him to talk about the match and the goalkeeper he had bought for me, but this was a complete shock. The entire staff was watching as he wielded the axe. I told him I didn't understand why he was doing it. He was firing me on the back of one bad result. I was upset and told him that I accepted his decision but didn't respect it, that if he didn't understand that these things happen in European football, he shouldn't get himself involved. I added that he was the first person to sack me in twenty-five years. I also enquired as to what he planned to do about my contract, and he told me that they would carry on paying me monthly. I wasn't at all happy about this because I didn't trust him and thought that if I went back to England I wouldn't see a penny of it, and I told him so. There was nothing honourable about this man as subsequent events were to prove: the club was pocketing the tax deducted from my pay cheque, as I discovered when I was personally presented with an Inland Revenue bill for the cool sum of £80,000.

The staff and the players were sick at the decision and the way it had been delivered. Sporting Lisbon were the best side in Portugal, looking to win the title that year, and the players and coaching staff were now watching their coach being sent home because they had had one off day. I was too stunned even to think of what I was going to do. All I wanted to do was get out of the ground and get back to my home in Estoril. I changed and cleared out my locker, and by the time I left the ground word had got out and already there were hundreds outside along with all the media who had been tipped off by the president. There was no joy among them; all of them were upset, although not as much as I was. I didn't say a great deal to them other than that I had been dismissed, that I was upset at the president's attitude and that I had no respect for him. It was generally seen as a foolish decision by a foolish president who did little to help the club.

There was, of course, a hidden agenda. Cintra's close friend, schoolteacher Carlos Querois, had just quit as coach to the Portuguese national team and he was available. He was seen as a prize catch because he was called a world champion, as is the custom in Portugal when any team wins any sort of world title. He earned this tag when his under-18 team won the World Championship with a very bright group of players in Saudi Arabia. He was an academic who had never played the game at a professional level. I knew he was around and I knew he was a great friend of my boss, but I hadn't seen him as a threat or a danger while he was national coach or even after because my team was developing so well.

The great irony of the whole situation was that only a week earlier Arsenal's vice-chairman David Dein, a friend of some years' standing, had telephoned me to pass on a message that Everton wanted a new manager and would I be interested. He gave me the chairman's name and telephone number, and when I called Dr David Marsh I told him, 'I have a fine young team here, I am enjoying my life in Portugal, I am top of the League and think I can win it. I am flattered you called me, but please forget me.' He thanked me for being straight and letting him know. It is amazing to think that three times in my career a club as big as Everton had come knocking on my door and I had turned them down each time. By the time I was booted out of Sporting, Everton were a long way down the road in their negotiations with Mike Walker and an appointment was imminent. Had they come in for me then I probably would have joined them. Timing is everything.

I also had an opportunity to join Wales as their manager while I was briefly out of work, but I didn't fancy their offer of a £40,000 salary against the £250,000 I had been earning at Sporting. There was a healthy bonus scheme, but for what? Winning the World Cup? In cold terms, it was two months' money for a twelve-month job. It would also have meant taking on a headache because the country was unarguably short of international-quality players. I had been at a high standard with England and still taken stick. I didn't need that sort of aggravation and heartache at my age, thank you very much. John Toshack took on the challenge, and resigned after one match. It was one decision I never regretted.

I didn't hide myself while I was on the outside looking in. I regularly went into Lisbon, sorted out a lawyer to look after my claims against the club, played golf and went shopping, and wherever I went people came up to me and told me how sad and angry they were and how much they were on my side and hoped I didn't think it was anything to do with the fans. But the really sad part of my departure was when the players decided to give me a farewell dinner in Cascais with all the players and staff. I was presented with Bulgarian and Portuguese national shirts and other gifts including the lion emblem of Sporting cast in bronze. It was all quite emotional, and after the dinner I went back to Stan Valckx's house with a few of the players and their wives for a cup of coffee, and went to bed quite late.

I couldn't have been asleep for more than a couple of hours when the telephone rang; it was José, passing on the awful news that young Sergei Cherbakov had crashed his car after the party and was in hospital totally paralysed. He had apparently left our party and gone on to a pub used by the Russian community, had a few drinks, stayed until the early hours of the morning and then shot a set of traffic lights and was hit side on. José rang me back an hour or so later to tell me that the news was getting worse by the minute. The lad was in a bad way and would never walk again. I immediately jumped into my car and drove to the hospital. There were already a lot of people gathered around the entrance, but I was immediately shown in and spoke to the surgeon who told me that tests and X-rays confirmed the player had lost all feeling in and use of his legs. It transpired that he had not been wearing a safety belt, and when the car had gone into a spin he was thrown about as though he was in a tumble dryer. The car was battered but not a write-off, and it was reckoned that had he been wearing his belt he would have come through with only minor injuries. The surgeon added that the player had broken his spinal cord, was a paraplegic and had no hope of recovery.

They allowed me in to see him. He was badly cut but conscious and aware of what had happened, where he was and who I was. He kept telling me he had no feeling. There was little I could do or say. It was heart-rending knowing the truth.

The club immediately stopped Cherbakov's salary and it needed the players and myself to chip in to keep him going. Sporting organized a match for him but they didn't put their heart and soul into it and it didn't raise a great deal. He went off to a special clinic in Italy but, despite their great reputation there for performing near miracles, they could do little for him. When I was in charge of Porto and we came to play in Lisbon I arranged for some friends to pick him up and he joined us for dinner before the game. That season we reached the Cup Final and beat Sporting in Lisbon. I think it was as satisfying for him as it was for me. I kept in touch with him until the end of the season before he returned to his home with his mother and father who had come to stay with him. He had arrived as an outstanding prospect with a brilliant future but went home as a twenty-one-year-old confined to a wheelchair for the remainder of his life. And I worried about getting the sack! His accident certainly put things in perspective.

I went home for Christmas and talked over my future with Elsie. We decided that as we had a nice house and a monthly pay cheque coming in, why not winter in Portugal with a little trip to the Caribbean as a sideline? The England cricket squad was on tour that winter, and I'd always wanted to watch England play cricket away against either the West Indies or Australia, so a friend of mine, knowing my ambitions, arranged for me to host a party of tourists for the *Daily Telegraph* in February 1994. It sounded idyllic. My first winter break since 1950, and what a break! A few weeks in the Algarve sharpening up my golf and a month with my wife in the West Indies talking to punters about cricket and football. It certainly beat managing Wales.

I had lifted from the depths of despair and was really looking forward to what lay ahead. I went back to Estoril on my own to sort out business when, a couple of days later, I took a telephone call from a stranger who introduced himself as the head of a travel agency in Porto used by the local club, a large shareholding which was in the name of Pinto Da Costa, the Porto president. I briefly wondered what all this had to do with me until he told me he was talking on behalf of the club and had the president sitting right next to him. He told me they would very much like me to go to Porto to become their coach. Would I be interested?

Obviously I knew all about Porto as a team. They were strong but underachieving, situated in the north of the country at the hub of Portuguese football. Most people assume the capital of a country is the most influential area, but there are fourteen top clubs in northern Portugal and Porto are the kings. I told them I was sufficiently interested to want to talk to them and they wasted no time, saying, 'Right, we will be with you in the morning.' Before I agreed to that, though, I asked them what was happening with their current coach Tomislav Ivic, who had taken the job after being sacked by Benfica following a defeat by my Sporting Lisbon side. I was still prickly about the way I had been kicked out to let in Querois

162

and I didn't want to be party to any skulduggery. They assured me that everything had been arranged; Ivic was leaving under happy circumstances and I would be going into a settled environment.

They got lost on the drive down the next morning and my first meeting with them was when I drove out to meet them and guided them in. There was no messing about. It was me they wanted and they immediately put a two-and-a-half-year contract in front of me that was worth substantially more than I was being paid by Sporting. I liked the money but not the length of the contract. I said I would take the rest of that season and the next because I had dreams of returning home, and in any case, after my recent bad experience I wanted to make sure I had a good relationship with the president before I committed myself to such a long time together.

I asked for twenty-four hours to think it over and took the opportunity to speak to José Mourinho in confidence. He was excited for me, telling me what a big club it was, about the excellence of the staff and what a strong guy the president was. He told me I would love the area because of the English influence, the beaches and the golf courses. He recommended it and jumped at the chance when I offered to take him with me, something I had already agreed as part of the deal should I accept. By this time I had fallen in love with the country and there was also the prospect of a wicked touch of revenge about the opportunity. How nice it would be to put one over on Sousa Cintra. I didn't really need the day's grace as I soon made up my mind and drove north to say yes; I signed the eighteen-month contract on the Monday, 31 January 1994, starting that day.

Under Ivic the football at Porto had become somewhat negative and stale and the gates had slumped to under 10,000 as the fans voted with their feet. I didn't have to change the personnel, just the style of play. I took away the sweeper and replaced a defensive midfield player with an extra attacker. We were a big club with great resources and didn't need the extra player at the back when we were playing lesser teams. I wanted more men up front so that we could play the ball forward and be more dynamic, creating and scoring goals. Our change of tactics reaped instant rewards. We couldn't stop scoring goals and I became known as 'Bobby Five O' because we kept winning 5–0, including a demolition by that margin of Werder Bremen in Germany in the Champions League. In my first domestic fixture we played Salgueiros away in the Cup and won 2–1 and then beat Maritimo 2–0, and I remember Louis Cesar, the old secretary at the club, coming up to me and saying, 'Mister, we haven't seen a game like that here all season.'

Nothing, however, seems to be straightforward in Portugal and in March the Das Antas Stadium was seized and closed by the authorities because of a £800,000 unpaid tax bill, forcing us to train in the car park as iron chains and padlocks barred our way. It was a crazy situation, especially as it was an ongoing one involving other clubs – but only our ground was closed down.

After our great surge we were soon back to gates of between 35,000 and 40,000 within five weeks, and in the end we almost pipped Benfica to the title having started off nine points adrift of them. It was only two points for a win, so it was a huge gap, but even so we finished just two points behind and that could have been one had I not put out a near reserve side to rest tired players in our last match, which we drew 0–0. I don't know what the president and his new coach at Sporting Lisbon thought, but they had been caught and overhauled by both ourselves and Benfica to finish out of the race in third place, having been top of the table when I left. Sweet justice, perhaps. We also reached the final of the Portuguese Cup that first season and, of all teams, we met Sporting in Lisbon at the Stadium of Light. I tried to be professional, but I have to admit that I had a terrific glow inside when we beat them 2–1 in the replay after a goalless draw in the first game. It was one of my most pleasurable moments in football.

Fate has funny ways of dealing with events, and the next time I returned to Lisbon to play Sporting was the night we won the title in my second season, 1994/5. The players threw me up in the air in the middle of the pitch in their joy and I didn't mind one bit. We beat Lisbon 2–0 and that meant we had ended any mathematical chance of their catching us. Even though we had denied them the title the home fans were incredible; they applauded me around the pitch and made it a very emotional and memorable night. Three nights later we came back down to earth with a big bump as we lost to Maritimo 1–0 in the semi-final of the Cup.

Over the first season and a half the club had been busy on the transfer market. We bought Brazilian Emerson, Louis Barras came back from Marseilles, Edmilson from Salgueiros, Vasili Kulkov and Sergei Yuran from Benfica and Walter Paz from Argentinos Juniors. We also made two sales: Fernando Couto to Parma and Emil Kostadinov to La Coruña. But although domestically Porto were winning trophies again, European success continued to elude me. In my first full season at the club we were put out of the Cup Winners' Cup by the Italians Sampdoria and once more luck was not with me. We won 1–0 in Genoa but they reversed the score in Porto and after extra time knocked us out 5–4 on penalties.

Tragedy was to strike me again at Porto at the end of August 1994, just as it had when I left Sporting. We had played Benfica on a Wednesday night and drew 1–1, with Rui Filipe scoring our goal. He was suspended for the match on the following Sunday and so was not involved in the build-up. The team assembled on the Saturday night, and when I came down after breakfast in my room Louis Cesar took me to the lounge and said, 'Rui Filipe is dead.' I couldn't believe what I was hearing. The news beat me over the head and left me gasping as I asked my staff to find out what had happened.

He had gone out with his family on the Saturday night and on the way back to his home he hit the kerb, the car slewed and he was ejected through the roof. They found his body a hundred metres away with the life smashed out of him by the stones he landed on. Once more there was no safety belt. It had happened again and I was distraught. Two young players in such a short time. With Cherbakov I felt that if we hadn't gone out for dinner it wouldn't have happened, but there was no way I could blame myself for this latest tragedy.

We played our game on Sunday, 31 August against Beira Mar under a huge cloud, observing a minute's silence and winning 2–0. It meant nothing to us. Everyone connected with the club was down, and the next day I went with the team to view Filipe's body and pay my respects. It was shortly after this that the president came to me to sign a new contract to help give the club a lift. By this time Porto was top of the table with big crowds every week. He wrote some figures on a piece of paper offering me another big pay rise. I was happy, in good health, I liked the city, enjoyed membership of the British club with its tennis and cricket, life was good, so I said yes. There was just one condition: I said that if I had an offer I couldn't refuse – say from Japan or AC Milan – I would want to go. He said in front of José that he agreed and if it happened all I would have to do was tell him and if I really wanted to go he wouldn't stand in my way. I was too trusting. I should have had it written down on paper. To me a promise is a promise and a deal is a deal, but some people see it differently.

It was to be quickly put to the test at the end of that season when, out of the blue in May 1995, Arsenal came in for me. George Graham had left in February under a cloud after the bung scandal and they were looking around for a new manager. When David Dein telephoned me to ask me what the situation was with my contract and would I be interested, my heart skipped a beat. For all Manchester United's recent success and the great years Liverpool enjoyed as the best club team in the world, Arsenal were, to me, *the* English club. It had always been my dream to manage or coach them and here was David Dein asking me if I was interested.

There were two jobs on offer – one as coach and the other as technical director – and I told David about the promise from the president and said we could do it quite openly. He came to Portugal at my invitation and outlined the two positions, thinking I would be more interested in the passive role of finding players, advising the coach, running the club and using my contacts. David even asked me to offer suggestions for the coaching position. I did – me. He was surprised that I was much more interested in staying at the sharp end; I told him I was not ready to give that up yet; he replied that if that was the job I wanted, Arsenal would be delighted. I said, 'If you are saying that I can have that job I will go and tell my president and I will be coming.'

I went over to England to meet the Arsenal board of directors and was very impressed with them. I knew David Dein, his chairman Peter Hill-Wood and managing director Ken Friar, but I also took an instant liking to Danny Fiszman and the Carr brothers. They were all top-class people, intelligent and polite. I was like a child at Christmas, I wasn't even bothered about the salary they would be offering. That was secondary. As far as I was concerned the decision had been made: I was joining Arsenal. All that was left was to hold Jorge Pinto Da Costa to his word and gain my release. I had to do the thing the right way as I have tried to do all of my career, and tell my president before signing a contract. I attended what I thought would be a farewell dinner in London that night at the English branch of the Porto Supporters Club.

When I returned to Porto I had a message from the president asking me to go to Switzerland with him the next day to watch the Swiss Cup Final, offering me the perfect opportunity to tell him of my decision. We saw the game and I told him the players he was looking at were not good enough for Porto and to save his money. Then, after the game, I told him I had received an offer from Arsenal and that I had accepted it as it was the right opportunity for me and the right club for me to go home for. Subject to our earlier agreement I was exercising my right to go. He and his wife Philomena went very quiet. It was his wife who was doing the translating and she was clearly not enjoying it, almost gasping for air as she told him. They talked, and she turned to me and said, 'My husband says that he cannot possibly let you go. You are very popular with our fans, it would be a terrible blow for the club and he is relying on you to take the team into the European Champions League. He has invested money in players on your recommendation and the whole of the future of the club rests on you. He begs you to please give him another year.' I asked her to remind him of our conversation after Rui Filipe's death, but he said he had only a vague recollection of it and couldn't remember exactly what had been said, and anyway he wasn't going to give me permission to leave the club at that moment. He stated, 'There is nobody to replace you and you have to stay.'

I rang David Dein to tell him about the sudden turn of events and he asked me what I planned to do. I had the option just to walk out on my contract, but neither he nor I was keen on that sort of thing which would tarnish the move. He promised me any help the club could give in resolving the situation. I went back to my president and asked him if compensation from Arsenal would help to change his mind, but he was adamant. He told me to forget Arsenal and to get on with my job at Porto.

I was torn between two loves, cursing myself and my position for not getting the agreement in writing. After George Graham's departure Arsenal wanted everything to be squeaky clean; the last thing they needed was a row about breaking contracts and poaching coaches. I was in a cleft stick. I could also hear what the president was saying about Porto for we were champions, we were in the Champions League, we did have an awful lot going for us and he had backed my judgement on players. We had sold Kulkov and Yuran, who was facing a manslaughter charge after yet another car crash, and we had brought in the Hungarian Peter Lipcsei and the Pole Grzegorz Mielcarski.

I didn't sleep a wink for two nights worrying about the situation. In the end I did the honourable thing and went against my instincts and my better judgement and decided to stay. Arsenal were as deflated and sad about it as I was but, as they were throughout our discussions, totally noble and fully understanding of my difficulties. It hurt me to turn them down. Elsie was looking forward to us going home so that we could be closer to our children, but at least I had something to look forward to with a good team and plenty to play for. Arsenal went on searching and eventually appointed Bruce Rioch.

As the press in England will confirm, I am not a man to hold grudges and my relationship with the president didn't seriously change, although he didn't have my total trust any more. Perhaps I am stupid to be so forgiving, but that is the way I am built and I doubt if I will change at my age. He compensated for his 'forgetful mind' somewhat when he showed great concern when, three months later, my malignant melanoma was diagnosed. He didn't put me under any sort of pressure while I was recovering.

By a strange coincidence the first game I went to see after my operation was Porto's European Cup tie in Nantes on 13 September 1995, and among the first people I met were David Dein and Bruce Rioch. I wished Bruce luck, and David must have been secretly relieved that I hadn't taken the job. I went back to managing in November, six weeks after my operation – much too early, but I felt the best way to recover was to get back to doing what I knew best. The scars on my face had healed remarkably quickly and certainly didn't bother me – I had no complexes about them.

It certainly helped my recovery that I went back to a good team which was seeking to retain the title. I must confess those first weeks back were a bit of a blur; it all went so quickly. I was happy to be alive and running totally on adrenalin. Neither Elsie nor my surgeon had wanted me to come back so quickly, if at all, but I had made a promise that if it didn't work out I would return home to England. It never happened. I was highly motivated and was immediately embroiled in my work on the pitch. I was lucky because the players responded really well to me. José and assistant coach Enancio had kept things ticking over well and we were nicely in touch. In my first game back we beat Campomaiorense, managed by my former number two Manuel Fernandes.

There was the odd problem with Vitor Baia, our international goalkeeper, who was suspended for two months as the result of an altercation *after* a game, forcing me to sign Lars Eriksson from Swedish club Norrkoping, and in early April 1996 we lost Vucavic for six months with ligament injuries. We had also lost Mielcarski to injury for five months, but despite this we pulled further and further away from our rivals, eventually finishing thirteen points in front of Sporting and seventeen ahead of Benfica to become Portuguese club champions for the second year running.

The only downside was, once again, Europe. After our masterly thrashing of Werder Bremen in the 1993/4 campaign we had drawn with Milan before eventually losing out to Barcelona, whose foreign stars Romario, Stoichkov and Koeman took us apart. For 1995/6 our group was tight: we drew twice with Nantes; managed a goalless draw away to Panathinaikos but lost disastrously at home 1–0; and drew away with the Danes Aalborg, who had replaced banned Dynamo Kiev, winning 2–0 in Portugal. Our 2–2 draw in France saw Domingos miss a penalty which would have secured our passage through to the next stage of the tournament, but it wasn't to be. Europe was fast becoming a monkey on my back. The club was confident and passionate about it and everyone wanted to do well, but when you meet top-class opposition you are always punished if you underperform or make mistakes. We were guilty of both and eventually received what we deserved.

It wasn't really my season for silverware and it was a big blow when we drew Sporting away in the one-leg Cup semi-final and lost. It was the second season in succession we had lost after being drawn away in the last four. The blow was somewhat softened by the phenomenal reception I was given by the home fans, heightened I presume by my return after illness. But we had retained the title comfortably and I felt I had done what I had to do for Porto. They were back into the money-spinning European Champions League and were going for a hat trick of titles for the first time in their distinguished history. I had given the president the extra year he had asked me for and I felt that all debts had been discharged when Barcelona called me in the spring to offer me a job for the third time.

The president knew I was serious this time because I told him I was leaving. He could see I was determined and that my mind was made up. This time he did not try to dissuade me but had his revenge by continuing to withhold part of my salary and bonuses for the year. It was a lot of money – a quarter of a million pounds in all – and I had in my possession a document in which they admitted the debt, but I still wasn't paid. After my experiences with Sporting and the non-payment of taxes, this latest episode didn't say a lot about the honesty and integrity of Portuguese clubs – after all, these were two of the top three in the country. It didn't end there, for as I went into my second year with Barcelona I received another Inland Revenue bill for £110,000! None of it made any sense as all my contracts were quite clear and in writing. Yet such was my love of the people and the country that I was tempted to return, not once but twice.

9

Barcelona Destiny

I always felt it was my destiny to coach Barcelona, one of the biggest football clubs in the world, if not *the* biggest. Twice before I had been forced to turn down the Catalan giants, but this time no number of protestations from Porto or warnings from my surgeons not to put myself under any extra pressure could divert me from fulfilling my ambitions.

But little did I know that I was pitching myself into the middle of a fierce political battle, a battle where I was always going to be the loser whatever I achieved on the pitch with the team. If I was used – as it seems clear I was – then I went willingly, and despite the obstacle course that stretched in front of me I emerged with pride and integrity intact and gave the club in return their second best season in a hundred years, the trophy cabinet bulging at the end of my time there as coach. I took with me to Barcelona a wealth of experience gathered from my playing days at Fulham, West Bromwich Albion and England and a managerial career which spanned club football in England, Canada, Holland and Portugal and eight years and two World Cup Final tournaments with the national side. I also arrived with my eyes clear following my confrontation with death that had left me with a different philosophy both on life and football. Had I taken the job on either of the two previous occasions it was offered me, who knows what might have happened, but this time I knew I was at least as well equipped as any other coach in the world.

The first chance to move to the Spanish club came while I was still at Ipswich. We drew Barcelona twice in European competition, once in the 1977/8 UEFA Cup where we enjoyed an epic tie, winning 3–0 at Portman Road only to lose 3–0 at the Nou Camp, eventually suffering defeat as much because of poor refereeing and bad luck as the result of the penalty shoot-out; fifteen months later we were paired in the Cup Winners' Cup and lost this time on away goals after winning 2–1 at home and losing 1–0 away. As a result of these games I came to know both the president, Josep Lluis Nunez, and Joan Gaspart, the long-standing vice-president of the club. Joan is an Anglophile, trained as a hotelier at the Connaught Hotel in London, and he was impressed with what we had done at Ipswich, which he knew from his experiences in the country was far from being one of the big players in the Football League. The friendship grew, and in the 1980/1 season he telephoned to offer me the job of managing Barcelona.

As much as I loved Ipswich I dearly wanted to go to Spain, take on a new challenge and test my ability, but I was in the midst of a ten-year contract and the Ipswich chairman John Cobbold exercised his rights to ask for compensation for the remainder of the contract. That killed any prospect of a deal because Barcelona felt they were too big a club to have to pay to fill their coaching position. I couldn't, and still don't, blame John for asking for the money; £200,000 was equal to the highest sum of money I ever paid for any player at the club, which is what England international Paul Mariner and Dutchman Frans Thijssen cost us. I thought that in view of what I had done Mr Cobbold should have let me go, but there are always two sides to a story and I bore no grudges against the man, nor did it alter our outstanding working relationship.

Joan Gaspart and I kept in touch during the intervening years and he often called me to talk about players they were interested in signing and asking my opinion of them. He and Barcelona came back for me again in 1984 when I was managing England and under terrific pressure. I remember the call well for I was actually with the international squad staying at our headquarters in Troon preparing for a home international match against Scotland. I took the telephone call at around 9.30 a.m. as we were preparing to go out for training, with players, coaching staff and the media milling around. We had a chat before he asked me what were the chances of my going to Barcelona; they needed a coach and needed one quickly. I told him at once that I couldn't even think of it. My mind immediately switched to the late Don Revie and the way he had walked out on England to coach the United Arab Emirates national team. Managing England meant far more to me than anything any club or country could offer me. The phone call didn't even reach the stage of talking money, as it had done in the first instance; I told him 'I am manager of England and the answer has to be no.'

That didn't finish the conversation, because Gaspart and his club were keen to have an English coach; because of our long and fruitful relationship, he asked me who I recommended. I told him that I thought Terry Venables could be the answer, that he was a bright, young, thinking coach who was destined to go a long way in the game. He was maybe a bit inexperienced but made up for this by being intelligent and progressive. Gaspart listened but told me he had never heard of Terry, and he even asked me to spell out his name. I suppose it shows the respect in which Gaspart held me because, after doing a few checks, they appointed Terry and he led them to the 1985 Spanish Championship and the 1986 European Cup Final. Terry had backed my judgement to the full and that did me no harm at all; indeed, it enhanced my reputation as a shrewd judge of football within the club. During our subsequent conversations it was often mentioned that one day I might be in a position to take the job myself.

As it happened, it was third time lucky. I was again under contract at Porto, and I remember receiving a call from Gaspart asking me where I stood in terms of that contract as Barcelona were contemplating changing their coach, Johan Cruyff. There is a somewhat sensitive dispute as to when I was first approached: some say it was in March 1996, while the club claim their first contact with me was in April. The difference was significant, for if it was the former then Cruyff was still very much in the job, but come April he was clearly on his way out because the official announcement of his dismissal came on 18 May. The club was trying to protect its image. In many ways it reflected my own position the following year when there were rumours of the appointment of Louis van Gaal long before I was told and it became official. Everyone in the world knew, but still the club denied it. I am afraid it is the sort of thing which happens all the time, not just in Europe but in England too. It is not nice when you are on the receiving end, but it is a simple fact of footballing life.

Later they called me again and said that they had made up their minds: Johan Cruyff was definitely going and was I available to fill the void? This time I was not going to turn down Barcelona under any circumstances. I had signed a new two-year contract with Porto after Rui Filipe's fatal car crash, agreeing with Pinta Da Costa that it would be the best thing to do to try to lift everyone at the club. But I put my name to that contract under the full understanding that if a big club came in I would go. I came unstuck on that point when Arsenal made a bid for me, but now I had given Porto an extra year's service, and the club was defaulting on my salary and bonus anyway.

I was ready to take my assistant José Mourinho with me to Barcelona, and after he had agreed to come we went in to see the Porto president. I didn't intend to ask his permission, I was simply going to tell him that I was going. I didn't even plan to tell him which club, but relented when he asked. He was very quiet when I told him of the offer and the fact that we were going to accept it. I told him that there were two reasons: the first that he had made his promise to me, and the second that he was in default with respect to my salary. Pinto Da Costa was clearly stunned at the news and said very little. He is a cool, calm, calculating person. He left me to do the talking and I tried to explain my decision, that it was my last chance to manage a club I had always wanted to join and, financially, it was an offer I could not refuse. He could hardly say no because in Portuguese football there is a ruling that if a player or a coach is not paid for three months they are entitled to leave the club for no fee. Some of the money that was outstanding to me had been due way back in August, giving me a legitimate and irrefutable reason for leaving.

It was sad the way things had turned out, but my respect for him as a person had not changed. For Porto he was an unbelievably good president who fought for the club at every turn. He didn't want to lose me because I had been good for his club; we were winning trophies, attracting big crowds and I was popular with the supporters. My leaving was going to reflect badly on him, particularly when it became known how much I was owed. Oddly, he did not try to persuade me to stay the way he had done when Arsenal had offered me a job. He didn't even ask me what I was going to be earning at Barcelona.

The next day I returned to the club to obtain my release, by which time the lawyers had become involved and had drawn up a document saying that the release would be granted on payment from Barcelona of 100 million escudos, some 25 per cent more than they owed me – a figure, incidentally, which was also fully documented. This took me by surprise and I told them it was nothing to do with me and that I was going anyway. Joan Gaspart had told me not to leave until I had my release and, on reflection, I should have torn up the papers and left. I didn't. I signed it and walked out, leaving it up to the two clubs and their lawyers to sort out.

It was completely out of order because all season I had been placating players who had not received their bonuses, telling them to hold on and not to run to the press with stories which would damage the club and our chances of winning more trophies. Imagine trying to motivate players who were not being paid properly! You couldn't see it happening at Bayern Munich or Manchester United. Pinto was embarrassed that he didn't have the money to solve the problem, and in the end he had to sell the Brazilian Emerson for £4 million in order to pay the players the bonuses they had earned at the end of the season, otherwise he wouldn't have had a team to play in the European Champions League for 1996/7. It was a messy departure and a sad one after two and a quarter years during which time I had won two Super Cups – the equivalent of the English game's Charity Shield – two Championships and the Portuguese Cup, taken Porto to the semi-finals of the European Champions League and made the players popular with their supporters again by playing attractive, attacking football.

One of the most pleasing factors of coaching abroad, I discovered right from my first days at PSV Eindhoven, was that I was divorced from the inevitable internal politics. I didn't want to have to soothe unpaid players, that was not my job, but it was foisted upon me at Porto so long as I sought to extract the best out of the players I was coaching. I couldn't wait to get to Barcelona and resume my coaching career at a club where the wages would be paid on time and contracts and bonuses would be discussed by the directors and not by me.

I was completely naive and unaware of the in-fighting that was going on at the club when I arrived. Señor Josep Lluis Nunez was trying to cling on to his presidency in the face of growing hostility and competition. Barcelona was a city divided with half of them on the side of the current regime and the other half backing sacked coach Johan Cruyff. It was my surprise party, and to many I was the unwelcome guest. I had suffered the *Daily Mirror* demanding my head when England won an international 1–0, but at Barcelona I was to be slammed by a section of the media after winning a game 6–0, and again after orchestrating what was described as the comeback of the century when we recovered from a three-goal deficit to beat champions Atlético Madrid 5–4 in a truly sensational Cup match.

I had signed a two-year contract with Barcelona which should have tipped me off that there could be problems ahead. When I read the small print, it stipulated that in the second year they could move me from coach to manager of the club. I read this and asked questions about it, but I was so confident that I would be successful that I dismissed any thoughts of changing roles, just as I knew that if I failed in any way at all I would be on the way out anyway. It didn't worry me at the time, but it might have done had I digested the story that appeared in *World Soccer*. Its editor Keir Radnedge wrote in

July 1996: 'One scenario envisaged by Nunez was that Robson would take over for next season, keeping the bench warm for van Gaal, then move up to the post of technical director in 1997/8.' Despite being so well informed, even Radnedge couldn't quite accept that such a deal could have been done without my knowledge, adding, 'The prospect of that can be no more than fifty-fifty.'

To understand FC Barcelona you have first to comprehend the city, the people and, indeed, Catalan. A casual visitor would not appreciate the depth of feeling for the region, and for most it is crystallized in the football club: when they play they are representing Catalonia against Spain, nation against nation. The supporters claim that FC Barcelona is more than a football club: it is the army of Catalan and its six million inhabitants. They are a proud and emotional people who will never forget that when Franco was in power he would not even permit them to speak their own language. Even when Franco died and Barcelona was returned to its people they retained the symbolism. Now all the road signs, airport signposts and menus are in Catalonian as well as Spanish, but the hurt still runs deep and many would prefer complete autonomy.

For visitors it is a wonderful, vibrant city, with stunning architecture and a culture all of its own, along with a lovely, balmy climate. Elsie and I lived on the Mediterranean coast in the charming town of Sitges, a holiday resort in the summer full of good restaurants and hotels and a sleepy, clean place in the winter. The club itself is sensational and the Nou Camp Stadium phenomenal, perhaps the best in the world, holding 120,000 with three levels of underground parking and not a single stanchion to obstruct the view – amazing, when you think that it was built forty years ago. It is not just a football club, it is a sports club and the focal point for young and old, male and female. Most sports are catered for and there is even an indoor skating rink; outside there are training facilities and a reserve pitch with a 'Mini Stadi' of 25,000 capacity which would hold its own in most cities as a stadium in its own right.

When the club travels out of the city, especially to Madrid, it is like an international match and Barcelona are always met at airports and hotels by hundreds and often thousands of supporters. Police are always needed to control the crowds when we fly in for an away game. I couldn't believe the way the club departed and arrived at airports in Spain – anything between two and five thousand people waiting to see the team off or watch them arrive. Without the police it would definitely be dangerous. Then, when we arrived at our hotel the night before an away game, there might be another two thousand fans waiting to catch a glimpse of the superstars. There were even more when Ronaldo played.

It got so bad that we were forced to send someone ahead to arrange security and police protection. When we played Real Sociedad in San Sebastian we were met at the airport and told that there were more than three thousand people outside the hotel on the sea front and that we were going to have problems simply getting through the door. I also remember going to a pre-season tournament in Majorca where we were to play Atlético Madrid. We booked a training ground the day before the game for a private session, but when we arrived there were at least five thousand fans waiting and it took us forty minutes just to get into the stadium. The fifteen policemen on duty couldn't handle it. I told them to open the stadium and put the fans inside so that we could reach the dressing rooms.

The city of Barcelona has been fed such a successful diet of football over the years that now winning is simply not enough; the club not only has to win trophies but do it with style and panache. Johan Cruyff did that for them both as a player and a coach, but even he ran out of luck and went without a major trophy for two years immediately before my arrival. The great Dutch master was like a black shadow looming over me for my first twelve months at the club. Half the city loved him for what he had done and the other half wanted something new after the two barren years; some were with the president Nunez but many were against him, supporters and media. It took a while to piece together the politics of this complicated situation but there was no doubt that I was following a much-loved legend.

Cruyff had created a very special style of football, adapting the Ajax way with his own ideas and weaving them around three of the world's best players in Ronald Koeman, Michael Laudrup and Hristo Stoichkov – and, later on, the Brazilian Romario. He had a group of Spanish and Catalan players who fitted in perfectly with fast, one-touch, total football, with the emphasis very much on attack. For six glorious years the people of Barcelona were thrilled and delighted with the football before the players began to age and the team stopped winning cups. In those last two years he won nothing but the Super Cup, although he did guide the team to the 1994 European Cup Final in Athens where they were humbled 4–0 by a great Milan side. I realized that I would have to match the best of Cruyff.

My second problem was the imminent elections. FC Barcelona is, I discovered, a very powerful political tool in Catalonia. All the local politicians in Barcelona like to be seen to be involved with the club, to have their pictures taken with the players, the coach and the president. There are many groups who would love to have the controlling interest in the club's affairs, and when Cruyff was sacked they used his dismissal to form opposition groups to take on Señor Nunez. Each of these rival factions had control of certain sections of the media – newspapers, radio and television – and these were used to attack Nunez through me from the very first day I arrived. Every perceived flaw or mistake was magnified out of all proportion to provoke a public backlash. It was the first time I had experienced such a thing, but not Nunez. Throughout, Nunez has remained the great survivor. He was appointed on the same day I won the FA Cup with Ipswich in 1978, and he now looks safe until 2002 unless results go really badly.

I was the president's choice to succeed Cruyff, so I was immediately seen as the enemy. I walked into a minefield. Before my team had kicked a ball I was attracting criticism which gathered pace, even though the club had its best start for thirty-three years with no defeats until a rainy day in November when we lost 2–1 to Atlético Bilbao in front of 46,000 fans in the San Mames Stadium, just two games short of the all-time record for matches without a defeat set by my recommendation Terry Venables in the 1984/5 season. Despite the start we had made, the goals we scored and the excitement we generated, all much of the media could do was moan. I was baffled and more than a little hurt because at that time I had no idea why it was all happening. We were criticized for not having a system, then for not having a system that the players could understand; then we were winning and scoring goals but not playing good football. As coach I could do no right.

On 26 January 1997 we beat Rayo Vallecano 6–0 at the Nou Camp, and despite being five up at half-time the 85,000 crowd were still giving the players a hard time. Our goals that night took our tally to sixty for the season, twenty more than at the same time the previous season with seven more points too; even so, the press slammed me the next day with the headline 'Barcelona win 6–0 – but don't play any football'. It was not just me and my Barcelona team they were taking apart, because by inference if we score six goals and we are no good, what is that saying about the losing team? All the time Johan Cruyff was there being photographed in the back of the stand, but to be quite honest he didn't bad-mouth me or write nasty pieces. He was always under pressure for a soundbite and he made the odd remark, like we ought to have more Spanish players in the team (which I found odd when I thought of Laudrup, Koeman, Stoichkov, Lineker, Romario, his son Jordi and the rest), but on the whole he treated me with a damn sight more respect than Sir Alf Ramsey when I superseded him as England manager.

I wouldn't want to criticize Johan. He would have been as disappointed to lose his job as I was when I had to step aside to let in Louis van Gaal. The fact that he was seen as a direct opponent of mine was because he was a figurehead for the opposition. We are all colleagues and criticizing each other does not help. I can even understand why some of the newspapers and some of the fans wanted him back because his record for Barcelona as a player and a coach was phenomenal. He was probably one of the four greatest players in the world during my years in the game, ranking right up there with Pelé, Platini and Maradona. He was a legend as both a player and a coach. It was not his intention to cripple me and I told the press that he was far too big for me to comment on adversely. That was one game I was not going to play, whatever the provocation. Perhaps the one area where Cruyff could have helped me out a bit more was to have stayed away from the ground more often. That would have helped me a lot for his presence served to perpetuate the incredible rivalry that existed between the two factions at the club. But, of course, as I said, he was innocent; he was there to watch the club he loved and the son he loved – and Jordi became my second Cruyff problem.

Jordi telephoned me when I took over from his father and said that he wanted to stay and play for the club under me and that he was sure he could do well. He stressed that being Johan's son had nothing to do with the situation and he hoped that I would base any decision I was going to take on technical merits and not be swayed by the politics. I promised him I would give him every consideration and would do what was right for the club. The truth was that it was the right time for him to move. It would have been an impossible situation for both of us. He would have gone back home and his dad would have asked him what had happened at the club. That is a natural father–son relationship, but if a story had leaked from the dressing room he would have been seen, unfairly or not, as the prime suspect. No, there was no way he could have stayed without the situation embarrassing either him or me and eventually the club, and I was delighted that I was able to find him a club as big as Manchester United, another of the world's best. Technically it was the right decision too because I also had players of the calibre of Ronaldo, Giovanni, Stoichkov and Figo in the squad, all fighting with Jordi for a place in the starting line-up. It was a no-win situation for if I hadn't picked him it would have been seen as getting back at his father and I couldn't let people think that way. Even though it wouldn't have been true, it would have been manna from heaven for the anti-Robson, anti-Barcelona brigade.

But the son of Cruyff was only a minor part of the difficulties of those first few months. The hardest part of it was not understanding exactly what was going on, why I was under such pressure day after day when results seemed to be going so well. Here we were top of the League, scoring stacks of goals, and into the bargain I had given them Ronaldo, a new hero to worship. I knew it was a big club but I was staggered that every day of the week there were dozens of journalists chasing every whisper and rumour and television and radio crews ready to stick microphones under my nose at the slightest excuse. It was like being at the World Cup Finals every day, where you have to arrange carefully controlled press conferences because of the huge demands of the foreign as well as the national press.

I genuinely thought it would ease off as we started by winning a pre-season tournament beating Inter Milan and San Lorenzo of Argentina and Atlético Madrid in the Spanish Super Cup, all this despite having our own pitch in an unplayable state. It was waterlogged and cutting up dreadfully, and after beating Espanyol 2–1, we had to move home temporarily to the Olympic Stadium in Montjuic. The pitch for that game against our neighbours Espanyol was truly incredible. It had been relaid and within minutes, as players swivelled and turned on it, great big chunks came out and by half-time it looked as though the entire area was covered with five thousand hedgehogs. There were great clumps in the way of the ball and with seventeen minutes to go we were a goal down and really under pressure from the fans and everyone else. Thankfully, Giovanni and Juan Pizzi saw us home with goals in the eighty-fourth and ninety-second minutes in front of 100,000 anxious fans. We played only one match at Montjuic, against AEK Larnaca in the European Cup Winners' Cup, before moving back home to the Nou Camp in time for the League game against Real Sociedad on 22 September.

That Espanyol match began to give me a clue as to what lay ahead if my team did not do the business. Some of the papers were immediately against me, others were on my side, but the national daily sports paper *Marca* was, rightly, independent. A paper called *Sport* had the knife in me while *As*, a Madrid-based paper, was aptly named as far as I was concerned. They had a couple of really evil journalists whose sole ambition in life was to dump on me and my club. What do you do? I did exactly the same as I did in England when the *Sun* and the *Mirror* were leading a nationwide campaign to have me sacked from the England job – I ignored it the best I could and battled on with my job. I couldn't read much Spanish at the time, so that helped to alleviate the problem, and it was only when it was picked up at home by the English papers that I really got to know about it.

The coverage of football in Spain, and at Barcelona in particular, has to be seen to be believed. The written media, radio and television are at the ground and the training ground every single day with three official press conferences every week and loads of minor skirmishes. Players are made available to them and are requested daily. Journalists had to fill acres of column inches every day and, as I had already found out to my cost, the simplest way of writing reams of copy is to take the critical, negative angle. Friday was the only clear day we had when we could work on free kicks and dead-ball situations without interference. They would have been there every day if they could, for the public thirst for information on the club was insatiable. Everyone seemed to want to know what happened in training, never mind in the games.

Both myself and José Mourinho were learning the language although José with his Portuguese was far advanced, and he was the one to put my point of view across, although the press officer Miguel Terres spoke good English and was a huge help. But I needed José in the dressing room, not a press officer. Louis van Gaal has a different outlook and uses Miguel everywhere, saturating the poor lad with work, but cut Miguel open and he would be red and blue right through. He is a super person and has coped brilliantly with the difficulties that both I and Louis threw his way.

The press didn't just limit themselves to questions on events at our club. I was regularly asked to comment on events at Real Madrid or on the latest exploits of Jesus Gil, the colourful president of Atlético Madrid. That was taboo territory as far as I was concerned and I always tried to keep the conversations centred around Barcelona. Señor Gil, a real character who has worked his way through a remarkable number of coaches over the years, was often a centre of controversy, taking on the Spanish Federation even to the extent of threatening not to allow his team to play against us in the quarter-finals of the Spanish Cup in March 1997. The game and its unusual build-up should have given the press enough to write about for the rest of the season after we came back from 3–0 down to win 5–4. I have personally never been involved in a game like it.

A subway strike kept the crowd down to 80,000 (!) and by half-time they were howling for my blood as we trailed by those three goals, all of them scored by Milinko Pantic. Just before the break I took a massive gamble by bringing off two defenders, my captain Gica Popescu and the French international Laurent Blanc, and throwing on the Bulgarian Hristo Stoichkov and Juan Pizzi. I was booed by my own supporters for doing that. At half-time I told the players to have a good look at the shirts they were wearing and to remember who they were playing for. I asked them to go out and win the second half by four goals. As it happened they had to score five in the half because Pantic grabbed a fourth goal. Sure enough Atlético were submerged with goals from Ronaldo (47, 50, 72), Figo (67) and Pizzi (82). I was exhausted just watching the game and afterwards I told the press to go away and savour it, to enjoy every moment of that incredible comeback.

Instead they went away and sharpened their knives. The headlines which greeted me the next day stated that *I* had lost the first half 3–0 and the *players* had won the second half. They had the effrontery to claim that the players, not I, had made the changes and that the team which played in the second half was the team I should have been playing all season. According to these incredible stories, I had remained silent during the break while the players made their speeches. Can anyone who knows me imagine my doing that when three goals down? I think not. Guardiola tried to put matters right with a statement in the press a couple of days later: 'People cannot blame the coach when we lose and then say it has got nothing to do with him when we win. He made the changes in the same way that he always does. It was Robson who told the players where to play and what to do – not the players. We are happy to resume our responsibilities on the pitch, but it is his job to decide the tactics. It is simply not true that we rode roughshod over his instructions. Robson is in charge, we limit ourselves to playing football.'

Stoichkov and Pizzi warmed up because I told them to, not because they decided they were going to go on. I decided the tactics, not the players. I was deeply hurt. Any other club, any other game and the coach would have been hailed as a hero; they would have labelled him a tactical genius for making those brave substitutions. I tore into the journalists at the training ground and for once told them what I thought of them and their own tactics. I told them I was prepared to bring the players in who had supposedly given them the quotes. I had already spoken to Stoichkov who denied everything, and they couldn't come up with anyone else. It was symptomatic of what had been happening. Fortunately this incident did not destroy the relationship between myself and the players.

Obviously when a coach has a squad as big and as talented as the one I had that season at Barcelona, there are going to be players who are left out and who will have a moan. That is true the world over, and the media are clever: they always go to the unhappy players to find their copy. I called the players in early on when I saw the direction in which things were heading and reminded them that we had a squad of twenty-four players of which only eleven could play with five on the bench. I explained that it was impossible to keep everyone happy every week but that because of our commitments, injuries and suspensions everyone in the squad would play their part in the season and therefore there was a need for patience.

To add to the pressures young players coming through the system were constantly being touted by the press and the fans for selection, particularly de la Pena, Oscar, Roger and Celades. De la Pena, known to the fans as the 'Little Buddha', was a particular favourite and there was a great demand for him to play, but I wanted to bring the youngsters on gradually and not rush them unnecessarily. I told the kids and the other players that if they weren't selected they had to keep their mouths shut out of respect for the players who were in the team, because those roles could be reversed at any time. They took that in and responded in the most positive fashion.

I gave the team that finished the Atlético match another chance in the next game away to Logroñes a few days later, the team which according to my detractors I should have discovered much earlier in the season, before the players found it for me. We struggled to win 1–0 with our substitute, the Nigerian Emanuel Amunike, scoring the only goal eight minutes from time. Nuff said!

This contretemps with the media after the Atlético game affected me deeply and certainly caused a shift in my relationship with some of the worst-offending journalists. In the meantime I simply carried on with my job of winning trophies for the club and helping the players and myself earn our win bonuses. I would start at nine in the morning to deal with messages and mail and to discuss with my training staff what was on the agenda for that day before starting training at 10.30 a.m. We always trained for at least ninety minutes and often for up to two hours, depending on what day of the week it was, and sometimes we would be back for training again between four and six in the afternoon.

Lunch is an important part of the day in Spain and people go home to their families or join them in a restaurant, rather than go to the pub for a pint and a sandwich as we sometimes do in England. I even got into the habit myself of having a proper lunch before going back to my office, often to be back at home by 8.30 p.m. If there was no training I could be by my swimming pool by 1.30 p.m., or if we were playing midweek I would stay at the club, skip lunch and be home by three. I was not expected back at the office and I was not expected to answer the telephones. I was the coach and that was it. I was there to train the team, not manage the club, and if I wanted to walk out straight after training I could do exactly that. It was a far cry from my days at Ipswich when I did just about everything apart from changing the toilet paper in the ladies' loos.

It was the same with transfers. I would sit down with Nunez and Gaspart to decide what was needed to improve the team and find out who was available. I might say that I needed a left-back and make a few suggestions; they would offer their choices but it would always be the one I wanted, if he was available. If it wasn't a well-known player I would have a look at the options, but basically I did nothing more until the new player was presented to me. I didn't have to be involved with transfer negotiations, that was someone else's task. It works well because it is not good for a player to be fighting with his coach over a new contract or wondering why the coach pays him less than a team-mate. On the training ground and on the pitch you look to build a mutual trust.

Preparation for the games was meticulous. For a match at the Nou Camp we would start with a short coach ride after the final training session from the ground over the road to the hotel. All the meals were planned and ordered by the doctor, so that the players ate the right stuff – plenty of carbohydrates and no red meat, although the occasional glass of red wine would be permitted. It is the custom here and does them more good than harm. Sometimes there would be a team meeting after dinner but players were asked to be in their rooms by 11 p.m. None was to be seen in the public areas of the hotel after that time, and never in the bar.

The culture on the continent is different to England. Even after we won the Cup the players didn't ask for and weren't offered an alcoholic drink to celebrate on the journey home. They drank mineral water or soft drinks. In England players go down the pub or the clubs after a game to get a few pints down largely because of peer pressure. In my experience in Spain, Portugal and Holland the attitude was far more professional. They knew how to look after their bodies. Obviously there was the odd exception – there is always the rebel – but generally top continental footballers would be horrified at the prospect of drinking seven or eight pints of beer on a Saturday night. I found the players easy to work with because of that attitude. They are dedicated performers who realize they have a short, highly rewarding career that they are not prepared to risk by playing the town.

I am not saying that the Barcelona dressing room was full of goody two-shoes, far from it. It was bristling with diverse characters such as Guardiola, who played in fifty-one out of our fifty-eight games in 1996/7 and was an outstanding player, but he was always ready to speak his mind. He had a strong personality and could influence other players. Amor was always correct, good with the press and said the right things in the dressing room if there was a wobble. He was the most perfect of people who worked hard to keep the dressing room happy. Sergi, Figo and Stoichkov would always have their say in any argument. Stoichkov had been portrayed as a sulky, moody player, but in the year I had with him he was a model professional. We were never in conflict, even though he had such a strong, fiery personality. In fact, there was not one of them I could point an accusing finger at. We only lost eight games out of fifty-eight all season, so that tends to keep a squad of players happy.

It was a magnificent performance in the midst of such a heavy schedule. Compare that record with, for instance, Real Madrid's total of forty-four competitive games in 1996/7; we had to fit an extra fourteen games in, so it was no wonder they were fresher than us come the end of the season. We had to play all the time, we couldn't just put off games because it was an international week, and we lost players like Ronaldo and Giovanni seven or eight times for Brazil friendlies, never mind the other absentees during World Cup qualifying weeks. Most of my squad were internationals of one sort or another and there were some weeks when we were very depleted.

As if we did not have enough problems with the fans, the press and the congestion of fixtures, early in 1997 the rumours began to grow about Louis van Gaal joining the club, fuelled by comments he made himself on Dutch television on 7 February. At first I didn't pay any attention and I thought the fuss would die down and go away as we were chasing Real Madrid in the League and well on our way to winning two cups – but it didn't. Not that the subject was ever brought up in my monthly meetings with Nunez and Gaspart, so I saw no reason to ask about the rumours until later in the season when van Gaal himself hinted strongly that he would be joining Barcelona from Ajax. Nunez told me that nothing had been decided, that I had my contract which guaranteed me a second year and I was not to let anything disturb me in the club's quest for trophies. Neither he nor Gaspart seemed in the least embarrassed about the situation, although on reflection they were never keen to prolong any discussion on the subject.

After a while I knew there was something going on, but I couldn't get to the bottom of it and there was no question of my throwing a wobbly and walking out. For a start there was that clause in my contract which mentioned the possibility of a change of status for the second season which I had all but ignored, but there was an addendum which stipulated that if I walked out on the club I would have to pay them double what they had paid me! Barcelona reckoned they were the biggest club in the world and that no one should be seen to be ditching them; it would be demeaning in their eyes. It would have cost me in the region of two million pounds. That never bothered me because I hadn't joined Barcelona to resign – only a fool would do that – and if things changed then my attitude was to let them pay for it. However, I still naively believed that my team would do so well that there would be no way they could replace me as coach for my second year at the club.

When I joined I was thrilled, honoured and privileged. I was also very confident that I would do well, and looking back on my year it was sensational. Facts show that I was the most successful coach in Europe during that season. The Barca directors were not to know that when they began covering themselves by lining up the successful Ajax coach to replace me. I had my contract – a document half in English and half in Spanish – notarized, translated and stamped by lawyers. Yes, they could get rid of me if I was seen to be unfairly critical of the club. The cards were well stacked in their favour but there was still nothing to concern me towards the end of the season. I was not looking for a war or even a conflict, I just wanted to prepare myself.

My reaction to the rumours was to roll up my sleeves and see how many trophies we could win. We finished the season well with only a couple of defeats in the last twenty-five games and, consequently, the hostilities abated and matters settled down as far as the fans were concerned, although there were still banners out now and again demanding 'Nunez and Robson out' and there was the odd demonstration at the training ground. It provided the newspapers with a picture and a story, as did 18 February when the players celebrated my birthday with champagne and cakes, singing 'Happy Birthday dear Mister' in English. It was all good fun, especially as it was on the day *As* had predicted would be my last at the club. Another one they had got wrong. The concept was something I had introduced to the players at Porto: the birthday boy bought champagne and cakes. I was the first to do it and the players carried it on because they enjoyed it. Presumably the players I had brought with me from Portugal had told the Barcelona players, and it was their way of showing their appreciation at a time when, I must say, it was very welcome. It was especially good to see Ronaldo singing away with a big smile on his face.

But that February generally was not a good month for me. Apart from the noises coming increasingly from Holland about van Gaal, we had a few bad results. We drew with Oviedo after leading 2–0, then, after a super 1–1 draw at the Bernabeu Stadium in the Cup, we lost 2–0 to local rivals Espanyol with Figo sent off and a dodgy penalty awarded against us by a Madrid-born referee. Then, after a 1–0 win against Racing Santander, we crashed 2–0 at Real Sociedad with another strange penalty decision going against us, oddly enough given by another Madrileño. I thought we had emerged from the bad run when we drew 2–2 with Atlético Madrid in the first leg of the Spanish Cup quarter-final, but then, on the first day of March, we lost 4–0 on the island of Tenerife with two of our players sent off and two penalties awarded against us. It was certainly this spell which lost us the title that season for it left us trailing nine points behind Real Madrid. It also prompted the press to predict short-term replacements for me to take the club to the end of the season, with names like Cesar Luis Menotti, the former Argentina manager, featuring strongly.

But we disappointed the critics again and in the long-run in to the end of the season we won nineteen, drew three and lost just two. One of those was a traumatic 3–1 defeat at Valladolid after leading 1–0 while at the same time Real were two down at Bilbao before coming back to win 4–2. Had the results stayed as they were in the first half it would certainly have made us favourites to win the League. Our final defeat was the most shocking: a 2–1 loss at relegation-doomed Hercules which finally handed the title to Madrid as they finished just two points ahead of us, despite our having won one more game over the season and having scored seventeen more goals.

Everyone now seemed to know that van Gaal was definitely coming except me; even as late as the second week in June the president was still telling me to keep at it, win what I could and then decisions would be made later. What could I do? I couldn't get involved in the speculation. They were my masters and I had to do what I was told. I wasn't looking for another role as I wanted to carry on with the job I had started, especially with a place in the European Champions League beckoning.

Apart from throwing away the League title we finished the season in glory, winning both the domestic cup and, much more importantly for a club of Barcelona's stature, a major European award. After that stunning 6–5 Spanish Cup quarter-final aggregate score over Atlético Madrid and our earlier triumph over Real Madrid, we simply could not lose that one. The draw was kind to us in the semi-final as we were paired with struggling Second Division side Las Palmas, and we clinched our place in the final in the first leg when we won 4–0 at the Estadia Insular with a couple of goals from Ronaldo. By a weird coincidence it was exactly twenty seasons before then that Ipswich had knocked Las Palmas out of the UEFA Cup! We may have made sure of a place against Real Betis in the final on 28 June with that first-leg win but we destroyed any hopes of a decent crowd for the second leg as only 25,000 turned up to watch the formality of a 3–0 win without a yellow card in view – a rarity in Spanish football.

The final at Real Madrid's Bernabeu Stadium was anything but a formality. It was to be my final game as coach and, with my British upbringing, the Cup was always special. The signs were ominous for us with Ronaldo and Giovanni on international duty with Brazil, Nadal missing through injury and the majority of the 85,000 crowd firmly against us. It was to get worse before it improved as Betis took a fifth-minute lead with a goal which came off Alfonso's head. We came back to equalize through Figo only for Finidi to put Betis ahead with just ten minutes remaining. That is when the character of the team really shone through. Remember, we were at the fag end of a long, tiring season but they found reserves of energy from somewhere and earned themselves extra time with a goal from Pizzi five minutes from time. Figo finally won it for us six minutes from the end. It was the fifth cup I had won out of five finals. As the man said, 'The harder you work, the luckier you get.'

Suddenly, it seemed there were a few Doubting Thomases out there who had belatedly realized that I could coach and that I was a winner. The realization had started to come on 14 May with the European Cup Winners' Cup Final when we beat Paris Saint-Germain 1–0 at the De Kuip Stadium in Rotterdam with a Ronaldo penalty thirty-seven minutes into the game. There was praise from the press, some of it grudging and some of it effusive, with *La Vanguardia* talking about the admiration for my team outside Spain, and even *Sport* said that I won my own particular war – whatever that meant. On the way to the final we had beaten the Cypriots AEK Larnaca 2–0 on aggregate with goals by Ronaldo in the first leg; Red Star Belgrade 4–2 over two legs; AIK Stockholm by the same scores of 3–1 at home and 1–1 away; and, in our best performance, Fiorentina 2–0 away from home having been held 1–1 in the Nou Camp in front of a full house of 120,000. There were not many backers for us to win the trophy after that first leg with the Italia side, but I fancied us because of the opposing styles of play and the fact that the Argentinian Gabriel Batistuta was suspended after being booked in Spain. I was right as first-half goals – a header from Couto and a free kick by Guardiola – settled it. So violent was the Florentine reaction – they hurled missiles and ignored repeated requests to calm down – that UEFA hit them with a two-match ban.

The celebrations after our triumph in Holland were satisfying and, for different reasons, those after the Cup Final even more so. The supportive *La Vanguardia* said I deserved nothing but praise after being the victim of fierce, unjustified and indiscriminate criticism. *Sport* admitted that I had set high standards for the incoming van Gaal and that it was a triumph for a man who 'had never lost faith in himself'. I had finished on the right note. Our third trophy was in the locker and there were a few people out there eating humble pie. I am not one to gloat, but the feeling was very, very warm.

When Betis coach Llorenc Serra Ferrer was appointed youth development coach it was announced that the new coaching team for next season was in place, but it was still the end of the season before the president called me in to tell me that Louis van Gaal was indeed coming, that they wanted to retain my services but in the new role of technical director. Nunez explained that they were bringing the Dutchman in for the long-term future of the club but it did not mean they wanted me to go and that I was part of the restructuring. What they were doing, of course, was softening me up after winning three cups and getting them into the Champions League. I honestly thought, even at that late stage, that there was no way they could remove me from my coaching position and that it would be van Gaal waiting in the wings the following season.

I was not shattered because I accepted the inevitability of it all after the rumours and stories. Quite clearly this had all been arranged for a long time and I was there on a short lease. They thought because of my experience I could hold it all together while they waited for a coach of quality and good reputation who was sixteen years younger than me. It may have been cynical, but it was a shrewd piece of business. It was a pity they couldn't take me into their confidence to make it easier for all of us, but they did what they thought was best, including honouring their contract with me, paying a huge amount of money for what was virtually a sabbatical year travelling around the world watching top players for transfer purposes. They also gave me the opportunity to leave without penalty if the right offer came along in the second year, even to the degree of making up my salary if the new club's wages fell short.

Despite everything that happened during that tumultuous 1996/7 season, my time at Barcelona did not diminish my enormous respect for the club, nor were there any major regrets on my part other than not being allowed to guide the team in the Champions League in the 1997/8 season or to challenge for the European Super Cup. I felt that I had earned those challenges, but in my role as technical director I respectfully kept my distance and made sure that I did not rock the boat for the new coach.

10

Two Players, Two Eras

One of the great joys of my year coaching Barcelona to three trophies was having the world's best player Ronaldo in my team. There is no doubt about the part he played in our success: in forty-eight starts he scored an incredible forty-five goals, thirty-four in the League in thirty-seven games and five in seven European Cup Winners' Cup games.

It was sad for the club that they lost him to Inter Milan, but that side of his career and the turmoil that went with it had nothing to do with me. I knew when I went to Barcelona that I needed either Alan Shearer from Newcastle United or Ronaldo from my old club PSV Eindhoven in Holland. I eventually identified Ronaldo as the player I wanted, and thereafter my only dealings with him were on the training pitch and on match days. He was portrayed as a greedy young man but I never had a problem with him or his attitude; in fact the biggest problem I had with the lad was getting him off the training pitch because he would always say, 'Please Meester, just a leetle longer, just a few more shots.'

Ronaldo is a sunshine boy from the beaches of Brazil. He learned his football playing in the streets and on the waste ground in Bento Ribeiro, a suburb of Rio. He was so poor that he couldn't afford the bus fare for a trial at Flamengo, who would not subsidize him. Their loss was someone else's gain.

Instead of heading straight for the dizzy heights he joined a little Second Division club, São Cristavão, before being sold on to Cruzeiro of Belo Horizonte at the recommendation of World Cup star Jairzinho, where he scored fifty-four goals in as many games. He attracted lots of European clubs, but PSV won the battle for his expensive signature and instantly knew they had a pearl, even though a knee injury curtailed the number of appearances in his two seasons with them, limiting him to thirty goals.

I had seen enough of him to know I wanted him, and I told Nunez and Gaspart he was the man the club needed and they backed me to the hilt. The trouble was that PSV, not surprisingly, didn't want him to go and even though we kept upping the price they resisted. I prepared myself to go in for my alternative. I had always liked Alan Shearer for his strength, power and goalscoring ability. I spoke to Ray Harford at Blackburn three times and he said he wouldn't sell him at any price and I promised not to rock the boat by pressing my interest any further. Ray said that money, with Jack Walker and his millions in the background, wasn't important, and I respected that.

There were other possibilities: João Pinto at Benfica; Alen Boksic at Lazio; the Argentinian Gabriel Batistuta; and even the option of bringing back Romario. But I really wanted Ronaldo, and decided to persevere in that direction. I spoke to central defender Stan Valckx at Eindhoven who confirmed my opinion of the player, saying that he scored goals for fun from all sorts of angles, distances and situations, and that he could also dribble and take players on. We started at ten million dollars and Eindhoven said no without a thought; we went to twelve million dollars and they still shook their heads. It went to thirteen, fourteen, fifteen and then jumped to seventeen. It was a lot of money, as Gaspart and Nunez kept pointing out, but I kept on saying he was worth it and they were brilliant in their backing. Gaspart himself at one stage said that it was no use dying and leaving the money to someone else.

We needed a change in personnel and the club wanted to win something. We had let Jordi Cruyff go to Manchester United, so we were one short on the staff and needed a replacement anyway with the frightening number of fixtures we were faced with. We decided that if they turned down seventeen million dollars we should ask them what it would take to persuade them while at the same time not committing ourselves. PSV took the bait and came back and told us twenty million dollars – a lot of money to any club, even Barcelona – a figure that was meant to frighten us away for good. It nearly did, for even Nunez gasped at that figure. But our quest for Ronaldo's signature had almost become an obsession. We agreed to do nothing for a couple of days – we knew no one else would pay that sort of money for a twenty-year-old who had been injured for three months. Having sat on things for a while we went in with a cheque for twenty million dollars, leaving PSV with little option but to cash in on their prodigy.

Some may say that we bought ourselves a parcel of trouble, but not me. He was a great player and a brilliant boy to work with. He liked a joke in the dressing room but he respected the senior players. He was a fine boy who trained well and, as far as I was concerned, he wanted to stay with Barcelona a lot longer. It was other people who decided his fate and his future and now I worry for him and his future the way the deal was orchestrated. Will he have to move every time his agents say so? Certainly one was quoted as saying that the whole world deserved to see him play, suggesting that he would be packing his tent and moving like a gypsy from country to country.

I have worked with some outstanding players during my

203

life, players from every corner of the globe, but he was in a different class and when you consider he was only twenty when he came to Barcelona it made him very special indeed. He is strong and quick over fifty metres, has a side-step that is lightning-quick with the ball at his feet, and he can shield the ball, turn and beat defenders in the twinkle of an eye. He has the ability, the talent and temperament to be not just the best in the world but maybe even the best ever. As good as Pelé and I cannot go any higher than that.

I was shocked when the troubles began to materialize because I thought we had signed him for eight years. What is more, he loved Barcelona and was a hero there. There was no indication that he wanted to leave or that he was in any way unsettled. But then this is where the job was so different to working in England. At Ipswich I knew every detail of every contract, but at Barcelona I only knew what I found out second-hand. I was looking from the outside in where players' deals were concerned.

It all began when the club wanted to change his contract in a bid to try to protect themselves. In Spain every player has a recision clause in his contract, a set and agreed figure for which the player can be sold and, obviously, the better the player the bigger that figure. Having signed for twenty million dollars it was decided that Ronaldo's recision fee should be a staggering twenty million pounds in a bid to put other clubs off even thinking about signing him.

The trouble is that it did not and soon top clubs like AC Milan, Manchester United and Inter Milan were sniffing around, forcing Barcelona into deciding that the figure should be upped even further. One of Ronaldo's three agents, Giovanni Branchini, was based in Milan and was a close friend of the Inter Milan president and they, the press reported, had already started negotiations to sign my top player. The problem for Barcelona was that the recision fee is contractually linked to the player's wages. Ronaldo was already on one million pounds a year *after* taxes, but after initial talks both figures were to be doubled: a two-million-pound annual salary and a guaranteed transfer fee of forty million pounds, breathtaking figures by any standards. This was all apparently decided in December 1996 according to reports, and the new contracts were to be signed later at an agreed date towards the end of February 1997.

Then a new problem popped up. The Spanish government made a dramatic change to the tax laws that had a serious effect on every football club, especially the giants like Barcelona. Much of the money paid to top players and, indeed, coaches is called 'image contract' – that is, the player or coach sells his image to the club for them to market and he is paid for that privilege direct to his company. The difference in the taxation rate was huge: normal salary carried 56 per cent and the image contract a mere 10 per cent. The new law changed all this by putting a ceiling of 15 per cent on the image contract leaving the remaining 85 per cent to be taxed at the high rate. This really did send Ronaldo's wage bill through the roof as far as the club was concerned and they suddenly found themselves needing some help. They tried to make an agreement with Nike and Catalan Television, but when the deadline for signing the new contract arrived the deals had still not been done. The agents immediately claimed they had been let down and reopened negotiations with Inter Milan, who already had a deal with Nike.

The agreement was eventually reached with Catalan Television in May 1997, but by then, apparently, the deal with the Italian club was a long way down the road. In June it appeared to be swinging our way again when, with Ronaldo in

Brazil, his three agents were in Barcelona and seemingly close to an agreement. It was on then off, then on again as they fought over small details. When his son was fifteen Ronaldo's father signed away his rights to his Brazilian agents Reinaldo Pitta and Alexander Martins and they, along with Branchini, were demanding fifteen million dollars for those rights, adding another massive amount to the bill. The estimated final bill, according to our local papers, would have been something like eighty million dollars. Even after Ronaldo finally went to Inter Milan there were complications. Barcelona turned the twenty million dollars into twenty million pounds plus a nominal two million dollars awarded to them by FIFA who were called in to settle the rows.

None of this seemed to affect Ronaldo himself or his attitude although it was very disruptive for the team because every day the newspapers would carry a different story that Ronaldo would go, Ronaldo would stay, then he was going again. My biggest problem with Ronaldo was his frequent trips home to Brazil to play for his country and to do other things. Here was one rich boy. I was told that while on one journey back to South America he bought an island off the Brazilian coast. Can you believe that? He popped home and bought an island. The last time I went home to England I bought myself a new tie. I spoke to him about the ongoing contractual wrangles but purely on the football front, reminding him that we still had a lot of football to play and a championship to win. I knew he was going to leave almost a month before the season ended because of his commitments with Brazil. I told him he had to forget what was going on between the club and his three agents and to apply himself to his game, to think of his mates in the dressing room. We needed to have the best of him while he was with us.

He played in the Cup Winners' Cup Final against Paris

Saint-Germain in Rotterdam, scoring the winning goal from the penalty spot, but he missed the Spanish Cup Final when we beat Real Betis 3–2 after extra time and, more significantly, the shock defeat by little Hercules. However you look at it, that last defeat cost us the Championship and a clean sweep of the titles. I have no doubt at all that had Ronaldo played in that game we would have won.

I just hope that all the high finance and the fantastic money he earns both on and off the pitch do not stop his natural development as a player. His ambition for money, presumably, is no longer a problem; he can probably live on the interest of what he is earning, and would find it difficult to spend everything unless he decided to buy more islands or began to pay off Brazil's national debt. I suspect that there will come a moment, if it hasn't already come, when he will subconsciously decide to stay on because he loves the game and wants to test his talents to the absolute limit. What makes Pete Sampras keep winning? What makes Colin Montgomery keep on chasing the big golf titles, or Evander Holyfield risk his life in the boxing ring? None of them needs the money, it is their competitive urge, their love for their particular sport, their devotion to it, their need to win. Few think of money while they are playing. If it is there in the sportsman's make-up money will not change it, and I sense that it is there in Ronaldo Luis Nazario de Lima, to give him his full name. He loves football and loves to play. He is never happier than when he has a football at his feet.

I believe only injury will stop him developing into one of the all-time greats, possibly the greatest of them all, and also if he loses his drive, becomes fed up with the game and looks for another side of life. In terms of potential he is a cut above anything else I have seen.

I spoke to him about his prospects one day, asking him if he really wanted to leave when he had the whole of Catalonia zipped up in his pocket. He was popular within the club, popular outside, girls would scream when they saw him and people loved him. He was bigger than any bullfighter or pop star. He took it all in his stride. I couldn't understand why he should even consider leaving. He had a magnificent house overlooking the Mediterranean in the richest area between my rented home in Sitges and Barcelona, he drove a fabulous BMW and he had no problem with the language. I told him I didn't want him to go and he replied that he didn't want to go either but his agents had told him he was here to play football and they were here to make money. 'I have to do what they say,' he told me.

It was a sad conclusion to a great year for him. I didn't even get a chance to say goodbye because he was with Brazil when the deal to move to Inter Milan was completed. It all, perhaps predictably, ended on a sour note with Ronaldo making disparaging remarks about the president. But in his short stay he had left an indelible impression on myself and the people of Barcelona. He reminded me of Diego Maradona the way he went past defenders. He was beautifully built for a centre-forward, big but certainly not muscle-bound. He was one of the quickest players I ever saw with the ball at his feet, strong enough to take a buffeting and a whacking. He can play with his back to goal or drive forward, stay on his feet and go past people. I have seen tough defenders bounce off him. Where Romario was lightning-quick over ten metres, this boy could sustain his pace for fifty, accelerating past his marker never to be caught. It means he can come deep to pick up the ball and see what is in front of him; then he can use his pace or his dribbling skills to take on defenders. With respect to Alan Shearer, who is not a dribbler and a feinter, Ronaldo can beat opponents just like George Best used to do in his great years.

It was marvellous just to watch him in training, practising his flicks, touches and techniques. I had to be careful he didn't burn himself out. He did have his odd quiet day and when he became static he would lose his effectiveness, but he was never moody, always full of respect. I knew that even for twenty million dollars we were buying blue chip. We couldn't lose on him. The investment was there for all to see and he was never going to be worth less than we paid for him. He was as good a buy as I ever bought in my career.

I would love to have seen Ronaldo up against my former Ipswich central defender Kevin Beattie. The Brazilian might have been the quickest forward but Beattie was the quickest defender I ever saw, and it is not wrong to discuss them in the same breath. Beattie used that pace to overhaul forwards and reach the ball first. We once clocked him over a hundred yards on grass in football boots at ten seconds dead and the further he went the faster he seemed to get. What's more, he had a left foot like a howitzer. I can pay him no greater compliment than to say he could have been as good as Duncan Edwards, the young Manchester United player killed in the Munich air disaster. I had the privilege to play with Duncan; my first game for England against France was his last before the terrible events of February 1958. I also had the misfortune to play against him. Too often all you could do was admire him as he steamed past like an express train.

I saw all the great English players over a long, long period, and while Irishman George Best at his best was truly remarkable and world class, I would say Beattie was the best English player produced in my time. He came out of Carlisle as a sixteen-year-old with no experience and even then he was a colossus, a natural. We took hold of him and developed him, taught him about intelligent play and responsibilities. Once he was taught the tactical side and positional sense, the rest came to him so easy because he had a genuine football brain. By seventeen years of age he had the body of a mature twenty-two-year-old and had established himself in the Ipswich team. He had a huge neck and thighs which developed as he used the weights. He was phenomenal in the air and so strong in the tackle that he quickly earned the nickname 'The Beast', but his other qualities were hinted at by his alternative *nom de plume*, 'Diamond' – albeit a bit on the rough-cut side!

He was in the England team at the age of nineteen, totally on merit. I will never forget his goal against Scotland at Wembley in May 1975. Gerry Francis brought the ball out of defence; Alan Ball went with him and got in an early cross from the right; out of nowhere came this figure who must have covered seventy-five metres in around seven seconds, powering the ball into the net from the back post. His football brain had seen the possibilities and he went so quickly that no one picked him up, or if they did they couldn't stay with him. This was a nineteen-year-old with such staggering vision.

Sadly, injuries stopped Kevin from reaching his full potential. He came back from an England game against Luxembourg in October 1977 with a twisted knee and was never the same again. He complained of pain on the Thursday while insisting that he would be fine to play on Saturday. He couldn't train again on Friday but he was still insisting that he would play when I made him take a fitness test on the Saturday morning. He failed. It turned out to be a badly damaged cartilage. It settled down but recurred and in the end we sent him to a top London specialist. There was other trouble around the knee as well and he never fully recovered.

Unfortunately he did not have the same mental strength as Ronaldo, as he displayed one day in 1975 when he failed to turn up for an England get-together under Don Revie in Manchester. I was somewhat surprised to see him when I arrived for work at Portman Road one morning, but he explained that he had forgotten his boots and had come in to collect them. He was running late and I actually drove him the short distance to the station to ensure that he caught his train to Peterborough, where he was to change for Manchester. So my surprise could be imagined when Don Revie telephoned me at lunch-time to tell me that Beattie hadn't arrived. I explained I had personally put him on the train and that he had probably been delayed. Half an hour later Don was back on the telephone saying that they had checked there had been no difficulties with the trains and he was still not around. By mid-afternoon there was increasing concern at both ends because of his mysterious disappearance.

He had never gone missing before and I knew he loved to play for his country. Was he in hospital? Was he ill? Had he been mugged? By this time it was me ringing Revie, and when there was still no sign after training at 5.30 p.m. I was really concerned and telephoned John Carruthers, our scout in the north-east, to tell him that we had literally lost Beattie. John, a good friend of the Beattie family and the man who discovered Kevin, went round to his parents' house where he was told that Kevin was in town but had gone out with his dad to play dominoes and have a pint of beer. John was flabbergasted, went to the pub and asked him what the hell he was doing. Kevin explained that he had arrived at Peterborough but had taken instead a train for Carlisle because he didn't feel right. He was nervous about joining England and wanted to go and see his dad to talk about it.

After that episode problems seemed to follow him about, none more bizarre than the day we entered him in the famous

Powderhall Sprints where the Professional Footballers' Association had been invited to take part with a race of their own to find the fastest sprinter in professional football. Every club was invited to enter their top sprinter, but only the very best were accepted. We felt we had a stone-blind certainty in Beattie because he was lightning-quick and so strong. It was accepted that there was no one faster around. This lad could have run in the Olympics. Because of the previous escapade with England we sent reserve team coach Charlie Woods with him up north with instructions to keep him handcuffed if necessary and under no circumstances to lose him. There was a book on the race so we all chipped in for a large bet, telling Charlie to bring back Beattie and the money. Despite the quality of the field, which included explosive runners like Malcolm MacDonald of *Superstars* fame and Alan Kennedy, we were convinced that this was money for old rope, and I told Charlie to ring me when it was over and tell us how far ahead he was of the field. We made sure he had his club shirt and shorts with him to run in and sat back to wait for the money to roll in.

Sure enough the telephone goes and there is Charlie, on the dot at the end of the race. But he had the worst possible news, telling me our thoroughbred had lost. I couldn't believe it. I thought he was winding me up until he explained how it had happened. It turned out to be pure Beattie. Everything had gone to plan as Beattie sped off from the gun straight into the lead, when suddenly everything fell out of his shorts and there he was, running against the fastest men in football, trying to preserve his dignity in front of the television cameras, the photographers and spectators by holding on to his not so private parts. He had forgotten to put on his jockstrap. The only time he had been out of Charlie's sight was when he was in the dressing room, and that had proved to be decisive.

It was typical of Beattie, and something we had to put down to experience. He was so good you could put up with most things he did but, sadly, his career finished desperately early because of his dodgy knee. We did our best to look after him with help and support but you cannot be with a player every minute. He was a lovely lad and very down to earth. He liked nothing better than to go down to the local pub and buy everyone in there a drink.

That's where the comparisons with Ronaldo stop. The Brazilian was a genuine hero and he couldn't go to a bar or even a restaurant without special arrangements because he would be mobbed by well-wishers. He, of course, had an army of agents, managers and minders to look after his every need and enough money to do whatever he wished. Ronaldo could afford to hire bodyguards if he wanted. Maradona in Italy had an entourage of a dozen people to cater for his whims and fancies. But they earned as much in a day as Beattie earned in his best year, which paid him about £17,000. That's how much the game has changed.

11

The Call Home

One significant effect the continual question marks placed against my future by the warring Barcelona press had was to attract a number of offers from home, none more intriguing than the one from the club I supported as a youngster in Durham – Newcastle United.

To say that the initial telephone call on 7 January 1997 from Newcastle's chief executive Freddie Fletcher stopped me in my tracks is to underestimate the situation, for at the time there had been no word in the media that there was any chance of Kevin Keegan leaving St James's Park; indeed, the former England captain was seen as the second Messiah on Tyneside and I, along with every true Geordie fan, had marvelled at the way he had transformed the club and enjoyed the devil-may-care attacking football his players produced at home and away.

Freddie called me at home in Sitges and said that he had some shock news. 'Kevin Keegan,' he said, 'is wanting out of Newcastle United.' I couldn't believe it. All I could say in response was 'What?' and then 'Why?' I thought that nothing in football could surprise me any more, but this was something else. There were no immediate reasons offered by Freddie because he came straight to the point. 'We see you as an ideal replacement. What would it take to get you to join us?'

I gathered my breath before I answered. 'You've shaken me, but I have to listen to what you've got to say. I have to tell you I'm on a very big contract at Barcelona. I honour contracts and I waited eighteen years to get here. To be honest I wasn't looking to leave. But Newcastle is Newcastle. My roots. My home. It was the club my father took me to when I was a kid, first in the queue to get into the ground. It was where all my childhood heroes played.'

My mind tumbled back to the days when I was offered the chance to go and train with my favourite club but chose Fulham instead. Don't ask me how or why, but I did. I jerked my thoughts back to the present and to the magnificent job I had, the fact that moving had not crossed my mind and that I was just six months into a two-year contract. I also felt that Barcelona were going to win things that season. Was I to give all that up to go back to my roots? I didn't tell Freddie about the clause in my contract which stipulated that Newcastle would have to pay back double my huge salary, but in the face of the fierce criticism I was receiving at the time, I guessed that given the opportunity Barcelona might let me go anyway.

A few days later Freddie Shepherd, the vice-chairman, Freddie Fletcher, Sir John Hall's son Douglas, a director of the club, and Mark Corbidge, the man they had appointed from the City to look after the flotation, arrived at a Barcelona hotel and offered me a five-year contract with a two-year option. My salary clearly didn't frighten them as they offered me a comparable salary. The next day Sir John Hall himself arrived to back up the bid. He was excellent. While emphasizing that I was the man he wanted, he did not try to exert any pressure at all and told me that he appreciated my situation at Barcelona and would understand if I could not accept Newcastle's offer.

I spoke to the Barcelona hierarchy five days after Kevin

Keegan's departure, on the night we lost to bottom club Hercules in front of 85,000 white-handkerchief waving, jeering fans. Real Madrid had dropped two points, and had we won we would have gone back to the top of the League. We went two up and the crowd were chanting 'Campeones! Campeones!' until it all went sour and we gave away three goals. Talk about omens. It was as if the fates were telling me my luck was out at Barcelona and I should take the money and run. Indeed, had I been fully aware at that moment that they planned to move me upstairs regardless of how I did or what I had won, I would have taken the Newcastle job.

Even so, I was sorely tempted at the time and asked Gaspart about the possibilities of being able to leave. I was torn in two directions. Everyone was shattered after that defeat by Hercules and if there was a time when the president might have said 'Good riddance', that was it. But he didn't. He told me that he didn't expect me to leave. Both Nunez and Gaspart were very consistent and firm. My feelings for the club were strong and there was a powerful bond developing. I did not want it to seem as though I was deserting a sinking ship.

Perhaps it was a good thing that I did not know what was going on behind the scenes because in hindsight I don't regret staying at Barcelona. No one can take away from me what my team achieved that season. It was a huge offer from a great British club and I was flattered that they thought I was worth it. Any other time, any other place and I would have snapped their hands off in my hurry.

Another option to offer itself to me during those chaotic months in Barcelona was Everton, also a massive club by any standards, who were underachieving and desperate to put things right. Once more it was *déjà vu* for this was not the first time I had been offered the job at Goodison Park. Indeed, I had previously shaken hands and actually agreed a deal to leave Ipswich.

In January 1977 I had gone up to Merseyside to meet the president Sir John Moore and chairman Philip Carter who ran the club and called all the shots. We agreed what was then a monumental ten-year deal which would have made me the highest-paid manager in Britain. It was the original 'offer I couldn't refuse' – and I didn't! All I asked for was twenty-four hours' grace before the deal became public to allow me to tell my chairman John Cobbold. He had been so good that I simply did not want him to learn it second-hand. Sir John had given me a rather large cheque as a gesture of goodwill and intent. Some gesture! It was worth more than my house and was several times my current Ipswich salary. When I returned home and showed the cheque to my wife Elsie, she said, 'That's the best day's business you have ever done in your life.' But within a day I had torn it up and thrown away a fortune because when I opened the *Daily Express* next morning I saw a shocking head-line screaming back at me: 'Robson Goes To Everton'. How could I accept a job with a club where they let me down on the very first day? If they could do that, what would happen in the future? I wasn't hanging around to find out.

Poor John Cobbold. The man who had given me such tremendous support and backing over the years first read about the whole episode in the newspapers after all. He deserved better than that and I went straight round to his house to tell him the full facts and to apologize. I was in a very humble mood when I arrived at John's home and I said, 'John, yes I have been approached by Everton, listened to their offer and agreed to go. I felt it was something I should take. I was going to tell you today and I am angry at the way it leaked out. It has cost Everton a new manager because in view of that I am not going.

If you will still have me I would like to stay with Ipswich.' John was pleased that I was going to remain at Portman Road and he laughed when I showed him the cheque, tore it up in front of him and threw it into the fire. Elsie thought I was barmy.

Now twenty years later, Everton had come back for me. Chairman Peter Johnson called me to say that he kept hearing reports that things were not so good for me at Barcelona. I had met Johnson earlier in the season along with the then manager Joe Royle when they were travelling around Europe looking at stadiums with a view to building a new home for Everton. They had already been to Amsterdam and Milan and were now in Barcelona to view the best. But now that Joe had gone Everton were looking for a replacement, with Dave Watson in charge as caretaker in the meantime. A delegation came over to see me at the end of April and told me they thought I was the one for the job and discussed the money that would be available for me to spend on players. It never went as far down the road as Newcastle, for no offer was made financially, but they left asking me to think it over.

Everton's approach was very correct, but what put me off in the end was that it was not a touch on the tiller job. Even from a distance I could see there was an awful lot to do at the club. I was not afraid of the assignment but I felt that I was the wrong age to take on a task like that. The club needed continuity and stability over a long period, and had I been younger I might have been more tempted. Let's face it, Everton are a magnificent club, every bit as big as neighbours Liverpool, and success would elevate it to the stars. You only have to look at their average gates when they are doing badly to see what it would be like if they were challenging for the top awards in the game again. The club is one of the gems in the English crown and Howard Kendall knew that better than anyone when he went back.

But there was more to come. At the end of May I was approached by Celtic via a letter from Fergus McCann, the president, which was sent to the club. It was a subtle approach containing a job description, which in itself was something of a novelty. I never actually met McCann although I did speak to him several times on the telephone. A good many of my friends really believed that I had agreed and was about to take the job; writer and broadcaster Roddy Forsyth, a Scot usually very much in the know, wrote in *The Times* that I had actually accepted the job and would be attending a press conference the next day for a formal announcement. It never reached that stage, although I admit I made several enquiries with friends to test the water. Ideally I would like to have spoken to Terry Butcher to get a feel for the club in Glasgow, but he was away on holiday. I did, however, manage to speak to Tommy Burns who told me I couldn't join a better club or find better supporters.

I never mentioned it to Barcelona and they didn't ask me what was going on, even when former Barcelona player Steve Archibald turned up out of the blue – or should that be the green – to try to persuade me, saying that Celtic were desperate for a top-quality coach. He was as good a salesman as he was a striker. He sold me a persuasive story on the club and how I was the man to make things happen. Steve had also done his homework and read the papers, and was guessing that I might be leaving the club. He wanted to know what was happening at his old club and whether I, as had been reported, would be replaced at the end of the season. He also told me of the appointment of Scotland manager Craig Brown's brother Jock to run the business side of things, and Steve emphasized that they were not afraid of the big salary I was earning at Barcelona. There certainly seemed to be no shortage of money in the old country.

It was tempting at the time in that the Louis van Gaal situation was reaching a head and I was now fully aware that he would be with us for the next season no matter what I achieved, but in the end I told them I was flattered, impressed with Steve and appreciated how big the club was, but Barcelona was even bigger and despite the pressure I was really enjoying the run-in to the end of the season and I would be making no decisions until then. Celtic continued to try to secure my services right up until the moment they appointed Dutchman Wim Jansen, but I always told them to forget all about me and find someone else.

I suppose that being in a high-profile job like Barcelona makes you a tempting target for all sorts of clubs, and apart from the British interest there were also offers from Besiktas in Turkey and, amazingly, my old club Sporting Lisbon and their even more famous neighbours Benfica. Besiktas were originally trying to tempt an old friend of mine, Gordon Milne, but he became involved in a wrangle between them and his old club and finished with neither. His club sacked him, Besiktas didn't want him and he was out of a job. They then came to me, via an agent, and offered me the job. I didn't even consider that one, it was an immediate no. I mentioned to them that John Toshack was available and he was a very good coach, so they appointed him. It was in fact the second time they had offered me the job – they had approached me while I was at Porto – and the second time I had turned them down.

No one could ever accuse me of having a big ego, but when Benfica made their bid I was touched and very tempted. After all, no one has ever managed the top three clubs in Portugal – Sporting, Porto and Benfica – and here was my opportunity to make a bit of history. I loved Portugal and its people and in truth I was sorry to leave Porto as the club had never won three titles in a row and it was a challenge I was looking forward to. Benfica were a different sort of club altogether, easily the biggest in Portugal with its six million fans nationwide. They are the Portuguese equivalent of Manchester United with supporters all over the world. Their approach came towards the end of the season in June, after they had lost the Portuguese Cup Final, leaving them empty-handed. They wanted a change for the next season and they wanted to know what I thought about it.

They were sounding me out, but I was in a state of limbo myself at the time waiting for Barcelona to tell me what my role was to be for next season, to discover whether I fancied the new position or not. After talking to one or two people who were close to me I decided to stay where I was and wait and see how things were to work out. I was still on my massive salary, and my decision was vindicated to an extent when the terms of my new role were defined: to travel around the world and identify the top players in each position ready for when the club needed to buy. I was also looking at emerging young talent around the globe, leaving Louis van Gaal to get on with the coaching.

Benfica decided then to keep things as they were at the Stadium of Light, but they had a disastrous start to the new season and clearly changes had to be made. The sitting president, Di Massio, wanted to take the club into the public sector to raise money to improve the team and pay off debts, but the members would have none of it and he resigned, putting the top job up for grabs. Three candidates appeared and one of them, Abilio Rodrigues, the favourite to win the election, telephoned me in August to ask if I would coach the team if he won the forthcoming vote. I told him that before I could commit myself to anything he would have to win the election. There was no way in the world I would let myself be touted as his running partner while still employed at Barcelona. What, I asked him, if you lost – where would that leave me?

I kept Joan Gaspart informed of what was going on and proceeded with his blessing to talk to the president-elect, and I duly met him in Lisbon and quite liked the man and his ambitions. I admit the thought of managing the third of the top trio of clubs in Portugal tickled my ego, and it would also have meant a return to coaching and going back to a country I loved, to a place where I was extremely popular. As it transpired Rodrigues didn't get elected and had I allowed myself to be tied to his bid I would have found myself stranded and in an untenable position at Barcelona. I was delighted when Graeme Souness, someone I had known for a long while, was given the task of trying to make the Lisbon Eagles a great club again.

But the Portugal connection did not end there. The regime that had sacked me at Sporting Lisbon when we were top of the League had been removed, and the new top man, Roquette, was a banker. While I was still at Porto he had invited me to Lisbon to sort out what the club still owed me from my earlier stay. They had deducted income tax from my salary but had not passed it on and I had been forced to pay my tax twice. He sorted it all out and repaid what I was owed. It was purely business and there was no mention of my returning to the club at the time. But then, in November of 1997, the coach Octavio Machedo resigned and my name was immediately linked in the Portuguese media with a return to the club. I was telephoned by one journalist who told me he knew I was on my way to Lisbon and when I told him I had not even been approached he responded, 'You will be.'

I was in Salisbury in England with my family when Roquette approached me again, this time to ask me to return as Sporting's coach, and by the time I returned to Sitges there were journalists on my doorstep. On 11 November I spoke to the Sporting Lisbon vice-president about the possibilities and implications without getting as far as talking contracts. My accountant John Hazell was with me in Spain at the time and they asked us what sort of figures we had in mind. We had a chat and wrote down some numbers and they didn't turn a hair. The Sporting representative reported back to his president to discuss the situation while I went to see Gaspart once more to avail him of the situation. Sporting promised me they would reach a decision within three days.

The president came back to me and said that because they were a public company they were limited as to what they could offer, and asked if they could talk to Nunez to see if something could be arranged between the clubs. Clearly they had somehow discovered that Barcelona were prepared to help out financially if I wanted to move, but this was an arrangement between me and Barcelona and I wasn't prepared for the two club presidents to meet and so refused to give my permission. Instead I told him to offer me what he thought the club could afford and I would discuss it with my president.

By the time the deadline came around I had decided not to return to Sporting and I waited and waited for Roquette's call to tell him. Nothing happened, so I called him several times, leaving messages with his secretary. He didn't return my calls and it was early evening by the time we spoke. He was extremely apologetic, telling me that his hands were tied, that the difference was too great and that the deal would fall through unless I was prepared to drop my asking price. I said that I understood that he could not compete and we parted on amicable terms.

Let's face it, if I had been out of a job and was offered £350,000 a year I would have jumped at it, as would hundreds of other out-of-work managers, but I wasn't out of work and I was reconciled to returning home to England when my contract expired with Barcelona. What was encouraging was the number of offers I was still receiving, not just clubs but national teams as well. At the end of 1997 both Nigeria and Saudi Arabia contacted me about managing their teams in the 1998 World Cup Finals in France. I wasn't too attracted to the Nigeria job, despite the quality of their players, but I was secretly quite disappointed when the talks with the Saudis came to nothing. It was the sort of challenge I quite fancied, taking on teams like the hosts France, South Africa and Denmark, especially with the budget available for preparations.

The interest shown in me served to blunt the disappointment I felt in not having a second year with my club team. I couldn't have done much more and the players put in a superhuman effort, keeping after Real Madrid despite the disparity in the number of games between the two clubs. I had managed to keep them motivated throughout a difficult season and I knew that a second season would have been so much better. Van Gaal would be thinking the same at the end of his first season.

12

From the Nou Camp Back to
the Future

I don't regret a minute of my two years at Barcelona. Very few coaches have the opportunity of working with this phenomenal club and I count myself as one of those lucky people. I would not have missed it for the world. It has been one of the great experiences of my life and I would recommend it to anyone with the ability and the strength of character to cope with the sometimes outrageous demands of a club of this size. In club terms there is no better entry on a curriculum vitae than to say you have worked with the Catalan club. It helps credibility, prestige and reputation.

What a place it was to work, what a city to live in. The sun, the sea and the golf at Sitges where I lived was just twenty minutes away from one of the most vibrant cities in the world, blessed with a wonderful climate and full of spectacular shops, brilliant architecture, thousands of top-quality restaurants, tourist spots, a magnificent port and an awesome football club whose stadium is a sight in itself, especially when it is packed to the rafters as it usually is for those big games. In many ways it should have been the place for me to finish my career, right there at the very top. My last match as coach was the day I won the Spanish Cup. If I wasn't so stupid and didn't still have the drug of football in my blood I would have politely tipped my hat and said goodbye with my three trophies under my belt.

One of the few problems you are left with after being at a club like Barcelona is, where do you go when you leave? It was easy to turn down all those offers in the first year because I had spent a football lifetime waiting for a chance to work at Barcelona, and having got there I was not going to walk out. I had been faced with a similar situation eight years earlier when I left the England job. Then I turned to Holland and PSV Eindhoven. Incredibly, it has happened all over again.

I was determined that, after eight years abroad, I would come home when my two-year contract finished. I even thought that at the age of sixty-five I might put my feet up if nothing came along in England to really capture my imagination and offer me the necessary challenge. I was beginning to think of watching a few Test matches against South Africa and maybe even going over to Australia for the Ashes, doing a few of the things denied to me over my adulthood by my total immersion in all things football. I should have known better. My passion for the game still burns as strong as ever and just when I thought of applying for my bus pass the offers began to pour in at an alarming rate of knots.

I talked once again with my old friend Sir John Hall at Newcastle United in March 1998 when the club was ripped apart by scandal and he said that there was the need for a stabilizing figure with football knowledge on the board of directors. That immediately caught my fancy. It wasn't simply a return to England, but a return home. At the same time I had a chance meeting on 21 February with my old PSV colleague Frank Arnesen in, of all places, Belgrade where I had gone to watch Red Star play Partizan, always one of the more technical of local derbies around the world, as the Yugoslav season reopened after its winter break. I fully expected that, in my role as director of transfers at Barcelona, I would be on my own. Some chance.

Such is the worldwide hunt for top-class players that virtually all the top clubs from around Europe were represented there. I looked around and saw people from Inter Milan, Olympique Marseilles, AS Roma, Valencia, Bayern Munich, Celta Vigo, Oviedo, Ajax – and those were only the ones I recognized! That's the sort of competition clubs are facing in the search for players. All the top leagues were represented with the glaring exception of England. In all my travels around the world in the past year I have come across very few English scouts.

I hadn't seen my old friend Frank because he had been sitting in another part of the ground with the former Yugoslav coach Miljan Miljanic.While we waited for the 70,000 crowd to disperse, I talked with the former Spanish star Luis Suarez who was doing for Inter Milan what I was doing for Barcelona. We had played against each other at Wembley way back in October 1960 when England won a splendid rain-soaked match 4–2. It was while I was talking about old times with the former Barcelona player that I suddenly spotted Frank.

It transpired that we were lodging at the same hotel, and when we returned Frank pulled me to one side and remarked upon the fact that it was a stroke of luck to bump into me because he wanted to speak to me. He explained to me the complicated position at PSV. Current coach Dick Advocaat was set to leave the club at the end of the season to take over at Glasgow Rangers and their chosen replacement, Eric Gerets, captain when I was at the club, was unable to obtain his release from Club Brugge for a year. PSV needed a replacement to keep the club at the top until Eric arrived and, Frank explained, my name was at the top of their list because they were aware I was going to be available. There was no salary mentioned at the time but I promised I would think about it. To be honest, I was more interested in seeing what developed for me in England and I promptly put it towards the back of my mind.

But it wouldn't go away. I couldn't help but think about it. I had loved my previous stay at the club, they had some good players and it offered me another crack at the Champions League. I knew the money would be good and it would only mean staying away from home for another nine months or so. They were obviously very keen because they came back to me a few weeks later, and when I began to express an interest they picked up their campaign. I had heard nothing from the other clubs who had expressed an interest, despite dropping a big hint both on television and in the media. By contrast PSV had been positive and decisive and were offering me a chance of coaching, which no other club at that stage had.

Money has never been an obsession of mine, but PSV really opened the suitcase to lure me back. The wage I was offered was well in excess of the vast majority of English Premier Division club managers plus the bonuses to keep them up with rivals Ajax were huge, especially if I left them again with the legacy of a place in the money-spinning Champions League. The challenge was there and so were the rewards. I knew from my talks with Frank that we were sure to lose a couple of top players. Jaap Stam was being hunted avidly by Manchester United – the original asking price was £15 million – long before I agreed to go back, but the club was ready to let me spend that and more to keep the team in a challenging position.

I took a couple of telephone calls from PSV players who had heard the rumours, and they told me personally that they would like me at the club. That was especially flattering and helped me to make up my mind, but there were other reasons:

the Champions League loomed large; so did winning a third title with PSV in the teeth of the challenge with Ajax, not to mention going back to a situation I was familiar with. I knew the standard and standing of the club, knew that they were a class act with a super stadium and that the chairman, Harry van Raaij, was a man I trusted (he was, of course, a director of the club when I was there the first time around). I liked working with Frank Arnesen, who would handle all the contracts and the business side, and there were players I admired like Stan Valckx, Vonk, Faber and others. I told Frank I would accept the job providing that my brief was to coach, train, select and motivate the team. I wasn't interested in any of the periphery like youth schemes and scouting systems because I was only going to be there for a year. All I wanted was to use my energy to get the results at first-team level and nothing else.

Unlike the Barcelona situation with Louis van Gaal I knew in advance that Eric Gerets was coming, and while I would keep him informed of what I was doing and the development of the team, he would have his own job to concentrate upon. Too much involvement and there could be a serious conflict of interest, as I discovered for myself when, soon after agreeing to go to Holland, Frank asked me to look at a certain player. Had I done so I would have been cheating on Barcelona and my work for them. Clearly there would be a great deal more contact with Eric towards the end of my tenancy when I would let him know about strengths and weaknesses, what the club had and what they needed, hopefully leaving him with a flourishing team when he eventually arrived. Until then it would have to be Bobby Robson's team.

In the midst of this Barcelona surprisingly asked me to stay with them and my old club Ipswich Town also made contact to discover what I was planning to do when my contract at

Barcelona expired. I met with the chairman David Sheep-shanks, who is also on the Football Association's International Committee, while I was in Berne, Switzerland in March to watch young Rio Ferdinand of West Ham United playing for England in the Wankdorf Stadium. He told me that the club would be interested to discuss a possible role where I could assist the talented young Ipswich manager George Burley. He told me that there was always speculation from the Ipswich public about bringing me back whenever the newspapers started writing about my next move. I spoke to George Burley about the prospect on a couple of occasions and he also told me he would be delighted if I eventually returned to Portman Road.

While the situation wasn't right at the time Mr Sheepshanks spoke to me, who knows in a year's time? If it is still of interest to us all, it might be the perfect job for me. After all, my house is only a short walk away and I have fourteen years of very happy memories there. Ipswich, with their tight budget, cannot compete with the sort of salary I have become used to, but money isn't everything. It would give me great satisfaction to help George and the club that gave me so much pleasure back into the top flight. I don't need the money. I can afford to buy a Rolls-Royce if I want one and I can look after my family. That is all that has ever mattered to me.

I was impressed with Mr Sheepshanks, and it is not so fanciful to think that returning to Ipswich is an option for me in the not-too-distant future. My ties to the area were, if it is possible, strengthened in October 1997 when the University of East Anglia at Suffolk College bestowed an honorary Master of Arts degree on me, specifically for the contribution I had made to the training of young people during my time at Ipswich. Attending the ceremony with me was Trevor Nunn, director of the National Theatre and the Royal Shakespeare Company, who was being made an Honorary Doctor of Letters. The two of us received a standing ovation from the 1,350 students and their guests, and it was all very emotional. Veterans of the event said they had never known a day like it. Trevor – a gifted, articulate man and an Ipswich supporter – made a speech and told the audience how his old dad would have enjoyed the day, and the fact that Bobby Robson was there would have made it extra special for him. They were charming words and I was able, for once, to enjoy it all because I wasn't obliged to stand up and say anything.

All this affection for and interest in me was overwhelming. Even after my deal with PSV had been done the phone kept on ringing, and one top English club was in touch with me on the very day I announced officially that I was joining PSV to ask if there was still time for them to intervene. It was a massive club and I would have been interested because they were also prepared to offer me the coaching position I craved, but it was too late, and although I had not at that time signed any legally binding documents I had given my word and I am a man of honour. Under no circumstances would I have reneged, any more than I would reveal the English chairman's name, having promised I wouldn't.

Here I was, at retirement age, back in demand. I have to confess it felt extremely good and caused me to reflect on the situation twelve months earlier when I felt that I was at a cross-roads having had what I thought was a successful year coaching Barcelona only to be left with the prospect of being shunted into another high level position. Any anger I felt at the end of that sensational year quickly dissipated though, because I could fully understand the logic of bringing in the younger man Louis van Gaal from Ajax who, if they hadn't snapped him up, would have gone to another top club to compete against them.

Once I had adjusted my mind to the fact that I wasn't going to be coaching for the second season and be with my players, I had to make a decision. I was left with several options: I could throw a sulk and let everyone know how unhappy I was to be sidelined; I could treat the second year as a highly paid sabbatical, swanning around the pleasure spots of the world, picking up my huge contract; or I could knuckle down, apply myself and do a proper job. The more I thought about the Director of Transfers post at the Nou Camp the more excited I became at the prospect of being the first man ever to undertake the job for such a fabulous club. Other top clubs around Europe, aware of the effects of the Bosman case and the increasing cost of football talent, had already set their plans in motion with high-profile directors travelling around the globe scouting the leading players. Obviously I would have to get used to it because it was so hugely different from the job I had done for so many years. I have always thought that if you are not flexible and prepared to adjust your mind and thinking you are nowhere in life. I decided I would give it a serious go and see what happened. I would watch which way the ball bounced. I was comforted by the knowledge that if a great offer came in for me to coach another leading club the president had indicated that he would look at it compassionately, but he also made it clear that he wanted me to stay and use my reputation and stature in world football to the benefit of Barcelona.

The first thing I needed to do was to draw up some guidelines and to this respect a meeting was arranged with Nunez, Joan Gaspart and, of course, the new coach Louis van Gaal. Without Louis' full co-operation the task would be a monumental waste of time and money. The existing scouting system was fine, but what was needed was someone with a high profile who could open doors, walk into clubs and be made welcome rather than furtively standing on terraces with the fans wearing a big hat and dark glasses. The game had moved on and transfers were often major international financial transactions involving big business, serious contracts, lawyers and agents.

The club was earnest about it and so was I. I was going to do the job to the very best of my ability. I decided I would set up a network of scouts around the world and watch the best players. It was decided that I would draw up a list of the top players in every position so that when the club wanted or needed to move into the transfer market they could target the very best there was around. It was not just established players but also the cream of the up-and-coming stars of the future, and to this extent I went to Egypt for the World Youth Championships in September 1997, and to Burkina Faso for the African Nations Championship in February 1998; I travelled to Germany, France, England, Italy, the former eastern Europe, to Brazil to see Flamengo play Vasco da Gama, and then went for nine games in six days in Argentina, watching over 200 players. It was a thrilling experience to be able to watch Boca, Riverplate, Velez, Sarsfield and others.

I used the job not as an extended holiday but as a great global adventure, watching outstanding players, making important contacts, setting up a worldwide network of scouts and actually going to games and countries I had always wanted to experience. While I was attending the African Championships I established a scouting system for the entire continent, encompassing Cameroon, Nigeria, Ghana and the Ivory Coast. Watching the Under-17 World Championships in Egypt was also an education, and out of thirty-two games in the tournament I managed to watch twenty-six of them live, sometimes two a day, and most of the rest on television during my three-week stay. I have reports and files on almost every player who played in that tournament, some of whom could be the top players of the future.

My job was busy, exhausting and exciting. I didn't just pick my own games; I would ask Louis what games he would like me to watch, which players he would like me to scout. He in turn supported me and I began to like the man who had taken over my job in mid-term. Although we were two different sorts of characters we had many things in common, particularly the desire for success and the capacity to work hard to achieve that objective.

I deliberately divorced myself from the players and, remembering the way in which Cruyff's presence at the stadium had unsettled me, went to very few Barcelona games, watching more games on Sky. The last thing I wanted was to be a negative influence, particularly during van Gaal's settling-in period, which is never easy in a club of that size. It was not all plain sailing for the former Ajax coach. He came through a rough patch in January and suffered the indignation of being dumped out of the European Champions League, but gradually he bedded the team down, the players became used to him and his tactics and success followed. Winning the double was superb and I enjoyed sharing in his success. It is not easy winning major honours in a first season and it only comes through dedication, application and hard work.

I heard and read of how I was hating my new job and yearning to be back at the sharp end, wishing ill to the man who had replaced me and the club I loved. It couldn't have been more untrue. I loved every minute. I was treated with great respect by everyone at Barcelona and at every club and country I went to. Far from feeling marginalized it massaged my ego. I had been working non-stop at the highest level for a long time. I love the industry but it is very demanding physically and mentally; my new role allowed me to stand back from the daily hullabaloo but still be involved at the highest level.

Clearly Barcelona liked what I was doing as well because in the middle of my negotiations with PSV Eindhoven I was summoned to a meeting with Josep Lluis Nunez and Louis van Gaal. I had no idea what it was about and neither did Louis. We travelled to the meeting together and we both thought it was the final farewell, the handshake and the long goodbye. We were stunned when Nunez said how well the year had gone and that he would like me to sign a new contract and stay for another season – in fact for as long as I wanted. Obviously they were not offering me the huge salary I had been paid as coach and as a 'thank you' for my second year, but it was still enough to make most Premier League managers sit up and take notice.

If the beast and the bug of football at the sharp end had not been within me I would have jumped at the chance of staying on, but I needed to be back with the players and working with a team again after my year away – but for anyone who finds the coaching job too stressful I can recommend the alternative. I made the job work and did it so well that Louis was very sorry that I was going because it gave him and the club a headache in terms of finding a replacement. In all modesty, someone with my experience plus my intimate knowledge of the club and its needs would be hard to come by. There is no doubt that doors swung open because of who I was. The red carpet was often rolled out at clubs, and in Africa I was steered to the front of the accreditation queue to receive documents in twenty minutes that were taking others up to seventeen hours.

The travel also expanded my mind. Too often with clubs you are whisked in and out of countries, seeing only the airport, the hotel and the stadium with no time to soak up the sights or the local culture. This was something I was able to do on my own and I found it immensely rewarding and often eye-opening. I had been to Africa before but, again, had been limited in what I saw. In Burkina Faso I witnessed at first-hand the poverty, squalor and filth. The average guy there earns twenty dollars a month; those without a job get nothing and virtually live in a hole dug in the ground with their fingernails. There is no anger and resentment for they know no other life, and while I was there I neither saw nor heard of any thieving or mugging. As far as I was concerned I was as safe as I could be, although I admit I took the precaution of not venturing out late at night on my own, but that would apply to a great many cities around the world.

There were, though, the occasional dangers involved. When I was in Egypt in September terrorists exploded a bomb outside a museum in Cairo which killed many tourists just 150 metres from my hotel. Fortunately I was between games and the only repercussion I suffered was to be caught in the resulting traffic jam. It was one of the places I wanted to go to, but although I did the Pyramids, the Sphinx, Alexandria, Cairo and Port Said, I was not able to go there. But you have to accept those risks as part of the baggage, just as you do the inherent problems with local food. I am lucky in that I not only have a cast-iron tummy but also adhere strictly to those rules we set for the Mexico World Cup of sticking to bottled water and keeping away from salads and unpeeled fruit. I also had all the necessary jabs, pills and potions to ward off the ills and evils of foreign travel.

Certainly the bomb did not deter me, nor did it spoil my enjoyment of a tournament where the standard of football was, in some cases, exceptional. A great many of the players were already established with leading European clubs. There were other players there who, had I been scouting for a lesser club than Barcelona, I would certainly have brought back, and there were a couple who could have played for Barcelona but for the fact that we had players of their equal in the same positions. I saw some outstanding young talent which looks sure to maintain the march forward of the beautiful game right across the world. The winners from Brazil were superb, but so were the runners-up Ghana, who maybe should have won it.

Once again, I was not there on my own. Many of the clubs were represented and there were agents swarming everywhere. Much of the scouting these days is done by agents who then sell on. I have great regard for many of the agents but you have to face the fact that they are in there to earn themselves money and you cannot trust all of them all of the time because they will sell you anything they can, at a cost to the club. I went to Africa to be able to say to Barcelona that players were either right or wrong for the club from first-hand experience. I brought back good names for the future when a player might suddenly be needed and, just as important, I was able to rule out players who were not good enough who we might have been tempted to buy on less evidence.

The seven-figure salary sounds a ridiculous amount of money for the job I was doing, but not when it is considered in its context. With transfer fees spiralling out of all proportion, a mistaken or wrong deal could cost a club millions of pounds. Then again, a well struck deal can earn a club millions. My advice, judgement and decisions earned far more for Barcelona than they paid me. My signing of Ronaldo was a prime example. There were many who thought I was mad when I recommended that the club should pay twenty million US dollars for the player, but in one year his value exploded and he was reluctantly sold to Inter Milan for a twelve-million-dollar profit. I suspect that more than made up for my high salary, not to mention the trophies he helped us win while he enjoyed that one sensational season with us.

One of my problems in this area was that the previous year the Barcelona B team had been relegated from the top league which meant that under the Spanish FA rules we were barred anyone from outside Spain in the team. That was a disaster for us in an otherwise great year. I could only watch it happen as I had nothing to do with the B team. Over the years the quality of our reserve players had been allowed to diminish and they simply weren't good enough to keep us in the top flight. It meant there was no point in bringing in talented young players from abroad because we would have nowhere to play them and bring them along.

The club addressed the problem immediately. They appointed top coach Serra Ferrer to look after what is called the 'football base' to make sure that the club go back to the top division again as soon as possible and that such a thing never happens again. Ferrer and his army of helpers look after the players from eight years of age upwards, their scouting, acquisition, training and development. Serra Ferrer was previously the chief coach at Real Betis, a top man who had taken the club to the Spanish Cup Final where they gave Barcelona a tremendous battle before we lifted the trophy. Such is his status that he would quickly have found a top job almost anywhere in Spain, but the lure and attraction of being connected with Barcelona was overwhelming. I have no idea what the club would have to pay to secure his services, but it clearly shows serious intent by having Louis van Gaal, Bobby Robson and Ferrer on the staff at the same time. That is forward thinking – if very expensive! – but the sort of investment which is needed at the top level of football these days, not solely for the top players but also for the leading coaches and managers.

Louis van Gaal will be a very rich man by the time he finishes at Barcelona, but as important is the fact that now the presidential elections are over the club can support him in the proper way and be strong for him. When it was going wrong early in the season they propped him up and looked after him. I had been criticized and attacked without reason, despite having the best start and scoring so many goals. I agree with the way the club supported Louis – that is the way it should be done. He is a long-term investment with, I understand, a five-year contract and a two-year option, and if he has a rough ride at the start, so what? He came through with their help and sailed on for the rest of the season. The reward was the Spanish title they craved, Real Madrid trailing in their wake. It was success through patience and understanding and van Gaal repaid their faith.

I know from the sort of money I was offered to return to England that attitudes are changing and coming into line here. Eyes have been opened, and after the influx of foreign players we now have top coaches like Arsène Wenger being attracted from overseas. The result is that the Premiership is top of the tree in terms of excitement, full houses, beautiful stadia and imported players. Alive with attractions, it is the place to be. The Premier League is right up there with the German, Italian and Spanish leagues. There is no league higher and there are no easy games, although I have to say that there is great depth in Spanish football these days. The former Real Madrid coach Fabio Capello is convinced that the Spanish League is tougher than Serie A overall. He admitted that Inter, Milan, Juventus, Roma, Lazio and Parma were big, big clubs but that the teams below them were weaker than the second half of the Spanish League. In that respect the English League is tough down to its very last club. In Spain we maybe had five or six easier games, but in the Premier League there is no such thing. Things have changed beyond belief since I departed the shores in 1990, and all for the better. Nothing has impressed me more than the way clubs and police have curbed hooliganism which was blighting the game, threatening its very existence. Every now and again we are nudged both at home and abroad with a reminder that the scum are still there, lurking in dark corners awaiting their chance to create havoc again, but the extensive use of video cameras, files built up by the police and the introduction of all-seater stadia have restricted the violence. There is nothing that would set the game back quicker than a resurgence of the sort of violence which saw English clubs reviled and hounded out of international competition in the mid-1980s. Free from the choking influence of the morons in hobnailed boots, football has been allowed to grow and flourish, and I doubt whether there is more exciting club football anywhere in the world. The Premier League stands up for comparison with the very best and I am not alone in thinking that it is at least the equal of Italian and Spanish football.

I understand that there are over 300 foreign players in the country. In 1978 when I brought in Arnold Muhren and Frans Thijssen there were only two others of any real note, the two Argentines Ricardo Villa and Ossie Ardiles, brought over from the World Cup-winning side by the farsighted Keith Burkin-shaw. Things have certainly changed, but clubs must beware that they bring in only the best to ensure that the standard keeps rising. Bringing in cheap players only serves to hold back the development of British youngsters and does nothing to improve the quality of the game.

It was argued that the arrival of the so-called foreign mer-cenaries would damage our young players' prospects and the international team. That couldn't be further from the truth, for our youngsters have been able to take the best of what the overseas players and their own local heroes offer and improve their own games. I cannot remember when England had such a fine crop of young players coming through, from the many at Manchester United through to Rio Ferdinand at West Ham United and the talented Michael Owen at Liverpool. They are all at clubs where there are a proliferation of foreign players, and I can only assume it has helped them improve their skills and their horizons.

The game has also benefited massively from the huge injection of cash from Sky television and, once again, the prophets of gloom and doom have been proved wrong. Far from affecting attendances, more and more supporters are going to games to enjoy the live entertainment having been fed a diet of two-dimensional football on television. It has certainly helped me keep in touch with the English game while I have been abroad and it has also meant that those unable to travel to games because of age or infirmity can enjoy the excitement of the live game. With football from around the globe also being shown it has stripped away the blinkers and the supporters at home know as much as many of the experts about the imports, having watched them in the Italian, Spanish or other leagues. Football has never been better served by television than it is in Britain at present, and I see no reason why that should change in the near future.

The change in the game's image has also attracted blue-chip businesses to come in with their investments and sponsorships, feeding the clubs with the money they need to attract the very best players in the world, enabling them to compete with the Barcelonas, Real Madrids, Milans, Bayern Munichs and the rest. The game is flourishing at home, but this in itself has brought with it other problems and questions that need addressing, not least of all the growing importance of the European League. There is no doubt that clubs like Ajax, PSV and Feyenoord in Holland, Manchester United, Liverpool and Arsenal in England, Rangers and Celtic in the Scottish League and Barcelona and Real Madrid in Spain are vitally important, and if you take them away and put them into a European Super League it would do terrible damage to the domestic game in those countries. We have to be careful. Taking the big teams away could seriously damage the Football League; the remaining clubs could wither and begin to die. We don't want to do that and be that greedy. The top clubs are still making good money and we have top-quality European football which is exciting and rewarding. Clubs like Manchester United and Liverpool visiting Leicester City or Derby County offer those clubs big days in their season. It stimulates the game and fills the stadiums. Take them away and there is a great loss for everyone.

I believe that the only way forward is to keep the top divisions around Europe down to a manageable number – eighteen, or no more than twenty – and extend the Champions League. I like the concept of four divisions of six rather than six of four. It gives the competing teams more games and therefore bigger pay days and allows the top teams to come through if they have an off day and lose the odd game. That way, too, the structure of the domestic league would remain the same, giving every team the dream of winning the title and making it to the big time. Who knows which teams will develop in the future? Look how Blackburn Rovers and Newcastle United have come through having found benefactors. Would those money men bother with the game if there was no chance of progress? Of course not. It also serves to help the big clubs, for would Manchester United not want to play their big rivals like Everton, Liverpool, Arsenal, Spurs, Chelsea, Leeds and Blackburn? Those are as big pay days as they would get if they were playing Real Madrid or any other big European side.

There is plenty of European football on offer for the bigger clubs in the Champions League and the Cup Winners' Cup, and there's the UEFA Cup which offers a massive carrot to the lesser lights. How important is it for Derby County, Coventry City, West Ham United, Aston Villa and others? It gives everyone something to play for rather than the season tailing off for half the league after Christmas. The Champions League, despite the expansion, will remain special and therefore will be out on its own in terms of a league, while the other two will and should remain as knock-out competitions. Make them all the same and we would lose so much.

But while the pinnacle of the pyramid is important, so are the grass roots. I was delighted for the game at home when someone as high profile and accomplished as Howard Wilkinson was appointed to sort out the problems from schools and youth football upwards. I have been beating the drum for years about the undue influence of the English Schools Football Association and the need for centres of excellence, academies and the like. Howard has started putting all of that into practice to bring us in line with the leading clubs abroad, and we must make sure that every professional club has its own school of excellence. Those who cannot afford to take that step must be helped, either by those who can or by a separate fund from the revenue coming in from television, or, if possible, from the National Lottery which is supposed to support all British sport. Our youth is our future and we must not be left behind by the rest of the world. They should all receive proper coaching, education and preparation. This should apply to girls as well as boys as the women's game, now under the

Football Association's umbrella, continues to grow. It is crucial that all youngsters are given the technical skills they need to compete rather than the biggest and strongest coming through as they did in the past. We are, after all, looking for footballers, not hammer throwers.

It requires sensible investment of some of the money pouring into the game, for it must be remembered that the vast majority of the flow of money coming in at the moment is generated from outside the game and, therefore, could be turned off as fast as it was turned on. Certainly you cannot cap wages or transfer fees. It is up to the clubs to make sure they have the right salary structure and spend their money carefully and within their budget. Paying out money they haven't got can only end in disaster, as it does in any business. Clubs would do well to remember the days of not too long ago when many clubs, big and small, were balancing on the brink of bankruptcy. These golden days should be used to underpin the game and the clubs, not to see how far things can stretch before the elastic breaks.

At Ipswich we bought what we could afford and still achieved success. We were a small club with small gates, but at the other end of the scale Alex Ferguson has done the same thing. He does not spend recklessly even though he has the money; he and the club are prepared to spend a lot on their youth development. Look how they have reaped the rewards from that farsighted policy. Ajax in Holland have also made their youth system pay to the extent that they can sell their best players and carry on winning their league and doing well in Europe. Those two clubs are an example to everyone.

There are an awful lot of players bought in a time of panic when things are going wrong, often purely on the evidence of an agent's video which, inevitably, is going to be highly biased in favour of the player he is trying to sell. How many foreign players have been brought into England without anyone from the buying club having watched them in action or having checked their background? The answer is both surprising and horrifying. In some respects the plcs, much criticized in some quarters, have introduced a sense of restraint by explaining to over-eager managers or directors that two and two do not make six in the real world. It may also curb some of the panic buying if there was a closed season for transfers during the season, one window of opportunity in much the same way as the Italian and Spanish transfer season operates. It would also give managers the chance of proving their managing ability rather than buying their way out of trouble or into success.

Fortunately I cannot see Sky pulling the plug on football because it has done so much for them. They know that football is their Rolls-Royce and they are not going to sell that and buy a Lada. No other sport will sell dishes as well as football. But it is important that the Premier clubs, who are getting richer by the season, do not forget those in the lower divisions. I repeat that they are our strength, the breeding ground for young players. They need support. Promotion and relegation between all divisions must be retained at all costs so that every club can aspire to greater things, not only the chairmen, directors and players but also the fans. Take that away from them and the interest would rapidly die. Stop that competition and you stop the very pulse of the game. Promotion and relegation increases the pressure and excitement, but if it was taken away it would not only hurt the lower clubs but also those in the Premier League who are keen to protect their own interests.

The game in Britain could soon achieve another big boost if we are awarded the World Cup in 2006, as I believe we might. I firmly believe that it is a straight fight between England and

Germany – I just hope they do not decide on a penalty shoot-out to separate the two! The competition has grown to such a dramatic extent that there are now only a handful of countries in the world who could possibly stage the tournament. The main competition for the two European competitors seems to comprise South Africa and Brazil. Both have undeniable rights to stage the tournament. The South Americans have established themselves as the great world force in football, and particularly in the World Cup, while Africa is the coming continent in the beautiful game and a World Cup there would be as big a promotion to their future as it was to the USA in 1994. But now that the World Cup has expanded to thirty-two teams it demands special qualifications, not least of all in the number of stadia required, hotels, security, travel networks and accessibility for supporters from all over the world.

Brazil has gone through a bad time economically and even its top stadium, the famous Maracana, is in a dilapidated state requiring an outlay in its millions to bring it up to date. The same applies to many of its other stadiums, spread over a massive country which would make commuting for teams and spectators alike very difficult. South Africa remains a political tinderbox that could ignite when Nelson Mandela goes. There is a great deal of violence in some of the main cities and apartheid still seems to exist in sport with the white population watching rugby union and cricket and the black people preferring football, even though they cannot afford to watch the top games as we witnessed in the African Nations Cup in 1996. I feel that at this time neither country would find it possible to stage the event.

I recall the security we had to have in Mexico, and that was for twenty-four teams. Now the hosts have to look after eight more and make sure they are secure and safe along with the supporters who travel to watch the world's biggest sporting event outside the Olympic Games. It has already grown to mammoth proportions as politics have embraced countries and continents who are inferior in world terms. It already means that some of the best teams do not make it to the finals. Are Jamaica, Iran, Japan, Saudi Arabia and South Korea better than Portugal, Sweden, Russia or the Czech Republic? Of course not. Can you imagine what it has done to Portuguese football missing out from a final list of thirty-two? Politics and in-fighting for votes have changed the face of the World Cup, but it would be disastrous if it were to decide the venue as well.

The other problem which FIFA must sort out very quickly is that of international dates. The situation is now completely and totally out of hand with clubs losing players to all manner of 'sanctioned' competitions, robbing clubs of the players whose wages they are paying, often at crucial times of the season. Dates have to be standardized so that everyone plays at the same time and leagues can arrange their programmes accordingly to allow players leave to perform for their countries.

I suffered terribly in my first year at Barcelona and to this day I reckon that the loss of my Brazilians cost me a clean sweep of the trophies. I played Atlético Madrid in a 3–3 draw without Ronaldo, Giovanni, Figo, Fernando Couto and Vitor Baia. Half my team didn't play and we lost two points, the same number of points by which we lost the Spanish League title to Real Madrid. That was just one example of the many times I lost players that season. Much the same thing was happening in England with South Africans, Australians and Brazilians being called away for all sorts of unimportant but sanctioned tournaments. Unless something is done anarchy will set in and damage the international game. That would be sad. For me there is nothing higher than playing for or managing your country, and one thing I missed in my time away was not being able to see all of the England games at Wembley, although I still managed to see most of them.

The other big void in my life for eight years was the FA Cup. It is still special and admired, respected and envied the world over. The Cup catches fire right from the start in England, but abroad I found that it was not until the final stages that interest really grew, and it was only the possibility of an entry into the Cup Winners' Cup competition which eventually brought it to the fore. Cup Final day in England is watched throughout the world. Try getting a ticket.

Our football industry is bigger in England with its many clubs, while most of the other European leagues have one or two major divisions at the most. In many ways I am aghast at why I left it and why I have stayed away so long. But it has been a marvellous adventure, not least of all my two years in Barcelona where I had a passport to travel the world and be the coach of the biggest and finest club in the world. As an Englishman abroad I have enjoyed almost every minute and would not have changed places with anyone. Life has been good.

Career Highlights

1933   Born on 18 February in Sacriston, County Durham.

1944   Joins Langley Park Football Club and within a few years is turning out for the under-18 side.

1948   Invited to trials at Middlesbrough and Southampton. Boro sign Robson on schoolboy terms.

1950   Rejects Boro's offer of a professional contract and journeys south to sign for Fulham, making his first-team debut at the age of eighteen. He makes 152 appearances for the club and scores 68 goals.

1953   Attends FA coaching course in Paddington Street with Jimmy Hill and Ron Greenwood after watching Hungary demolish England 6–3 at Wembley.

1955   Marries Elsie after returning from a close-season FA tour to the Caribbean.

1956   Makes his debuts for England U/23 and B sides while still at Fulham, scoring a goal in the former against Denmark. Signed by Vic Buckingham at West Bromwich Albion for £25,000. Robson makes 239 appearances for the Baggies and scores 56 goals.

1957   Full international debut under Walter Winterbottom in

November against France. England win 4–0 and Robson scores twice. He is awarded twenty England caps with four goals for his country.

1958   World Cup Finals in Sweden with England, who lose out 1–0 to the Soviet Union in a play-off for the quarter-finals. Winterbottom sees promise and urges Robson and Don Howe to go to Lilleshall to qualify as FA coaches.

1961   Gains full coaching badge.

1962   World Cup Finals in Chile with England, but Robson is injured and is replaced in the team by Bobby Moore. England lose 3–1 to Brazil in the quarter-finals. Robson asks for a transfer in August after payment talks with WBA following the abolition of the maximum wage. He moves back to Fulham under Bedford Jezzard for £20,000; in his second spell there he makes 193 appearances and scores nine goals.

1965   Coaches Oxford University to the first of two successive wins in the Varsity match. Robson also becomes a staff coach with the Football Association.

1967   Southend make it known they want Robson to be their player-manager; Arsenal also interested, but Robson quits Fulham and leaves England for Canada to become player-coach of the Vancouver Royals.

1968   The Vancouver job having fallen through, Robson rejoins Fulham as manager in January. He is sacked by the board for bad results the following November.

1969   Chelsea manager Dave Sexton asks Robson to do some scouting at Ipswich and Nottingham Forest. Robson writes to both after the games offering his services; Ipswich respond and Robson moves to Portman Road as manager in January.

1971   Ipswich slump to the bottom of the First Division, but Robson is offered an extension to his contract.

1973   Everton, Derby County and Atlético Bilbao make offers, but Robson stays put.

1974   Receives more tempting offers from Sunderland and Leeds United, but declines. Ipswich Town top the First Division for the first time since 1962 when Alf Ramsey won the title, but finish the season in third place.

1977   Saudi Arabia seek Robson's services as national squad manager, and Everton try a second time.

1978   Ipswich finish just three points clear of the relegation zone but beat Arsenal 1–0 in the FA Cup Final. They are then thrashed 5–0 by Nottingham Forest in the Charity Shield.

1980   Barcelona make the first of their three bids for Robson.

1981   Martin Edwards seeks to secure Robson's services for Manchester United shortly after Ipswich Town beat AZ 67 Alkmaar of Holland 5–4 on aggregate to win the UEFA Cup, but again he declines and Ron Atkinson is chosen instead.

1982   Ipswich, hit by injuries, finish second in the First Division behind Liverpool. Robson takes England B to Iceland in May, scouts for Ron Greenwood during the World Cup Finals in Spain and in June is appointed England manager. He is vilified by many for Keegan's omission from his opening squad to face Denmark in September.

1983 England lose 1–0 to Denmark at Wembley and fail to qualify for the European Championships, Robson's first major tournament in charge.

1984 Barcelona come back for Robson, but he recommends Terry Venables.

1986 Offers his resignation after England are defeated by Argentina at the quarter-final stage of the Mexico World Cup by the Hand of God and a sublime goal, but the FA don't accept it.

1988 Tenders his resignation a second time after England lose all three group games in the European Championships, but again it is not accepted.

1990 News leaks prior to World Cup that Robson is leaving for PSV Eindhoven, causing a stink. England improve with every game during the 1990 World Cup in Italy but lose on penalties in a tense semi-final to the eventual winners, West Germany. The squad wins the Fair Play Award and returns home to a rapturous welcome. Robson takes up position at PSV.

1991 Despite going out in the early stages of the cup competitions, PSV are Dutch champions. Robson goes to Buckingham Palace to be made a CBE.

1992 PSV again pip Ajax to the title, but lose out in the Champions League to Anderlecht. Robson is not offered an extension to his contract, and moves to Sporting Lisbon at the end of the season.

1993 In December Robson is suddenly dismissed by Sporting president Sousa Cintra after a disastrous UEFA Cup defeat at the hands of Casino Salzburg, despite the club being top of the League.

1994   At the end of January Robson signs an eighteen-month contract as head coach at FC Porto. Porto beat Sporting 2–1 in a replay to win the Portuguese Cup, and beat Benfica to win the Super Cup. In September Robson agrees to an extension to his original contract.

1995   In May Arsenal make a bid for Robson, but Porto president Pinto Da Costa refuses to co-operate. Porto are crowned champions of Portugal and retain the Super Cup, but European success continues to elude Robson as Sampdoria win their Cup Winners' Cup tie. In August Robson has a malignant melanoma removed from his face, but within a few months he returns to the helm at Porto.

1996   Porto retain the title, but crash out of the Champions League at the group stage and lose the Cup semi-final to Sporting. In the spring Barcelona again approach Robson as a replacement for Johan Cruyff and he accepts, unaware he is walking into a minefield.

1997   In February rumours begin to circulate that Ajax coach Louis van Gaal is to replace Robson at Barcelona. Some bad results in the middle of the season lose Barcelona the Championship, but the club beats Paris Saint-Germain to win the European Cup Winners' Cup and Real Betis to win the Spanish Cup in successive months. Despite this success Robson is made a technical director in charge of transfers and van Gaal moves in. Robson remains at the club throughout the year in the face of tempting offers from Newcastle United, Everton, Celtic, Besiktas, Sporting Lisbon, Benfica, Nigeria and Saudi Arabia. Made an Honorary Master of Arts by the University of East Anglia.

1998   Barcelona win the Spanish title. Robson has talks once
        again with Newcastle, and Barcelona and Ipswich, but
        agrees to go back to PSV on a one-year contract to fill
        the void left by Dick Advocaat.

Index